THE
THIRTEENTH
APOSTLE

by EUGENE VALE

Published by Jubilee Press, 1983

First editions published by Charles Scribner's Sons
        8 printings

Reprints: Fawcett/Crest Giant

Copyright © 1959 EUGENE VALE
Library of Congress Catalog Card Number 59-11660
Published simultaneously in Canada

Printed in the United States of America

        ISBN   0-9609674-0-0

WHO IS THE THIRTEENTH APOSTLE?

For the U.S. Consul, stationed in a colorful Central-American port, the search to discover the thirteenth Apostle began unexpectedly. An encounter with a mysterious painter, who disappears, compels the Consul to track him down. Setting out to cross dangerous jungles, he is drawn inland by tantalizing clues, past exotic villages, toward the high mountains. The spur leads him to risk the perilous ascent of a gigantic peak. As he fights his way upward, he inwardly progresses to adventurous discoveries of his own self, until he recognizes the identity of THE THIRTEENTH APOSTLE.

"BRILLIANT, POWERFUL, SIGNIFICANT," wrote Robert R. Kirsch in the *LOS ANGELES TIMES,* adding: "There are a hundred passages I would like to quote but I must settle for one:

"'The mystery of our role on earth. The great questions at the beginning and at the end of our existence. Where did we come from? Where do we go? And in between: why are we here? What is the meaning and the purpose? Questions which cannot be answered with that absolute proof which has become dear to our hearts. So we proceed to live as if the basic mystery did not exist.'"

"TANTALIZINGLY SUSPENSEFUL"
"Not in years has a novel so excited readers as has EUGENE VALE's unusual story of physical and spiritual adventure."
"A MAGNIFICENT PERFORMANCE"
THE NEW YORK TIMES

"VALE is a compelling storyteller."
THE WALL STREET JOURNAL

"A GREAT BOOK. It is a *Pilgrim's Progress* of our age . . . A book of brilliance, nobility, and beauty. A remarkable performance in the literature of self-discovery."
Edmund Fuller in *THE CHICAGO TRIBUNE*

LIBRARIES

"As writing of magnificently sustained imaginative force, as an engrossing journey toward self-discovery by way of a physical adventure of the most dramatic and dynamic sort, it is a towering rarity in modern fiction. Those who go in courageous quest of their own souls will find it a Himalayan experience."

WILLIAM ALLEN WHITE LIBRARY

"An intense and compelling novel."

LIBRARY JOURNAL

"One of the rarest of publishing phenomena is the book which earns and deserves both critical and popular success. Such a book is THE THIRTEENTH APOSTLE, and its author, Eugene Vale, immediately achieved recognition as a major figure in contemporary American literature.

"THE THIRTEENTH APOSTLE is a book to own, for it merits frequent rereading. But the rereading is always a pleasure, for the author has a master's skill in the use of the English language.

"Because THE THIRTEENTH APOSTLE is clearly destined to be a landmark in twentieth century American letters, the University of Southern California is proud to add the manuscript to its special collection of Contemporary American Literature. The author's notes are certain to be of interest to the scholar of the future. The manuscript is, therefore, an especially important addition to the extensive holding of manuscripts, letters, and first editions of outstanding American authors since 1850."

UNIVERSITY OF SOUTHERN CALIFORNIA LIBRARY

INTERNATIONAL PRAISE

Published in 17 countries, translated into 8 languages

FRANCE

Albert Camus: "I was extremely interested by its striking qualities."

La Croix: "A great American novel. It deserves to be reread many times."

Marie France: "A magnificent book. The emotions reach a rare intensity. This is a very great novel, powerfully original."

ENGLAND

London Observer: "This novel never lets one down. The battle with the mountain is extremely exciting."

Christopher Fry: "A novel of real importance."

The Times Literary supplement: "It makes an exciting story, filled with fine descriptions and sensuous awareness."

Sir Victor Gollancz: "I am confirmed in my opinion that THE THIRTEENTH APOSTLE is one of the very finest novels written in English."

Dame Sybil Thorndyke: "The book wonderfully expresses the attempt of humanity to break through into another form of existence."

SPAIN

"A literary master"

HOLLAND

"Splendid".

AUSTRIA

Volksblatt: "A powerful epic ... An excellent novel ... A beautiful work."

BELGIUM

Le Phare: "An achievement in the strongest sense of the word, a work where a writer unveils the secrets of his soul and at the same time engages in an urgent dialogue with his country and his epoch. The author follows in a line which includes Hawthorne, Conrad, Joyce, and above all Melville. From now on this book takes its place and date in American literature."

Revue General Belge: "That this book is a bestseller does not astonish because it touches the core of that disquietude which, since Melville and Thoreau, constitutes the major theme of American literature. This is a book with which one has not finished after one has read it."

SWITZERLAND

Neue Zuercher Zeitung: "This novel accredits Vale as an important novelist, a well deserved honor. There is no doubt that this is an outstanding book."

Tribune de Lausanne: "A triumph."

Der Bund, Berne: "A monumental work, of which the beauty of the language gleams up, sentence by sentence."

Lucerne: "One rejoices that this work has such a great success."

FRANCE

La France: "American literature offers us a happy discovery with this great book by Eugene Vale . . . The voyage is described with the admirable precision of the greatest American novelist."

Courier Francais: "The work has an extraordinary power . . . One wishes that France would not remain behind in this area where she was once unchallenged."

ITALY: "Profound"   **POLAND:** "A beautiful novel"

MEXICO: "Inspired"

to my son—RONALD DAVID

JUBILEE PRESS, INC.
7906 Hillside Ave.
Los Angeles CA 90046

CONTENTS

PART ONE

IROZCO

CHAPTER I

DONALD C. WEBB, the consular official whose duty it was to investigate the death of the painter Franz Crispian, clambered onto the saddle of the burro and followed Padre Paolo into the jungle.

The green, watery heat engulfed them at the edge of the sun-baked village where Webb had been stranded after his car broke down. There had been no possibility of repair; and it had seemed that the jungle had brought Webb's journey to a premature end, when Padre Paolo had come along on one of his missions of mercy which kept him travelling from one to the other of his widely dispersed parishes. The famous mountain priest had offered to guide Webb, at least to Irozco. And he had arranged the loan of a burro from an Indian trader, whose daughter he had once saved by primitive surgery, performed under flickering torch light.

They were riding side by side, Webb stiffly erect in his white tropical suit, his cramped body clashing at every step with the unfamiliar jogging of the burro; while Padre Paolo, his black robe flowing over the saddle in easy, relaxed lines, was merging his tall, lanky frame with the small animal in perfect unison, his shoulders absorbing the rocking jolts with supple acceptance.

"I assume, Senor," the Padre said in his groping, uncertain English, "you will have need to go beyond Irozco. It is, perhaps, only the first station in your search?"

"I'm afraid so," the Consul said. "I have to follow his trail to the place of his death."

"And you have information where he went after he left Irozco?"

Webb shook his head. "Only rumors that he was seen in different places. For some time, he must have taken quite an erratic course. Until he reached Santa Rosa."

The priest nodded gravely. "It was, perhaps, to be expected that he would find his way to the mountains."

"He didn't intend to. He told me he wanted to avoid them."

"And yet he went there." For a while, the Padre rode in silence.

15

"Why? You cannot know. There may be many reasons. But if there was fear in his heart to go to the mountains, I doubt that he died in Santa Rosa."

"You think he returned to the plains?"

"No." The Padre paused. Unaccustomed to speak during his lonely travels, he did not express himself with ease; his mind was attuned to think in poetic images rather than words. "The town hangs high on the breast of the mountains," he said pensively. "But he could have gone higher still. And probably did." He turned to Webb. "It is so, is it not?"

"I don't know." Webb broke off, thinking of the cryptic message which Hal Barrie, the American engineer in charge of the Santa Rosa mine had sent him. The message specified neither the cause of death nor the circumstances. Considering that Barrie was always very precise and methodical in his reports, this lack of detail indicated that he was avoiding, or perhaps refusing to give explanation, possibly because he was unwilling or unable to shed light on Franz Crispian's fate.

"With your permission, Senor," Padre Paolo said at length, "I will change my itinerary to accompany you all the way." He hesitated. "Unless, Senor, I can persuade you to turn back."

Webb sat up, startled. "Why should I?"

"You are a man of the city," the Padre said. "It would be difficult for you to imagine the hardships and dangers of this wilderness."

"I've heard enough about it," Webb said, suppressing any indication of the fear that had haunted him since he left the safe confines of the harbor city.

"Just the same," the Priest persisted. "The reality of it is more than the description. There are many terrors of the body and the mind." He scrutinized Webb with a sidelong glance. "It may be wise for you to reconsider."

Webb bit his lips. For a moment, the Padre's warning, joining forces with his own persistent anguish, threatened to tip the scales. "I have no choice," he said curtly.

The burro, treading softly, was carrying him deeper into the jungle. The road had narrowed, suffocated by the encroaching vegetation that strained greedily to reduce the walls of the tunnel hacked across its tangled mass. Suddenly, behind the fleshy fronds of a young palm, they saw Webb's car, lying tilted on the side of the road, its axle broken.

Neither of them said a word as they passed the glistening, helpless machine, tumbled among the triumphant growth of giant leaves. Webb was staring straight ahead, fighting off the eerie feeling that the last bond with civilization was receding into the hungry shadows of the jungle. When he looked back, the car had disappeared behind a cluster of trees, and Webb was touched by a sense of doom as briefly as by the silent wingbeat of an invisible bird. And he knew then that it was too late to turn back.

"With your permission, Senor," the Padre said, resuming his probing, "may I ask if Senor Crispian was your friend, perhaps of close relation?"

"No. Why?"

"It seems a cause of wonder that you will undertake so difficult a journey, merely to track a man to his grave."

"He was an American citizen. As his Consul, it's my duty to inquire into the circumstances leading to his death. My government extends its protection to our citizens wherever they go." He broke off, wondering whether his explanation was formal enough to conceal his own burning interest in Crispian's fate.

"Surely, it is too late to protect poor Senor Crispian."

"But not too late to find out what happened to him. Where he went. His reasons. Whether he was killed in an accident, by disease, or murdered. In short, the cause of death."

"It may be difficult," the Padre mused. "Men die of many causes —sometimes of themselves."

"Do you mean—suicide?"

"No, Senor. A man would not journey for weeks and months to take his life."

"Then there must be some cause."

"Surely. But the evidence may not tell you enough. Because the truth of the soul is not that of the body."

Fleetingly, the image of Crispian's gaunt, intense face passed through Webb's mind. And he felt gripped unaccountably by the urgent need to resist his inclination to agree with the Priest. "I have to state facts in my report," he said curtly.

"I understand," the Padre continued. "But what are facts? A man dies. The physician chooses his facts, perhaps the police, or you the Consul." He smiled. "And the priest, too. I also have to make a report. Only I seek different facts. At the grave I look back on a man's life, and perhaps I will say 'Pedro was a good man. He was poor, because he did not like work, but he loved his children and made bows and arrows for them. And when his wife left him, he did not touch food and did not speak until she came back! Facts that are not facts, and yet are important. But such things about Senor Crispian would not interest your government." The Priest fell silent. "Though they may be important to you," he added all of a sudden.

Webb looked up, startled. He was sure that he had in no way betrayed his own need to discover what happened to Crispian. "What makes you think I have any personal interest in the matter?" he asked, almost sharply.

Padre Paolo smiled. "Your government would surely be satisfied, if you went directly to the place of his death. There would be no need to find out what drove him to Irozco. It is a detour, Senor."

Webb stared at the burro's bobbing head, no longer attempting denial. After a pause, the Priest continued, quietly, as if he were thinking out loud: "It must be a very powerful interest that draws you into this jungle. You hate the wilderness—it is against your nature. Yet you proceed. Is it allowed to ask why?"

Webb groped for an answer. Trying to formulate his motives, he realized they could not be understood by an outsider. The truth was that he could still not give a satisfactory explanation. Not even to himself. Not even now, no matter how often he had struggled with Crispian's memory. There seemed to be no way to grasp the impact of this strange personality.

"If I could answer you, Padre," Webb said with a thin smile, "I might not continue the trip."

The road had tapered off, forcing them to ride in single file, each man lost in his thoughts.

The Padre's question continued to linger in Webb's mind, haunting him. How was it possible that he, a sober-minded, practical man, could have been drawn from his well-ordered life into this jungle; how could a dead man force him to follow him to his grave? What was it about Crispian that had cast such an irresistible spell over him?

Recalling his first impression of the frail, little man, he saw the paradox in an even sharper light. He had judged Crispian to be an utterly insignificant person; there was nothing in his appearance that could have led Webb to suspect the extraordinary influence this man would have on his life. He was, in fact, so unobtrusive that Webb did not immediately notice him when he slipped into the office of the consulate.

Webb, at that moment, had to devote all his attention to a Mr. Bradley, a Massachusetts shoe manufacturer, whose yacht had limped into the harbor, in need of repair. Some parts had to be flown in from Chicago, and the Bradleys expected the consulate to help them get fixed up in a hurry. The man was as impatient as his wife; it almost seemed that he was pursuing the pleasure cruise with the energy of a business trip. Webb assured them of every assistance. Though resenting the visitors' imperious manner, Webb retained his polite, even deferential attitude, until the restless Bradleys, appeased though not reconciled to their misfortune, departed.

Only then did Webb discover Crispian, seated quietly on a bench in the corner. A quick glance at the man's ill-fitting suit assured Webb that he was not consequential enough to demand immediate consideration. Anxious to get the Bradley matter on its way, he dispatched the cable. He was about to turn to a visa application, when he remembered the man, who had made no effort to call attention to himself, waiting as patiently as if he were accustomed to be overlooked.

Webb had to call him twice before Crispian looked up, torn from his thoughts, trying to find his way back into reality. In Webb's opinion he did not succeed too well, because Crispian looked more lost, as he approached the desk, than he had in the world of imagination.

"What can I do for you?" Involuntarily, Webb dropped the 'sir' from the opening question he had asked innumerable times in twenty years of foreign service.

The answer was incongruous. "I arrived yesterday. On some steamship." Crispian smiled apologetically. "I forgot the name."

"The S.S. Lucia," Webb said, dryly. It happened to be the only ship in the harbor, a converted tanker with accommodations for tourists. For a moment, Webb wondered whether Crispian could be classified as a tourist, but a swift, furtive scrutiny of the emaciated face convinced him that the man could not be relegated to that category.

Crispian smiled, as if he realized that he had been judged and was found wanting. "I just came to ask if I had to register with the consulate," he said, humbly. "It's my first trip abroad. And I don't know much about legalities." He shrugged, helplessly. "But I always do my best to comply."

The words reflected a pathetic eagerness to fit himself into established order, which, as Webb had just begun to suspect, was bound to reject him, if for no other reason than his lack of easily identifiable labels, so necessary for common acceptance. No doubt, this was the sort of man who would fail wherever he tried to join, a perpetual remnant, the useless left-over for which there was no room on the standardized shelves.

The conclusion made Webb wary. He did not like the irregulars, because they usually turned out to be troublesome, particularly in foreign countries, where the consulate was responsible for them.

"Where are you from?"

"Detroit. I'm an American citizen," Crispian said eagerly, proud of his legal link to a vast community, almost clutching at this cherished bond to his fellow men, perhaps his only one.

"What is the purpose of your trip?"

Crispian seemed momentarily confused. "No purpose."

"I mean, are you here on business?"

"Oh, no. Just a tourist. I'm on my vacation." After a pause, he added with a strange intensity, which did not escape Webb's notice: "I needed a rest."

Webb hesitated. He could have told Crispian that a tourist did not have to register. But he decided against it. There was something disturbing about this man. It would be safer to have a file on him, just in case.

Reaching for the standard questionnaire, Webb started to fill in the answers which Crispian gave without hesitation, but somehow in an oddly detached manner, as if he were speaking of a stranger. He told Webb that he was approximately 39 years old;

birthplace and date unknown. He explained that he had been left on the doorsteps of a hospital, and further volunteered the information that he was raised in an orphanage. Later he had been apprenticed to an engraver, but had not stayed with his trade.

"What is your present occupation?"

Crispian seemed undecided. "I paint," he said humbly, too modest to call himself an artist.

The pen scratched reluctantly. To Webb most painters were bohemians. When he saw them clutter up the pier with their easels, walking around unshaven and sloppily dressed, he often suspected that they had drifted into the arts because they were too lazy to take a decent job. Also they were known to drink too much, and sometimes they ran out of money and had to be shipped back at government expense. A distinct possibility in Crispian's case, whose cheap suit revealed him to be an unsuccessful painter.

"You have your return ticket?" Webb asked.

"Of course," Crispian answered, amused, as if he had read Webb's thoughts. "I intend to go back."

Webb moved uncomfortably under the stare of the penetrating eyes. They were buried in deep hollows of the gaunt face, almost hidden beneath bushy eyebrows, as if they were not to be looked at, but only to look out with. At one moment, when they were fixed on him, Webb caught a glimpse of their extraordinary, luminous sheen; he felt as if a spotlight had been turned on him, and he shrank back, busying himself with the questionnaire, nervously asking the routine questions. But remembering the piercing glance, he could not escape the incongruous sensation that Crispian was finding out more about him than he, who was asking the questions, was able to learn about the person he interrogated. At any rate, it was quite evident that Crispian supplied the information with the patient indulgence of a man who knows that the biographical data reveal nothing about him.

When Webb had reached the bottom of the page, he looked up and saw that Crispian was smiling at him. "Anything else you want to know?"

Flustered, Webb turned back to the sheet. He had run out of questions. For filing purposes the record was complete. He could no longer hold the man.

"That is all. I hope you'll enjoy your stay."

"Thank you. I know I will. I've been wanting to come here for a long time."

After Crispian had left, Webb resumed his interrupted routine. There were three visa applications, which required some checking. Then he made a report on the pressing business of the yacht. The shoe manufacturer was an important man, probably very influential. His request was definite, straight to the point. It was the sort of task that gave Webb pride and pleasure in his work.

He worked later than usual. When he got ready to close up the office, he came across Crispian's questionnaire, which he had forgotten to file. Before dropping it into the cabinet, he surveyed the data once more. Usually, his long experience enabled him to construct a fairly comprehensive personality picture from the cleverly designed questions on the form. But in this case, the biographical blue print did not project a matching image of the structure that had arisen on the ground plan, as if the man were standing apart from the determining factors of his life, detached from the outer reality of his environment. Strangely dissatisfied, Webb buried the questionnaire in the file and went home.

He was crossing the crowded Paseo, when he saw Crispian at the Cafe del Torro, a sidewalk restaurant which was the gathering place of tourists at the cocktail hour. Oblivious to his ill-fitting clothes, with the shirt collar a size too large, Crispian seemed to be endeavoring, quite earnestly, to play the role of the tourist, sipping his coffee with a kind of unhappy determination to do as the Romans do, apparently quite unaware of the gulf that separated him from the rest of the chattering, boisterous crowd.

When Webb passed his table, Crispian's face lit up, as if he had found a friend in the wilderness. "Can I buy you a drink?" he asked, almost pleadingly.

Webb felt eyes from all corners turning in their direction. "Some other time," he said, flustered. "I have to go home."

Crispian threw a coin on the table. "I'll walk with you. If you don't mind?"

"I'd be delighted." Strangely enough, it was true; Webb welcomed the opportunity to question the man further, this time in the subtle context of casual conversation.

They turned into a sidestreet, where Webb was less likely to run into any acquaintances. "I'm taking you through the old part of town," Webb said. "Very colorful. As a painter, I'm sure, you'll be interested."

Crispian nodded, absent-mindedly. Soon they were passing underneath low balconies, treading among naked children playing under their feet, side-stepping dripping laundry hung in bright blotches of colors across the narrow lanes. Webb kept up a steady stream of explanations, imperceptibly mixing questions with his information about local customs.

By the time they had approached the residential section along the glistening blue bay, Webb had learned a good deal about Crispian. An unknown artist, he earned a bare living by painting murals on the walls of bars and taverns. With a shrug of his shoulders, Crispian dismissed the prostitution of his talent which was offered to public view, while the paintings he had created in the drafty attic of his boarding house remained stacked against the wall. Webb could not detect as much as a trace of bitterness; in fact, it was not even clear whether Crispian had ever submitted any of his canvasses for sale or exhibition. He seemed inexplicably indifferent to his work once it was completed; but not while he was creating it. A passionate, almost obsessed drive rang through his casual description of his working hours, frightening in its intensity. Apparently, he never stopped before exhaustion, seeking, as far as Webb could determine, neither relaxation nor the company of friends.

"I'm beginning to understand why you needed a vacation," Webb smiled. "But may I ask how you obtained the funds?"

Crispian chuckled. "The boarding house burned down. The insurance paid for the damage."

"You mean, your paintings were destroyed—?" Webb exclaimed.

"Most of them," Crispian nodded, without any apparent sign of regret. "The rest I stored in a warehouse and left."

For a while, they walked in silence past the neatly kept white villas, shadowed by fragile palms. In a way it was fortunate, Webb reflected, that Crispian had realized some profit from his work, which, in all likelihood, he could not have sold anyway. Still, it did not explain his utter indifference to the destruction of his paintings.

"And what made you decide to come here?" Webb asked.

There was a long pause before Crispian answered. "I once saw a photograph of the harbor. In an old magazine which somebody had left on a bench in a park. About three years ago. Or more. But it stayed in my mind. There's something about that mountain range in the background." He turned to look inland. "Tried to paint it twice, but it wasn't right. I had to see it." He studied Webb with a sidelong glance. "Interesting formation, don't you think?"

Webb's eyes remained fixed on the ground. "It seems to be rather intriguing to most tourists."

"And to you?"

"When you live in a place you get so used to the sights, you forget them," Webb said, starting to walk faster. He was suddenly getting impatient, anxious to get home. The walk had served its purpose. He had successfully drawn out Crispian, without arousing suspicion; if he tried to get more information, the man might become reticent, and perhaps altogether uncommunicative.

"I regret," Webb said, as they approached the steps leading up to his villa, "that our walk has to come to an end."

"You do?" Crispian gazed at him with a glint of amusement in his piercing eyes. "If you haven't asked all your questions, go ahead."

Webb felt the blood rise to his cheeks. "I hope you don't think I was prying?"

Crispian smiled. "Oh, I didn't mind. In a way it made me happy that someone was interested enough to try. Usually people don't even take the trouble."

There was such a disarming quality in his frankness that Webb's anger evaporated, leaving him helplessly groping for an apology.

Crispian's hand closed around the wrought-iron fence. "What are you afraid of?" he asked with unexpected directness.

Webb drew back; there was no telling how much Crispian might have learned about him, while he was proudly pursuing his subtle inquiry. "What makes you think I'm afraid?'

When Crispian faced him, the humorous twinkle had disappeared from the dark hollows of his eyes. "I noticed that yours is the only house with a fence."

"Very observant," Webb said with growing irritation. "But I have to disappoint you. It's no clue to my character. The fence happened to be built before I rented the villa." He broke off, remembering that he had chosen this home in preference to another which had seemed more convenient. An unconscious choice that seemed to justify Crispian's conclusion. Unable to withstand the silent gaze, Webb turned away. "Goodbye," he said harshly, as he passed through the gate.

He did not look back until he was inside the house. Through the window of his study, he saw Crispian walking down the street, his small shoulders hunched, a lonely figure outlined against the glittering expanse of the ocean, wandering forlornly past the shuttered villas. At that moment, Webb was gripped by regret, and he was tempted to call him back. But his annoyance persisted, and he went upstairs to the terrace, where he usually had his cocktail before dinner, relaxing in the cool evening air.

As soon as he was stretched out on the comfortable chaise-longue, his mulatto maid brought him his customary rum drink. A fat woman of bustling vitality, she seemed even more restless than usual. Remembering that this was the evening when she attended the voodoo ceremonies, Webb, smiling at her impatience, let her go. As usual, she tried every trick of persuasion to get him to meet her voodoo priest, and Webb went through the polite ritual of promising to join her the next time.

Actually, he knew that he would never go. The mystic aspects, embodied in magic rites, did not interest him. And his curiosity in the folklore was not strong enough to overcome his aversion to any spectacle of inflamed passions, of wild dances and chaotic emotions; in short, of self-abandonment in any form. He considered order the supreme law of the universe, and consequently the highest goal of man. Accordingly, he had arranged his life in patterns of strict regularity, to which he adhered with formal discipline and disciplined formality.

As far as he could detect, there was no flaw in his philosophy. And yet there were times when he felt vaguely disturbed, as if his flesh were drying up inside the rigid shells he had imposed on himself. Whenever the pleasantly safe routine of his days would begin to weigh on him as a burden rather than a protective device, he would reassure himself by contemplating his substantial achievements. He had worked himself up to a solid position; he was respected; he was a trusted civil servant, who would some day be entitled to a pension; in short, he had won for himself a secure place in an orderly universe.

But this evening, he failed to gain the expected satisfaction from the review of his circumstances. Not even his drink, carefully mixed in accordance with his instructions, tasted as well as usual. His discomfort, as he well realized, was due to Crispian; a stranger often stumbled blindly into carefully guarded private domains from which even friends of long standing were excluded. Before Crispian could further upset the delicate systems of checks and balances, it would be best to keep away from him. He was, after all, of no importance to Webb. An unsuccessful artist, without means, drifting into town on a vacation. An insubstantial particle of the great country Webb represented. No need to become involved with him.

The drink was beginning to taste better. He gazed at the distant mountain range, that shimmering streak suspended above the roof tops of the city. Sometimes, he would contemplate their blue haze for hours, wondering how it could cast such a spell on all non-residents. Tourists, arriving with no other intent than the desire to have a good time, would at first be puzzled; after a few days they would find their eyes drawn from their rum drinks more and more frequently; and soon they would come bustling into the consulate, clamoring to include a trip to the mountains in their grand tour, pressing him to arrange transportation inland. Even more remarkable was their common reluctance to discuss their motives, either because they were unaware of the strange fascination or too confused and ashamed to admit it; rarely did they state any other reason than the wish to see 'what those things look like from close by.'

Webb, of course, had to discourage them. Forbidding heat, impassable roads, poisonous snakes, fever, and swamps made it next to impossible to traverse the jungle. The few who had attempted to penetrate the wilderness were forced to turn back before reaching the foothills.

Even if the reports they brought back had been less harrowing, Webb would not have been tempted to leave the narrow territory bordered by the consulate on one side and his villa on the other. He was content to contemplate the blue mountain haze from his terrace; if anything, he was glad that they were so far away and guarded by an inaccessible wilderness.

And now, here he was, fighting his way through the jungle, as if the mountains, after years of impassive watchfulness, had suddenly reached out to pull him from his apparently safe retreat. That they had chosen him among the many who were eager made it no less unexpected than the fact that he had been led, step by step, to undertake this journey, coerced by an inexorably concrete and logical chain of circumstances.

The links were deceptively simple: an old magazine left in a park in Detroit; a fire in a boarding house which, three years later, supplied traveling expenses for Crispian; an erroneous notion that he had to register as a tourist; even Webb's accidental meeting with Padre Paolo, without whose guidance he could not have proceeded. Strangely inconsequential happenings; and yet it seemed as if an unseen hand had started to weave long ago unrelated events into an inextricable net.

Webb's burro had come to a halt. The sudden quiet disrupted his thoughts; looking up, he saw Padre Paolo waiting for him at a fork of the road.

"This trail—it leads to Irozco," the Padre said, pointing at a thin crevasse in the foliage. Webb saw that the path rose at a sharp angle from the gently mounting road they had travelled. "It is steep," the Padre said. "Also, it is wild." Webb's glance tried to penetrate the laced shadows, but the path disappeared shortly in an opaque darkness which was barely rippled by faintly stirring leaves. "There is yet time to choose, Senor. You may prefer the short cut to Santa Rosa."

Webb wiped the sweat from his forehead. For the first time, he noticed that his white suit was soiled and drenched; his sleeves were ripped in two places, and the neat creases of his pants had become crumpled; at the same time he grew aware that his legs were wounded from the constant rubbing of the stirrups.

Webb sensed that the Priest's dark, wide eyes were reading his fear of losing himself even further in this wilderness. "I've chosen to go to Irozco," he said, stiffening at the thought that he might be considered a coward.

The Padre's eyes stayed on him a moment longer. Then he nodded, bridling his burro up the steep incline. As the animals penetrated the receding, intangible dusk, their hoofbeats grew increasingly uneven on the outcropping of granite slabs across the trail.

Webb's glance searched the bizarre groupings of twisted trunks; and soon he realized that it would be as impossible to unravel this entwined growth as it would be to detect a thread of fate in the planless multitude of life's accidental happenings. The eerie sensation that the invisible hand which had planted the magazine in the Detroit park was now gliding alongside behind the thicket was surely as absurd as his previous attempt to string disconnected events on a thread of destiny like pearls on a string.

If such a thread existed, it could not be found on the outside, for the same factors might have been displayed to a multitude of people, leaving them indifferent. It was only by choosing among them what was pertinent to each that people created their own fate, just as Crispian had done when he retained the impression of the mountain range, waiting until life's fitful progress offered an opportunity to pay for the trip, unknowingly shaping a destiny that led him to his death on the mountain.

And similarly, Webb had just now made his own choice at the crossroads to Irozco, obeying a set of impulses, the origin of which would have to be traced even farther back than the magazine in the park. So far back indeed that the borderline between choice and circumstance became obscured by the mist that clouded the past.

Because even his first meeting with Crispian at the consulate was not in itself decisive. He had not been obliged to pay more attention to him than to any of the thousands that drifted into his office. But there was something in Webb that responded, though he did not immediately realize it. In fact, in the days after brusquely leaving Crispian at the villa gate, Webb had braced himself against Crispian's next visit at the consulate, which, he felt sure, was inevitable; and he had resolved to make it clear to the shabby painter that his consular duties did not require him to become a friend to every tourist.

But the days passed, and Crispian did not show up. Gradually, Webb grew disturbed, even apprehensive; and soon he was no longer following his habitual route on his way home, but strolling about, trying to find Crispian in one of the places frequented by tourists. However, Crispian had disappeared, and Webb was increasingly impelled to track him down, until, one day, he discovered him, seated on an eroded wall by the harbor.

Webb was struck by the change in appearance; apparently, Crispian had realized the futility of his attempt to appear as just another tourist. Having shed his stiffly padded suit, he now wore corduroy pants of a rusty color, a sailor's striped sweater that left his thin arms bare, and a tattered straw hat, probably acquired at a second-hand store in the native quarter. This time, it was camouflage rather than masquerade; for now he was blending so perfectly with his environment that Webb had almost failed to notice him in the crowd that filled the docks and piers. Sitting immobile, he was a part of the scene and yet not of it. The hidden incavations of his eyes did not reveal whether he was drinking in the kaleidoscopic disorder of wild colors, or studying the sweating, toiling, quarreling, shrieking, and laughing humanity around him.

When two naked children emerged from behind the wall, climbing out of the water, Crispian turned slightly. They tapped him on the shoulders, making him their playmate with instinctive trust. He held their hands, gently and without presumption. He laughed with them as they clutched their noses and jumped back into the oily water below.

"Enjoying your vacation?" Webb said, tipping his new panama hat to the unshaven man in a gesture of inbred rather than specific politeness.

Crispian's gaunt face broke open in a joyous smile. "I was hoping I'd see you again," he exclaimed.

Aware that his past rudeness had not earned him such warm friendship, Webb wondered whether this cordial welcome could be attributed to the loneliness which, as he had often observed, seems to befall Americans in foreign countries, driving them to clutch at each other like survivors in a sea of blank faces.

But Crispian's next words quickly shattered the illusion that his interest and affection were directed to the representative of his homeland, rather than to Webb, the person. "I was just thinking about you," he said with his disarming smile.

"Really?" Webb said, swiftly on guard against another intrusion of his privacy.

"Yes. About your extraordinary self-control. I mean, the way you keep yourself a prisoner."

Webb drew back, almost angrily. Apparently, there was no way of dealing with this man on an impersonal basis. Crispian simply refused to respect the shield of polite formality, behind which civilized people allowed themselves, by tacit agreement, an area of seclusion. Ignoring anything irrelevant, Crispian seemed to insist on brushing aside all ornamental decoy, heading straight to the core of the matter.

"I'm afraid I don't understand you," Webb said coldly.

"You don't?" Crispian's tone expressed surprise as well as genuine concern.

"No," Webb said. "And I'm not inclined to pursue the matter further."

There was a long pause, while Webb tried to recapture his balance. Regretting his sharp rebuff, he groped anxiously to pick up a thread of conversation. "I've been wondering how you were getting along," he said finally, gazing at the children splashing around in the water. "Have you been sight-seeing?"

Crispian nodded, absent-mindedly.

"I suppose it's a fascinating locale for an artist." Webb was warming up to the subject. "Let me show you my favorite spot." He led Crispian past a row of dilapidated warehouses to a narrow pier, where a herd of fishing boats was riding at anchor. The gayly-tinted sails were flaming against the pale evening sky, their fire nourished by the brown bowls of the hulls. Crispian gazed at the splendorous tumult of colors, and said nothing.

"If I could paint," Webb said, carried away, "here's where I'd put up my easel. As a matter of fact, most visiting artists do. They love this romantic corner of the bay." He surveyed the scene with a proprietary interest, permitting himself the satisfaction of local pride. "Isn't it beautiful?"

Crispian nodded. "It's picturesque all right," he said, if not disdainfully, at least indifferently.

Webb turned sharply, as if his good will had been rewarded with a slap in the face. But when he saw Crispian's expression, he realized that no offense had been intended. Crispian's attitude seemed to be that of a man preoccupied with infinitely more important work; of a man who has to forego the pleasure of playing with toys, because he is struggling with enormous tasks.

"If a sight like that does not inspire you," Webb said, "may I ask what sort of subject you enjoy painting?"

Crispian seemed to shrink into himself. "I don't enjoy painting," he said. A faint tremor passed through his frail body like a sudden gust of wind shaking a solitary tree on a mountain top.

"Then why did you choose to become an artist?"

"I didn't choose." His shoulders sank, as if he despaired of explaining.

Webb was gripped by a strange excitement; he sensed that he had unexpectedly broken through the surface and was approaching the region where the key to Crispian's perplexing personality might be found. "I'd like to see some of your work," he said.

Crispian shook his head. "There's nothing I could show you. What's left of my paintings is stored in Detroit." After a pause, he added cryptically: "I travel light. Never take any excess baggage along."

"What about the new work you've done since you came here?"

"I haven't touched a brush."

"You're going to?"

"No."

"Not even sketches?"

"Nothing."

Webb frowned, bewildered. He had taken it for granted that artists came to Puerto Carribas to paint the forlorn, dilapidated beauty of the harbor town. He could not conceive that any real painter could remain unproductive among the unceasing stimuli of these romantic surroundings.

"Any reason?"

"I told you. I needed a rest."

"You've been here two weeks."

Crispian turned away, his eyes scanning the horizon. "The fact is, I've given up painting. For good."

"Why?"

Crispian remained silent. His lips closed tightly; he did not want to talk about it. His hands pushed deep into his pockets, he walked along the pier, ignoring Webb who had fallen in step beside him. When they had reached the outermost plank, Crispian drew back as if he had just realized that one more step would have led him beyond the edge.

For a while he stood irresolutely, swaying with the creaking pier. And suddenly he did talk about it. Haltingly at first, in disconnected sentences; then rapidly, as if his pent-up anxiety found relief in confession; and finally the words came tumbling out, like rocks breaking loose in a partial landslide of the soul.

He could not say how it first happened that he had turned to painting. He had simply obeyed a need like hunger or thirst, which had to be stilled. It was, in the beginning, a joyous experience; a toying with color and form, satisfying the desire for self-expression, common to everybody. But gradually the hunger increased as it was fed, doubling its ravenous appetite. Driven, Crispian learned that the overflow of experiences could be channeled into art; soon it became a necessity to banish the phantoms of his stirred-up imagination into frozen forms. The contest took on an unsuspected urgency; he was swamped by images when his eyes, which he had trained to see, grew increasingly aware of the impressions impinging from all sides of the world around him. Before long, he started to fall behind, and the weight of unabsorbed experiences rested on him as an added burden. Trying to keep up with himself, he withdrew more and more from any distraction; and even so, he was teetering at the brink of exhaustion, until finally he broke down.

As abruptly as he had started, Crispian fell silent; only the shadows nestling in the deep hollows of his cheeks continued to quiver with the turmoil of his alarmed nerves.

It was then that Webb, for the first time, read the full meaning of the deep lines in Crispian's face. In the eyes, too, he detected something that affected him strongly; it was more than torment; it seemed like an intensity too great for the small frame in which it was held.

Webb felt swamped by a helpless compassion; his previous annoyance at Crispian's disregard of polite formalities had evaporated. The man could no more protect himself against his own intensity than others; he was defenseless against the blunt impact of all that was important, unable to resort either to the subterfuge or the evasion of the irrelevant, helplessly condemned to live with greatness.

"Do you really believe," Webb asked at length, "that you can stay away from painting?"

"I have to." Crispian's voice was almost inaudible. "It's my only chance to get well."

"Suppose you learn to control it? It may be easier for you than to give it up altogether."

"I can't. Not enough strength for moderation," Crispian said softly. "It's a sickness with me. A passion that leads to excesses."

"Couldn't you limit your working hours?"

"Probably." A harassed smile appeared on Crispian's lips in response to Webb's naive question. "But that's not the point. It's not the quantity." A haunted expression clouded the smile. "It's where you're heading. I'm afraid of it. You can only go so far, and then you get frightened, and you want to turn back."

"Turn back? To what?"

"Safety." Crispian was gazing at an old fisherman, who climbed from his boat into a dinghy, a basket full of sparkling, writhing fish on his black shoulders. "I just want to be like everybody else. That's my only wish."

There was so desperate a longing in his voice that Webb could not bring himself to point out its obvious futility. For a while, the silence hung between them. "I'm not going to stay here much longer," Crispian said suddenly.

"What happened?" Webb was surprised. "I thought you liked Puerto Carribas."

"I did. Enormously." Crispian's eyes sparkled. "I was completely happy. At first."

"And now?" Webb asked, struggling against an inexplicable anguish.

"It's not as peaceful as I'd imagined the tropics." Crispian gazed from the teeming crowd on the dock to a long line of sweating negroes, filing up the gang plank of a freighter, their muscles bulging under heavy loads of bananas. "Instead of a sleepy port, I found a city, bustling with activity, noisy, restless."

The deep-throated whistle of a steamer came between them, roaring up in the distance, its echoes vibrating past them like a trail of smoke.

"It's, of course, no resort."

"Too civilized," Crispian said, unaware that he was contradicting Webb's meaning. "Perhaps I could find a more primitive place. I've been thinking of going inland."

Webb, wheeling around, saw that Crispian's eyes were searching the glimmering streak of the distant mountain. "I hope you're not intending to head toward the mountains?"

"On the contrary." Crispian smiled. "I want to get away from their sight."

When Webb arrived at home, he found a message from the Bradleys. The restless pair was about to return from an aimless tour of the neighboring countries; unable to sit still, they had chartered a plane, hopping about like a couple of fidgety grasshoppers. And now that the parts for the yacht had arrived, the millionaire shoemaker was rushing back, in one long leap, to supervise the job.

Without enthusiasm, Webb arranged to invite them to a formal dinner party, inwardly fortifying himself against the onslaught of their energy which was as tiring as it was tireless. Later, on his terrace, the coolness of the soothing drink touching his hand, he compared their compulsive need for activity to Crispian's drive. The analogy, though falling short in some respects, was amazingly justified in others; at any rate, it helped him gain a far better grasp of Crispian's conflict than he had expected.

The creative field was alien to Webb; he had never quite understood what motivated a gifted man to forego material rewards for the imponderable joy of self-expression; to give up security for the dubious results of the search for truth; sometimes even to surrender established success and applause for the hardships of yet greater achievements.

But now, as he drew the parallel between Crispian and Bradley, he realized that the painter's demoniac drive was not an isolated phenomenon. He himself had known many businessmen of Bradley's type, whose need for money increased as they grew wealthier. But money, as he had often suspected, was merely their excuse for an otherwise inexplicable fanaticism about work. Some had admitted to him, almost embarrassed, that they were not motivated by greed; to them, their balance sheet was a tangible scoreboard of their efforts, abilities, and accomplishments. Others had conceded that they plunged into work to escape from themselves.

In this important aspect, the nature of the painter's drive differed. In its direction, as Crispian had mentioned. For Crispian was drawn into himself. Like the sorcerer's apprentice, he was struggling with the inner forces he had innocently awakened when he tapped the sources of his talent and imagination.

Satisfied with his analysis, Webb regaled himself with the quiet enjoyment of his drink. But soon, he became disquieted; as a partial answer it was undoubtedly correct; yet, there was more to it; there was something, he dimly felt, that was of great concern to him. His eyes were drawn toward the mountains, and he grew increasingly disturbed by his own response to their alluring glitter. Though he knew himself to be immune to their suggestions, he wondered if he had warned Crispian emphatically enough against leaving the city. At their hasty parting, just before the four o'clock rains which daily drenched the city, Crispian had promised to reconsider. But when Webb had looked back before turning into a sidestreet, he had seen that Crispian's eyes were again fixed on the mountains, watching them while they became obscured by the sheets of rain racing toward the ocean. Remembering Crispian's expression, Webb knew that it would not be long before he would be advised of the painter's departure.

The call came three days later. Crispian's voice sounded gay and unconcerned. He invited Webb for a drink. Webb could not spare the time, because the Bradleys were coming for dinner that evening; but when he heard that Crispian was leaving the next morning, he hurried to the dismal tavern, wrought up, anxious, and determined to seize this last chance to dissuade the painter.

"I don't intend to go very far," Crispian said, when Webb sat down at the bar. He seemed exhilarated by the prospect of the adventurous trip. "Only to Irozco. From what I've heard, it might be just the right place for me. Primitive. Yet, it can't be too wild. I've been told they even have a trading post."

"An impressive name for a shack, that's all. According to my reports, you won't even find a place to stay. The tribe lives in hovels. Aboriginal hunters and fishermen. Unbelievably elementary."

"Good," Crispian nodded. "That's what I want."

"Why? What do you expect to find there?"

"I don't know." Crispian frowned. "Maybe the uncomplicated, child-like existence of the savage." He smiled shyly. "You know, back to nature. Back to the sources of life."

"A romantic illusion. It's as impossible for a civilized person to turn into a primitive as it is for a savage to master the complexities of our high-powered culture."

Crispian nodded, but said nothing.

"There's no going back to childhood," Webb persisted.

"I'm not even tempted. But when you've lost your way, you retrace your steps to beginnings. You look for your roots."

Webb looked away, bewildered. In his simple manner, Crispian had suddenly illuminated for him the recent trends of rootless generations toward folklore, primitive art, history, even archaeology. Apparently, there was an awareness in people that in their unbridled progress they had lost their way.

"Why do you keep warning me against the jungle?" Crispian asked abruptly. "What's it like?"

Webb, seeing his chance to impress on Crispian the folly of going inland, gave him a vivid summary of all the frightening tales he had heard about the vast, dark, uncanny landscape behind the tree border. He doubled his efforts when he sensed that Crispian was as unshakably determined as a man who, unknown to himself, has an appointment with fate.

Crispian absorbed all the information, listening raptly, his eyes fixed on a paper napkin on the bar. Without relaxing his attention, he reached for the pencil the bartender had left behind and started to doodle.

Webb was struck by the nervous, greedy trembling of the hand, moving over the white napkin with the wild exuberance of a prisoner escaping from jail during a lapse of the guard's watchfulness. And indeed Crispian did not seem aware that he was drawing a face. His frequent questions, with which he both interrupted and prodded Webb, revealed that his thoughts were focused on the trip.

Meanwhile, the face took shape on the napkin with increasing rapidity. The acceleration reminded Webb of a reformed alcoholic's mounting abandon after the first few drinks. Crispian's passion was breaking through, a tormenting thirst—not for the drink that stood untouched beside the trembling hand—but for the blank space that could be filled, for the void that craved creation.

Suddenly, Webb broke off in the middle of a sentence. The face was leaping at him in a burst of recognition. His own image. But it was so badly drawn that it seemed more like a caricature than a likeness.

"Are you drawing my portrait?" he asked with angry irony.

Crispian, torn from his thoughts, drew back, gazing at the napkin as if he noticed the sketch for the first time. He dropped the pencil. "You don't see any similarity?" he chuckled.

Webb shook his head. He was shocked to discover that Crispian's passion for painting was not supported by talent. The fumbling attempt to capture his personality had resulted in the very opposite of what Webb knew himself to be. The sketch gave the impression of a dreamer, absurdly romantic; the eyes dilated with unstilled longing, the hair tousled, the sensitive lips parted as if they were on the verge of forming the words of an impassioned prayer.

"It's you all right," Crispian said, watching him with an amused glitter in his eyes.

Webb looked from the drawing to the bar mirror, comparing the sketch with the reality; and he found immediate reassurance in the impeccable image of the distinguished-looking figure flashed back at him. A rather impersonal face, quite lean, almost dry, the perfect mask for the civil servant; fleshless, unemotional lips, gray, steady eyes, a high forehead crowned by silvery hair, its patina adding the dignity derived from long, and therefore successful service.

Relieved, Webb turned back, and saw that in the meantime Crispian had, with impish humor, transformed the sketch into a cartoon. By circling the face and adding a few lines, he had made Webb into a barrage balloon, straining to soar to the heights, but held down by ropes fastened to filing cabinets on the ground.

The addition, incredibly expressive, upset Webb's painfully restored equilibrium. Now that Crispian had provided, in blunt strokes, a key to his concept, the sketch seemed no longer as absurd as before. Webb even had to revise his judgment of Crispian's lack of talent; though still rejecting the interpretation, he could not overlook the masterful assurance of the lines, unquestionably drawn with superb craftsmanship. And the longer Webb looked at it, the more he felt compelled to acknowledge its justification, against his will, overpowered by something that surged up from deep inside of him, clamoring for attention.

Hastily, he reached for his drink, gulping it down to steady his nerves.

"Have I upset you?" Crispian's question betrayed a friendly interest, but no apology.

"It's not a very flattering picture."

"What do you expect from a cartoon? I hoped it would amuse you."

"I don't find it amusing."

"I suppose not," Crispian nodded. "One's personal tragedy never is. In a way, it's fortunate that we don't really understand it—except when it's shown to us in the light of comedy."

Webb pushed his drink aside. This uncanny, and seemingly effortless insight angered him beyond belief. "What makes you think you know so much about me?"

"Do I?"

"Apparently more than I."

"That's quite possible," Crispian said cheerfully, unaware that he was adding fuel to Webb's hostility.

"Don't you think it's rather presumptuous?"

"Not at all. You see, it wasn't difficult for me to understand you. Because we're so very much alike."

Webb stared at him, incredulously.

"I suppose it's not very obvious. But I recognized it right away, the first time I saw you at the consulate. We're of the same mold, like brothers; different sides of the identical coin." He smiled apologetically. "Does it shock you to hear that?"

"Why should it? I'm sure you don't expect me to take you seriously." The notion was indeed too ludicrous. At that moment, Webb saw their eyes meet in the mirror, which confirmed, with glaring clarity, the sharp contrast between the shabby painter and the distinguished government official.

"I apologize," Crispian said, reading Webb's thoughts. "I didn't mean to force myself on you. I imagine it can't be pleasant for you to consider me your brother. So let's just say, I'm a poor and forgotten relative, who suddenly turns up from nowhere." He looked away, keenly aware of Webb's rejection. "I didn't expect to be welcome. I merely wanted to explain why I felt drawn to you. It's not often that one finds a kindred soul."

"I suppose not." Webb had meant to add warmth to his cautiously non-committal statement, but it had remained dry, when actually he was moved. He had felt that the pathetic yearning to be accepted as a friend came from the depths of this man's loneliness. His hopeless search to find family ties could have started in the days of the orphanage; and his shy offer to act the role of a brother might have been made many times before. But the fact that the misguided result sprang from a true need made it no more acceptable to Webb. And yet there remained in his mind the slight apprehension that Crispian, who had surprised him so often, might again turn out to be right.

"You don't have to agree," Crispian smiled. "It doesn't really matter what you think of me. In any event, there's nothing either of us can do to cut the bonds between us."

Webb looked at his watch; he had to hurry home to meet the Bradleys. For a brief moment, he considered inviting Crispian to dinner. No doubt, it would mean a great deal to the painter. But the man's clothes were too shabby. The Bradleys might consider it an insult.

Webb dropped some money on the bar.

"You're leaving?" Crispian asked, looking up.

"I'm late."

A quiet sadness had seeped into Crispian's eyes. And at that moment, Webb was suddenly seized by the irrational conviction that he could save Crispian by inviting him to dinner; that this small gesture of extending the hand of friendship would restrain him from going inland, thus succeeding where all the warnings had failed. But Webb could not say the words. Instead he stuttered: "I'm sorry that I could not change your plans."

"You've done your best," Crispian smiled. "In fact, you couldn't have argued so well if you hadn't felt the need to beat down your own wish to come along."

Webb looked up, startled, searching Crispian's face to determine if he was serious. "I assure you," he chuckled, "nothing could be further from my mind."

Crispian's solemn expression was not affected by Webb's smile. "If I don't see you again," he said quietly, "let me give you this as a parting gift." He handed Webb the sketch on the crumpled napkin.

Webb was about to push it into his pocket, when he saw that Crispian, with a few erasures, had cut the ropes holding down the barrage balloon. Webb shrank back; his hands trembled.

"I wish I could give you more," Crispian said, his eyes resting on Webb with a warm, luminous glow.

These were the last words Webb ever heard from Crispian.

CHAPTER II

THE BURRO slipped. Desperately struggling to gain a foothold on the wet ground, the frantic animal leaped forward, broke to its knees and threw Webb into the mud. For a moment, he lay there panting; the last threads of his will power snapped; he slumped back, sprawling in the oozing slush, utterly defeated.

But, at that second, the Padre's burro came splashing to his side, showering his face with slimy mud; a wild grip sent a searing pain through his arm; he felt himself dragged over the ground, and dropped. Scrambling to his feet, he saw the Padre gazing at the swaying head of a snake, poised to strike over the imprint of Webb's body.

"She is angry, senor," the Padre whispered, "because she is frightened. If we don't move, she will go away."

Slowly, the fer-de-lance slithered back, disappearing in the undergrowth; but the deathly pallor did not leave Webb's distorted face. The damp earth was dripping from his hair, and when he saw the soiled white of his suit, he surrendered to the sobs that shook his shivering body.

The Padre avoided looking at him, discreetly leaving him to himself in this moment of abject panic. "You will feel stronger than before," he said, as if he knew from experience that a breakdown of this kind was necessary to sift the fear from a man's courage.

He led back the second burro and helped Webb into the saddle. "We go not far and then we rest," he said. "Beyond the pass there is a river."

As Webb followed him up the slope, he sensed that the Padre was right; he felt a new confidence rising from the depth of his being like the mist steaming from the drenched ground. The four o'clock rains had passed over them in a short, violent burst; and when Webb reached the rim of the slope, he saw the clouds

41

racing toward the ocean, trailing sheets of rain behind which the jungle was steaming up like smoking fire.

Far away, beyond the tightly woven tree carpet, was the pale white of the ocean, was Puerto Carribas, and the terrace of his villa from which he used to gaze at the mountains. Step by step, as the burro traversed the pass, the landscape sank down, mile after mile of the plains swallowed up by inches of the rising crest; and soon there was nothing but the sharp line of the hill against the sky.

A cool breeze was pressing against his wet shirt as they descended into the narrow valley, covered by low trees that rounded its contours like moss. When they had reached the shallow, clear river winding its way through the center, the Padre led the two burros to a shady spot with tall, rich grass. Dropping to the ground, Webb watched him enviously; the Priest showed no signs of fatigue, while Webb's limbs were aching; his cramped tendons felt like ropes coiled over contracted muscles.

"When you have eaten," Padre Paolo said, returning with a loaf of the black bread baked by the mountain Indians at monthly intervals, "you will not tire so quickly." He broke the bread in half, with the solemn reverence of the poor, and also divided a flat oval of gray, hard cheese.

When they had eaten, the Padre gazed at the descending sun, as if he were troubled by the need to reach Irozco before nightfall. Yet, he made no preparations to leave. A few times, he seemed about to say something, growing increasingly tense with each false start. He shifted repeatedly from one side to the other, evading Webb's glance, until finally he overcame, almost vehemently, his resistance. "Perhaps, senor, I should have told you that I can be of some assistance to you." He paused. "I knew Senor Crispian."

Webb sat up, startled. He had wondered how Padre Paolo could have failed to meet Crispian on his travels. Now he had the answer; and at the same time he understood the Priest's strange reluctance to reveal that he knew the painter; he too had been deeply disturbed by his contact with Crispian.

"Where did you meet him?" Webb asked tensely, almost hungrily, anxious to fit additional pieces of information into the jigsaw puzzle of his search.

The Padre gazed at a spot behind Webb. "The first time—right here."

Webb did not turn. He felt as if Crispian had joined them, forging an unexpected bond between his two friends, a link that would grow more intimate as they exchanged their knowledge.

"He was standing there," the Padre said, "with a basket of clay he had gathered at the foot of the hill to your right. He told me he was using the clay for the pottery he helped to make at the village. Since money was useless to the hunters of Irozco, it was the only way he could pay them for their hospitality. He was most grateful to his Indian friends. And also to me, when I offered to let him ride part of the way on my burro. But he insisted on walking beside me; he was a much humble man."

"And he was quite free with his conversation?" Webb said with spontaneous sympathy, when he saw that the memory had etched a deep bewilderment into the Padre's bronze features.

"More so than I," the Priest said. "I was much confused. Perhaps, because of all I had heard about him."

"Before you met him?"

"Long before. I was told of his arrival the very first day after he crossed the jungle border. Do not ask how news travels in this wilderness. All at once, everywhere, it springs into existence. The forests whisper: a stranger is among us. Even your approach, senor, by now is known in Irozco."

"And what did you hear about him?"

"It was most remarkable, senor. First I was told: white, crazy man lost in jungle. A few days later: a friend has come to live with us. I was amazed. Never before had I heard the Indian word for friend used in connection with a white man."

Webb nodded; it did not astonish him. "Did they wonder what he was doing among them?"

The Padre gazed at the glittering river, his eyes following the soft ripples gliding past them. "They had a surprising answer. I'm sure it must have been as perplexing to Crispian as it was to me. But to them it was not; it was as natural as if he had come to paint their village."

"What? What was their answer?"

"White man has come to find God." Noticing Webb's startled reaction, the Padre smiled. "You must understand, senor, that they saw nothing unusual in that. They thought it quite possible that God might be hiding under some shadowy tree of their wide jungle."

Webb shook his head. "But how could they arrive at such an absurd interpretation? I'm sure Crispian did not mislead them."

"He did not tell them, for he did not know himself. In their simple manner, they discovered the truth by themselves."

"The truth?" Webb stared at him, incredulously.

"Indeed, senor, the truth." When he saw Webb's utter disbelief, he smiled. "Unless you have a better answer?"

"I have his own. He wanted a rest. And I'm convinced he meant it."

"Quite so, senor. But was it fatigue that troubled him, or was it unrest? There is a distinction, senor. For to be restless is not the same as being tired." He paused. "Though it is a common confusion with you Americans. Exhausting yourselves in your noisy cities, you think you need rest, when actually you seek peace."

On a first impulse Webb wanted to deny the Priest's conclusion. But then he thought of the Bradleys; and when he reviewed in his mind the many American tourists who had arrived in the tropics with the romantic desire to shake off, at least temporarily, the complexities, the burdens, and responsibilities, the haste and relentless exhaustion of their driving industrial civilization, he began to agree with the mountain priest. He had often wondered what motivated these level-headed businessmen, these staid and civic-minded lawyers, these responsible manufacturers and bankers to turn themselves into quixotic travellers, impelled by unknown and undefinable yearnings.

"Did Crispian tell you the cause of his unrest?" Webb asked, wondering if the painter had mentioned to Padre Paolo his need to escape from his work.

"He did not have to. For I knew. There was no other cause than that which is common to us all. Only in him it was stronger. Because he had no defenses."

"Defenses? Against what?"

"You will forgive me, senor," the Padre said, "if I speak of that part in all men which is entrusted to me, the Priest. Just as the other half is in your charge, as the Consul who represents government and law."

"Are you referring to our immortal soul?" the Consul asked with involuntary irony.

"No, senor. I will not demand of you belief which you can oppose by doubt. I will speak of that which can be pushed from our minds, but cannot be denied. The mystery of our role on earth. The great questions at the beginning and at the end of our existence. Where did we come from? Where do we go? And in between: why are we here? What must we do? What is the meaning and the purpose? Questions which cannot be answered with that absolute proof which has become so dear to our hearts. Therefore, we push them aside and proceed to live as if they did not surround us on all sides like the very air we breathe." For a while, he sat in the quiet repose of meditation. "As if, senor. As if the basic mystery did not exist. For man must act and knows not what to do. Imagine a man running and he knows not why or where to. And all the while he thinks, but the answers that would guide him are withheld. And he must make decisions; he must choose directions at the many crossroads of his life, and he knows not his goal." He turned to Webb. "I ask you, senor, can such a man find peace?"

A flock of birds was passing over the river, raucously chattering among themselves.

"He cannot," the mountain priest continued. "He tries, he seeks; he fails and tries again. He invents answers, and doubts them. He ignores the questions and is disturbed. He proclaims his running a natural law, and finds that he has invented a word, no more. So then, resigning himself, he creates a limited world within the other, for he must get on with the business of living. He calls it the realistic world, when actually it is not. And everywhere he runs against the borders, for they are not far away, all around him. He pretends not to see them, and yet he does." The Padre smiled. "Even you, senor, who are in charge of that limited world, must be perplexed at times. When you file away the documents that state the plans, the motives, and the reasons of the busy people who pass through your consulate, you must have wondered. Have you not?"

Webb did not answer. He was lying on his back, his glance fixed on the white patches of sky breaking through the tree tops. He experienced the same quiet uneasiness he had felt when gazing at the distant mountains; and now he knew what they had meant to him.

"Poor Senor Crispian," the Padre said after a while, "was too honest with himself. He could not learn to pretend, and could not live as if."

Webb shifted uncomfortably. He was strangely reluctant to accept the Padre's interpretation, which did not coincide with his own impressions of the artist. "Did he tell you that?" he asked, propping himself on his elbow.

"No, senor. He didn't have to. I could see his God was very strong in him."

"He might have denied it."

"Possibly. There are many who do. But to deny," the Padre continued, unshaken, "means as little as to proclaim one's faith. Vanities both, no more. For what exists can neither be banished nor flattered by our opinion. The truth is, senor, one way or another we all have to live with our God. Or, if you prefer, with the mystery of our life. How? It is up to each of us. We may choose to evade, to rebel, to ridicule, to hate, to believe. Only one thing is impossible, the very thing most people try—to ignore."

The sun had descended behind the crest. Feeling a sudden chill, Webb got up, rubbing his stiff arms. "When we set out on our journey, Padre, you asked what drew me to follow Crispian."

The Priest, who had started toward the burros, turned back, gazing at him, uncertainly.

"Why did you ask, Padre," Webb said, holding his glance, "when you knew the answer. The same reason that made you join me. You, too, want to know where Crispian went. In fact, I suspect it is as important to you as it is to me."

Without looking back, Webb crossed to the river bank.

When he bent over the water to wash his face, he recoiled, jolted by the shock of a frightening recognition. The image reflected in the water was no longer the familiar picture he had of himself, not the respectable mask of the well-groomed official. The unshaven face, the tousled hair, the haggard eyes had taken on an unmistakable similarity to Crispian's sketch.

At the approach to Irozco, the jungle suddenly flared up in a burst of flowers. A creeping vine, which Webb had not observed before, hung its luminous ochre blossoms like lanterns over the dark green of the trees. As they rode through the rapidly gathering dusk, the vines behind the blossoms, almost invisible in their ghostly pallor, brushed against their faces, curling at once to entwine and embrace them. And it was not until Irozco came in sight that the flamboyant net, which both ornamented and strangled the trees, spread open, surrounding the dismal arena of the village clearing with deceptively quiet beauty.

The Indians, as the Padre had predicted, had been informed of their approach. But they gave no outward sign of recognition, watching them with stoic indifference as they rode through the village. Only gradually did the scattered inhabitants permit themselves to show their curiosity. By the time the travelers had stopped before the chieftain's hut, they were encircled by ragged children, gazing at them with wide, earnest eyes. And from all sides, small groups were approaching, young men in the vanguard, who took charge of the burros when Webb followed Padre Paolo into the hut.

The chief, flanked by his council of wise men, had not only expected them, but, inexplicably, he also appeared to be aware of the fact that Webb had come to make inquiries about their friend "Little Beard," the name they had given to Crispian, because he had ceased to shave while living among them.

The Padre, acting as translator, conveyed to Webb the chief's greeting. Any friend of Crispian's would have been received with open arms; but Webb was even more welcome, because the Indians believed him to be the painter's brother.

"Tell them I'm his consul," Webb said hastily. Noticing the Padre's astonished glance, he added in some confusion: "At any rate, you can explain that I'm not his brother."

The Padre translated, but the chief seemed to ignore the correction. With a gesture of simple dignity, he invited Webb to squat in their circle and share their meal of braised meat.

While they were eating, Webb grew envious of the Priest who was able to communicate with the Indians in their language; he felt as if he were not only excluded, but might be missing out on some vital bit of information, despite Padre Paolo's detailed summaries. As far as could be determined, Crispian had adapted himself perfectly to the primitive existence in the village. Apparently, he was so content and happy that he had intended to remain in Irozco for the rest of his years, and his friends had built him his own hut, for which he rewarded them by making pottery of a more practical and handsome design than had ever been known in the village.

Proving it, the chief pointed at the bowl in Webb's hand, a beautifully rounded form, ornamented with a design of striking simplicity. When Webb learned that it was shaped by Crispian's hands, he drew back, chilled by an eerie sensation; and gradually he found himself studying the decorative lines as if it were possible to read their hieroglyphical language.

The chief noticed his interest and clapped his hands; soon an old woman brought in a strangely shaped jug, its neck elongated in a curve of incredible elegance, but so narrow as to become useless. The chief explained that toward the end of his stay Crispian had come to ignore the practical purpose of the things he shaped. Soon they were no longer objects of utility, but creations of independent beauty. The villagers had failed to understand what he was doing. Ascribing some unknown magic to the unfamiliar shapes, they had preserved them in Crispian's hut as objects to be venerated rather than used.

Webb, of course, guessed what had happened. The handicraft, starting so innocently, had become imbued by the creative passion, sweeping Crispian along until the hands that were forbidden to paint were kneading and shaping and molding the clay into exquisite forms, irrespective of their intended purpose. Webb also concluded that Crispian's intense preoccupation with pottery must have stopped abruptly.

The Padre confirmed his assumption. "The chief says that Crispian, shortly before he went away, began helping them weave their mats. When they visited him, they found that he had destroyed his pottery tools."

"Do they know why he left?"

The Padre seemed to freeze up. Stricken by a strange helplessness, he said: "I doubt it."

"Have you asked them?"

The Padre shook his head. Webb had to prod him twice, before the Priest questioned the chief. After a few brief exchanges, Padre Paolo reported the negative result. "It seems—one morning he had suddenly disappeared." The Padre hesitated. "The chief used the word 'fled' or 'escaped.'"

"Do they know where he went?"

"No. As a matter of fact, I think by now they have told you all they know."

The Padre was right; no further information could be obtained. At the end of the meal, the Indians led Webb to Crispian's hut, which was to be his shelter for the night. The Padre excused himself; the sick of the village had been waiting to be examined; though it was late, he could not disappoint them.

Exhausted, Webb dropped on the straw; but the stifling heat did not permit him to fall asleep. He listened to the haunting chants of the young Indians, gathered at the river banks both to welcome and to pacify the full moon. Before long, the weird shadows of Crispian's elongated, strangely shaped jugs, jars, vases, pots, and bowls, surrounding Webb on all sides, were beginning to sway in the sing-song rhythm, dancing within their frozen forms, as if at last they had found their liberation which Crispian, their creator, had refused them. And indeed Webb was beginning to see figures and faces within the rounded distortions of the clay, outlines as dimly discernible as prisoners in the shadows of tightly barred windows. One shape in particular tormented him with its painful familiarity, until he recognized, with a sudden shock, the similarity to Bradley, a tragically unhappy face barely visible, suppressed, almost submerged in the coarse grain of a pot's massive belly.

Almost panicky, Webb scrambled to his feet. Unable to determine whether his visions were real or mere tricks of his stirred-up imagination, he sought refuge in the cooler air outside.

The peaceful glimmer of the tropical night calmed his nerves, but did not relinquish the magic of its spell. Gazing at the deserted village, Webb wondered how the same sight might have appeared to Crispian. On the surface, the reality matched Webb's dismal expectations: a desolate, sordid scattering of primitive huts, squatting clumsily in the soft moonlight that poured on the gutted, encrusted mud of the clearing. Pungent smells clashed with the magnificent, intoxicating odor of the vine blossoms glowing in the dark folds of the jungle; silence embraced by myriad noises; peace surrounded by dangers. There were so many contrasts that Webb could not organize them into a dominant impression; and his question, what Crispian had found in going back to the sources of life, remained unanswered.

At that moment, he heard footsteps. The lonely figure of the Padre was crossing the square, heading toward the hut that had been assigned to him for the night. Apparently, he had just left his last patient, and he looked so weary that Webb did not hail him, letting him seek his well-earned rest.

There was something about the Padre's remarkable personality that disturbed Webb; in fact, the strange mountain priest had grown more puzzling to Webb in the course of their journey. Padre Paolo's fame had preceded their meeting; for a long time, reports of his incredible accomplishments had seeped down across the jungle, reaching not only the consulate, but eventually even the United States. Two years ago, a visiting reporter from New York had written an article, describing the many duties which the Padre had taken upon himself, acting as teacher, advisor, judge, even messenger; and above all, as the only physician in the vast territory. The article must have been widely syndicated, because donations and pharmaceutical supplies came pouring in from all parts of the U.S. For a while, Webb was kept busy forwarding packages to the Padre. Then the torrent slowed down to a trickle, finally ceasing altogether, and the forgotten Padre continued his work unaided as before.

In those days, Webb had formed a picture of a priest so deeply devoted to his deserted parishioners that he had shouldered his heavy burdens with a calm serenity, attainable only by a man who had dedicated his soul to God and his life to charity. But now, after meeting the Padre, Webb had to reverse this picture. Padre Paolo was indeed exhausting himself in his holy mission; but he was a man torn by a deep conflict.

At that moment, the Padre stepped outside; perhaps he too had found the heat in the hut too oppressive. For a while he stood irresolutely in the pale light of the moon. Then he started to cross the square, approaching Webb's hut.

When he discovered the Consul in the shadows of the entrance, the Padre stopped, surprised to find him outside. "I was coming to wake you, senor." His hands clenched as he gathered his courage. "There is something I have to tell you. Something I should have told you before, but it is a heavy thing on my heart."

He broke off, and remained silent; and Webb grew apprehensive that the Padre might not continue unless assisted. "It is about Crispian?" he said gently.

Padre Paolo nodded. "I did not tell you all. I did not tell you that I met him a second time. Here in Irozco." His breath came in short gasps. "Also I know why he left. Perhaps, senor, it was my fault. For I was too troubled to extend the hand that could have held him back."

Webb looked away, avoiding the Padre's eyes, as if he were afraid to see in them the mirrored image of his own guilt.

Having disposed of his self-accusation at the outset, the Padre found the rest easier. He spoke slowly, dredging up the events of the past from the depths of his memory. But so vivid were the images he evoked that Webb not only visualized the scenes, but became part of them. Indeed, as he looked at the deserted square, it seemed that the ghostly population of the Priest's tale materialized before his eyes; he saw the Indians crowd around the fire; he saw Crispian, waiting desperately for Padre Paolo, who had been called back from a village upstream. A roar of welcome greeted the Padre, as he pushed through the circle of wailing women, approaching the ten year old boy, whom Crispian was holding in his arms.

The boy was convulsed by the poison of a deadly snake. And when the Padre examined the small, shivering body, he knew that his expert incisions would be as futile as the magic chants of the Indians, rising to the dark sky in a plaintive clamor.

The scene, for some reason, etched itself into Webb's mind with brilliant clarity. The smoke, spiraling up, losing itself in the insatiable void of the black night, carrying with it the magic sing-song of the old men and the wailing cries of the women; the arena of the crowded village clearing, its glow barely holding its own against the dark forests pressing in from all sides; the Padre cutting into the trembling flesh of the boy, locked in a hopeless struggle with death, not only one being's death, but with death itself, the death that had sprung from the folds of the night, towering over the village, so vast and hard, inexorably squeezing the small life from the child's wilting body with an iron grip.

And in the center—Crispian, the most helpless of all, for he had neither magic incantations nor medicine to contribute. Only his love and his rebellion and his compassion. Long after the

Padre had ceased his efforts, Crispian kept the child in his arms; and even after the Priest had pronounced the boy dead, Crispian would not surrender him, so that finally they had to wrest the cold, lifeless body from his embrace.

"Senor, I cannot describe his expression," the Padre said. "It is something I will never forget. In his face was the terror of one who had been gathering flowers in a paradise, singing and dancing; and suddenly he stares into the glittering eyes of a tiger."

"Was he so devoted to the child?"

"The boy was his friend. I had seen them together when they were gathering clay. But that was not the cause of his terror."

"What was?"

"He had seen death. Not the concealed death you know in your cities. Death as it can only be seen in the jungle." His voice trailed off, and Webb, feeling a chill on his damp skin, waited in the silence, vainly groping for a hold. The night had lost its stillness; something was lurking in the shadows, small pinpoints of danger that could swirl up into gigantic clouds.

"He had come here," the Padre continued, "to seek refuge in the primitive existence of the jungle. He did not know what he would find at the sources of life. For in your cities, the secret of life's innermost nature is hidden from sight. You are so busy earning a living, trying to enjoy living, learning and postponing and longing or complaining about living that you know all but life itself; you cannot see beyond the thickets of your many doings." He looked down, groping for words. "But when you come here, like Crispian, to embrace life in its true being, you find that you clutch death in your arms. As we, who are close to the jungle, could have told him—life in its nakedness is hounded by fear; for at its core—is death."

Wrought up, the Padre broke off, listening to the plaintive song wafted up from the river bank in a surge of rising urgency. Webb waited for the Priest to continue; so far Padre Paolo had not mentioned anything about his personal involvement in Crispian's flight from Irozco. But the Padre did not add anything; instead, he pointed toward the river: "You may want to watch their ritual."

And without awaiting confirmation, he led the way down. There was no distinct path; the entire tree-covered slope had been cleared of brush. Suddenly, Webb's foot got caught in the hollow bark of a fallen tree. A cloud of dust rose up as the dead trunk collapsed, exposing swarming hordes of pale termites, their subterranean activity arrested in a flash of frozen time. The pallid sight, terrifying enough in itself, lashed Webb with its sudden resemblance to the Padre's description of death in the jungle; he leaped up and rushed after the receding silhouette of the Priest.

At the river, the yellow moon, incredibly near, almost searing the tree tops on the opposite shore, had divided itself on the rippled surface of the stream into thousands of small globes, which rolled with the waves, rocking back and forth in the bowls until the ball was passed over the crest to the next hollow, or dissipated in a dying oscillation of flaming gold. As far down as Webb could see, nothing remained still; all parts of the landscape seemed to have joined in a dance as ecstatic as that of the Indians, swaying below them in two concentric rings. At one moment, when the rings broke open, Webb saw in their focal point what appeared to be a little dog, strapped to a plank.

"A pagan sacrifice," the Padre muttered bitterly. "I have not been able to stamp it out." He closed his eyes, trying to repress the resurgence of a terrifying memory. "Soon they will surrender the animal to the river." Again he paused. "Like they did that night with the dead child."

The Padre's terror communicated itself to Webb, as he visualized the body of the boy strapped to a wooden board.

"They do not bury their dead, nor do they burn them," the Padre said, his eyes fixed on the distant wedge where the river disappeared into the night. "They let the waters float them away."

"Was Crispian here?"

The Padre nodded. "He had followed us at a distance. But then he could not let it happen. He was a man insane. They had to hold him; he lashed out at his friends; he fought them, as if they were killers, when in truth his anger was directed against God."

At that moment, the dancing rings of Indians splintered into the separate entities that had composed them; and the fragments swarmed into the river, where they froze into immobility, half-submerged, while the strapped animal, pushed into midstream, began its awesome journey into the vast hunger of the night's emptiness.

"Imagine, senor," the Padre said hoarsely, "a child's small, soft face, very still and white, gliding past you on the river, its broken eyes turned upward, not so much frightened as bewildered; its little body strapped to the wood; and the power of the leather, and the strength of the river, and all the forces of nature combining and working to carry it to destruction. Why? A boy ten years old. A boy who wanted to play some more with Crispian, who had a right to breathe and play and sing, for he had done no harm. So you may ask 'why?' Where is God?" He was breathing in stifled gasps. "And here was poor senor Crispian, rebelling like Job, and I, standing at his side, I failed him."

At that moment, the little animal, squealing and whimpering, was floating past them. Struggling to free itself, it overturned the plank, but came up again, steadily moving downstream. The Padre did not look at it; his eyes were fixed on the distant wedge where the waters streamed into the void. And it seemed to Webb, in that instant, that the flickering light of the torches was illuminating the whole tragedy of this Priest, who was locked in a hopeless struggle with God; for the rebellion he had attributed to Crispian was his own.

His anguish had at last exposed the cause of his restless exertions. A promethean defender of Man against divine injustice, he aided the sick and the stricken and the poor, protecting them, alleviating their pain, pleading their case before the God he loved with all his heart, the God who was so unquestionable a reality to him that he could not even seek refuge from his tormenting questions in the drastic solution of disbelief.

"I knew, senor, that Crispian was standing behind me," the Padre said. "I knew there was time until the child disappeared in the night to say the words a man has a right to expect from his priest at a time like that. I should have said: 'God has taken this child unto Himself.' For truly I believed He had. And then I should have added: 'God is just.' But I could not. I said nothing." He paused, until suddenly his voice surged from his strangled chest: "For I know not God. I love Him, and know Him not."

PART TWO

SANTA ROSA

CHAPTER III

SHORTLY after dawn Webb and the Padre resumed their journey. While they traversed the valley, a gray mist was rising from the ground, gradually thinning out as they ascended the steadily mounting slopes. And, by the time they had emerged from the jungle, the white heat of the sun was modulating the landscape with increasing intensity.

Neither of the two men referred to the events of the night, shyly avoiding to touch on the secrets of their souls which had been exposed in the turbulence of the Witches Sabbath; the ghosts, which had been exhumed from their graves, had wilted in the light of day and had been re-buried, though not in their former separate tombs, but in the shared sepulchre of mutual insight.

Since it had proven impossible to follow the painter's trail from Irozco, Webb had decided to head straight toward Santa Rosa. As far as could be determined, Crispian had disappeared in the jungle, crossing, and possibly criss-crossing the wilderness without any other aim than to escape, and not to stand still. He had certainly not remained anywhere for any length of time, or else word would have reached the Padre. And yet, Webb conjectured, the fugitive must have suddenly come into clearings from which he could see the mountains; and though he might have plunged back into the protective shelter of the entangled trees, the fear of the mountains' vicinity must have followed him.

For the mountains were everywhere. All day long, Webb and the Padre traveled in full view of the endlessly spreading range, which stretched its arms from horizon to horizon. The bluish haze, which Webb had contemplated so often from the roof of his villa, had at last descended from the sky, revealing its roots in the earth. Slowly crystallizing into tangible form, growing firmer, heavier with every weary hour, its contours became more distinct as stronger colors poured into the molds, painting plastic forms into the flat silhouettes. And gradually, in the course of the trav-

57

elers' approach, the mass splintered into individual peaks, crests and valleys; yet, even these tangible delineations did not retain their final shape as mountain would push in front of mountain, or a jutting promontory would recede, revealing unexpectedly a peak rearing behind it.

There was indeed no stillness in this living mass, but a gradual unfolding as new perspectives were opened and others concealed. But, nevertheless, in all this unceasing shaping and kneading of the mass, there was no uniformity. At first imperceptibly, and then more and more distinctly, one towering summit began to loom above the others, reaching out from behind them; and unlike its predecessors it did not surrender its prominence. In fact, it grew, the closer they came, inexorably rising above the rest, drawing domination toward itself, until all the other peaks were relegated to the subservience of foothills, streaming together to raise the giant on their flattened, straining shoulders.

And then, suddenly, as the Padre led the way into the last gorge before Santa Rosa, the titan had disappeared; and even after they emerged on the high plateau, it remained concealed from their view, hidden in a side valley, behind slanted hills which it had gathered about itself like the folds of a gigantic cloak.

The trail crossed the plateau, rising like a curved cable to the village cluster, which was precariously perched on the slopes cascading down from a craggy crest. It was truly, as the Padre had described it, a fragile ornament hanging high on the breast of the mountains. Its houses and huts were scattered like pebbles strewn by a colossal hand in one careless sweep; and it seemed that they had rolled down until they had found a hold, some on the upper meadows, more in the triangular kettle, with the thickest conglomeration coming to rest at the bottom of the hollow, except for the few that had spilled over the rim.

And above it, slightly to the right, Webb saw Barrie's mine, a pale wound torn into the flesh of the mountain, touched by the red glow of the descending sun which trickled from its jagged edges like blood.

It all looked strangely like a stage setting, as many mountain villages do; and Webb felt like entering a theatre where the curtain had not been lowered, so that the scenery remained offered to public view, stimulating the curiosity of the onlooker, without revealing the content of the drama and the conflict of its absent characters.

For there was no doubt in Webb's mind that the crisis of Crispian's odyssey had been enacted within this mountain kettle, which rose on all sides to prevent escape. The very fact that Crispian had dared to approach it proved that finally he had been stopped in his tracks, an exhausted quarry realizing the futility, or perhaps the impossibility of further flight. Turning, he had decided to meet the challenge; and when he approached Santa Rosa, it was not to surrender but to attack. His arrival in the mountain kettle was a gesture of ultimate, impassioned, and perhaps desperate defiance.

Webb realized well enough how difficult it would be to chart the course of Crispian's contest with the intangible influences of the mountains; it might be impossible to reconstruct all the erratic moves of a man fighting shadows. But there was one concrete piece of evidence which would help him in his search, a vital fact which marked the breaking point of Crispian's resistance. Suddenly, one day, an urgent request for paints and canvas had arrived at the consulate. And before Webb had managed to obtain the specified supplies, impatient inquiries, protesting the delay, came pouring down from Santa Rosa, unreasonably frantic, as if Crispian, once he had made his decision, could not afford to lose another day. After the supplies had been dispatched, there was silence. When Webb slipped a casual inquiry into an official letter to Hal Barrie, it was ignored. And an indirect message to Mona, Hal Barrie's daughter, produced nothing but a vague and unsatisfactory answer.

The two travelers found the engineer in the mine's administration barracks, which squatted above the town like an angry fortress. Their arrival added to the general confusion, in the center of which Barrie was shouting orders. A dynamite charge, badly calculated, had collapsed a shaft, wounding two of the Indian laborers. Though their lacerations were not too serious, Padre Paolo was welcomed as a savior by their two sobbing wives; clinging to his arms, they led him toward the boiling clouds of grimy smoke still lingering over the mine's entrance.

After the crowd had rushed from the office, Barrie shut the

door, apologizing for the turmoil. Though he made an attempt to be friendly, Webb sensed that the tall, sturdy, square-shouldered engineer was even more upset by the consul's unexpected arrival than by the accident. Listening grimly to Webb's carefully stated reasons for his inquiry, Barrie's weather-beaten, granite face remained unresponsive.

"You could have saved yourself the trouble," he said in the end. "If there had been any facts for an inquiry, I would have reported them."

"I'm sure. Nevertheless, you may have overlooked something."

"Maybe. But it wouldn't matter. Not a bit. If I had to hold an inquest, I'd write at the finish: good riddance. That's all. As simple as that." His wiry crop of iron-gray hair, cut close to the angular skull, bristled at Crispian's memory. "He was the kind of fellow who's no use to anybody. No use at all. A troublemaker."

"Suppose you just tell me what happened."

"There's nothing to tell," Barrie said stubbornly. Webb could not quite determine whether the engineer was merely adamant or so deeply confused that he could not honestly convey in what way the painter had provoked him. Yet his anger was no less fierce because it was vague.

Swatting at a fly that had landed on a chart of the mine shafts, Barrie barked: "He didn't do any real harm—if that's what you mean. Just a nuisance. One day when I looked out the window—there he stood, all of a sudden. With that funny little beard the Indians had told me about. After a while he came in and started to ask me a lot of questions. Never did find out what he wanted. In the midst of our talk, he left. Just like that. Didn't show up anymore either. Until I called him in."

"Why?"

"Can't have a white man associate with the Indians. Not up here. Or they'd soon lose all respect. Especially a funny-looking white man. You know, disorderly, like all those painter fellows. With his beard and all. Made him shave it off. But I doubt that it did any good. There was just no authority in him. Not the type of man those savages could look up to."

"Nevertheless, they loved him?" Webb interjected, pointedly.

Barrie hit at a fly. "I will admit, he had a way with them. Maybe because he didn't keep his proper distance. Even worked with them. You know, went out to their fields, like a common laborer, toiling with them. That's when I sent for him. Told him I wouldn't tolerate it. But on that one thing he got stubborn. Couldn't shake him, even when I lost my temper and started to shout. He said he had to exhaust himself. It was necessary. Because it kept him from thinking; if he was all tired out, he could sleep nights."

Webb looked out the window, remembering a period in his youth when he, too, had escaped into exhausting work. Trying to endure the tragedy of his wife's death, he had anesthetized by fatigue every fibre of his being which was capable of feeling pain.

"And suddenly that Crispian fellow stopped," Barrie growled, shuffling the papers on his desk, then locking them up in the top drawer, as importantly as if they were secret documents containing the strategy of his future attacks on the mountain. "Never explained why he got tired of working. At first, I figured his true nature had come out. A loafer—that's how I'd sized him up right away. The kind who never does a decent day's work. But maybe I was wrong after all." He shook his head, frowning with that puzzled expression which, as Webb had observed, would incongrously appear at his most active moments.

"He wasn't sitting still, either," Barrie went on. "They told me he was climbing all over the hills. One day, I saw him myself. Way up high. He was walking fast, not like somebody who enjoyed it; but as if he had to get somewhere. Though maybe he was just trying to tire himself out. Because some days, when he came here, he looked all worn out. Or he'd show up at the house. Just to sit around. Didn't want to bother anybody, just wanted to be there, as if he needed the company, even when nobody was paying any attention to him."

Barrie shook his head, still perplexed. "Then again he'd follow me up to the mine, like a dog that you couldn't chase away. Or he'd be waiting for me here, sitting on the doorsteps, like this office were a village store where people could congregate for a round of small talk. Never said anything much, except once, when he let loose and started to rant about things he didn't understand at all, rambling on and on, until I shut him up."

"What did he say?" Webb asked, suddenly alerted.

"I'd just got a circular from my home office in Baltimore. Some tariff restrictions those bureaucrats in Washington had thought up. I may have used one or two rough expressions. I guess that's what set him off. Though he didn't say a single thing that was to the point. Just rambled on about our country. How much good will there was in its people. How idealistic they really are—you know, that kind of talk, as if nobody had ever heard about dog eat dog, or chasing a dollar, or getting ahead of the next fellow. He got quite angry when I told him. He said, I misunderstood. There wasn't one of us who could ever do enough for the great dream that was alive in our land. No matter how much anybody did, he'd still fall short of the love that vast, good earth had given to us." He turned to Webb. "To be perfectly honest, I didn't like that kind of talk. I mean, not from him, anyway. Not from the kind of a fellow who had never done anything for his country, except maybe live on relief, or what-have-you. I told him that, too, and he didn't argue with it. He couldn't. Just sat there, kind of guilty-like."

A deep anger rose in Webb; at that moment, he actually hated Barrie for his brutal lack of insight.

"I sure had him there," Barrie chuckled, unaware of Webb's reaction. "He even admitted that I was right. Though he protested he had tried. In his way. But he wasn't sure if he had done enough. He'd have to do something more to repay for all the good he had received."

"Did he say what he would do?" Webb asked, swiftly connecting the fragmentary sentence with Crispian's sudden request for paints and canvas.

"No," Barrie chortled. "It was just talk. After all, what could he do? What could a guy like that accomplish that would be of use to anybody?"

The question still hung in the air, when Barrie was called outside by his foreman. Through the open window, Webb heard him bark orders at the man, who listened as silently as if he were accustomed to being intimidated. Barrie, apparently not dismayed by his miscalculated dynamite charge, which he considered no more than a minor defeat in his battle against the mountain, gave instructions for a new attack. At first, the commands sounded reasonable enough to Webb; the details were realistically thought out. But there was a jarring note somewhere, perhaps in Barrie's sense of proportions, which was bewildering to Webb.

Until now, he had known Barrie only through their correspondence. And from the precise reports, often bolstered by graphs and charts, Webb had formed a picture of a hard-headed realist, of a man as methodical as he was practical. But meeting him in the flesh, Webb was surprised to find that the picture, which he now saw in the larger setting of its surroundings, had taken on weird shadings. In fact, precisely what had seemed most reasonable, now seemed to turn Barrie into an increasingly fantastic figure.

As he listened to the strange undertones in Barrie's instructions, Webb could not fend off the impression that Barrie was so involved in his small labors that he had lost sight of all relative dimensions. Angrily hacking, boring, slashing into the mountain, he seemed to consider it a major triumph when he had driven a shaft a few feet deeper into the colossal base. Indeed, he acted as if the mine were a battlefield, and his work a personal contest. Digging pebbles from the immense stone masses, he considered himself victorious because he had robbed his adversary of some small glittering treasures. And it did not enter his mind that he could not even keep those pitiful ounces of gold, but had to pass them on to the invisible stockholders far away.

Barrie's battles became even more disturbing to Webb, when he stopped in front of the window and gazed at the mountain's majestic splendor displayed with infinite generosity. It occurred to him that Barrie was utterly unaware of the wealth so freely offered. Perhaps, for that very reason, he was angrily attacking what he could not understand. Dimly aware that he was in the midst of more than he could grasp, he lashed out blindly at the beauty around him, hating that which he could not see.

"We're pretty busy these days," Barrie said, as he returned. "I'm opening a new vein." A grin of happy expectation slashed his face, and Webb had to turn away, because he could not bear to see it. For at that moment, it occurred to him that Barrie was not the attacker, but a self-condemned prisoner, locked into the jail, which he himself had dug into the mountain; held by the chain and ball of his narrow ambitions, while he was whipped by his petty hates against all he could not understand. And the mountain, far from being wounded by the little man's pathetic attempts, was offering him a particle of its substance so that he could punish himself more surely.

"Let's have a drink at my home," Barrie suggested.

On the way to the house, which was perched high above the village in an almost feudal manner, Barrie talked of business matters in connection with his administration of the mine. The same methodical, reasonable tone which had characterized his memorandums, prevailed in his words; only now, Webb also heard an accompaniment of diabolical laughter. But Barrie was utterly deaf to it; he discussed his work in terms of cost and output. Only once did that occasional expression of vague bewilderment reappear; it broke through when he admitted to Webb that the mine was running dry; in fact, about two years ago, he had reported to the head office that the costs of operation were beginning to exceed the returns. The order to shut down, which he had expected, had not yet arrived. And so he continued the unprofitable operation, not knowing whether the deficit was overlooked in the labyrinths of the corporation's larger and far more important holdings; or whether he was exerting himself on behalf of a tax deduction.

"You take a fellow like Crispian," Barrie said, while mixing the drinks in the living room, "and you wonder how he can go through life without taking a decent job and making something of himself. Of course, by the time he got here, it was too late. If he'd been younger—maybe. Maybe I would have taken him in hand and straightened him out."

"Provided he would have asked you to," Webb said crisply, his resentment breaking through.

"He did," Barrie said, unaware of Webb's surprise. "Came here one night, and asked me for a job. Anything. Just ordinary work. Regular hours. Pay-check at the end of the week. He had it all figured out."

Webb's shoulders sagged. It was to him the most tragic moment of Crispian's struggle. He visualized the painter's small figure in front of the hulking engineer, pleading for sanctuary within the shelter of conventional living, begging for a chance to escape from the tyrannical demands of his consuming genius.

"What kind of work did you give him?" Webb asked.

"None."

"You mean, you turned him down?"

"Of course."

"How could you?" Webb exclaimed.

Barrie looked at him, astonished. "I couldn't have used him to haul water. It's hard work at the mine. Can't hire just anybody; certainly not a guy you can't depend on."

When Webb turned away, Barrie continued in a sudden growl: "Besides, that's not all he wanted. Not just a job." He broke off, regretting that he had started on something which he had intended to hold back. For a moment, he seemed to be seeking a way to extricate himself. But then, suddenly carried away again, he burst out: "He also wanted to get married. Settle down and raise children. Just like everybody else. He was walking up and down in this room, all excited. He had it all planned. There was only one thing he had overlooked; he hadn't asked the lucky woman. So he asked me instead. He asked permission to marry my daughter."

Webb waited in stunned silence, while Barrie stirred the drinks with a hard clicking of the spoon.

"I want you to know," Barrie said, suddenly facing Webb, "that she had not given him any encouragement. He might have amused her with his crazy ways. A girl gets lonely up here. Maybe she went along on walks with him a few times. But no encouragement." He glared at Webb. "You can ask her yourself!"

He crossed to the door and called Mona. She must have been listening to them in the adjoining room; when Webb turned around, she was standing on the threshold, framed by the door, as immobile as a painting. She was tall, with large dark eyes that reflected an occasional spark from her silver earrings. Her long hair, of a soft, somber brown, fell back from her face which, in repose, had an extraordinary, almost timeless beauty.

"Tell him," Barrie demanded.

Her eyes sought out Webb. He felt sure that he detected a strange plea in their dark glimmer. She was obviously afraid of her father; and yet, there was also something indomitable about her; her silence seemed expressive of a submerged fortitude rather than submission.

"It's true," she whispered.

Barrie approached Webb, triumphantly. "You see!"

"Yes, I see," Webb said, holding Mona's glance a moment longer, as if to assure her that he had entered into the conspiracy.

"I sure told him what I thought of him," Barrie growled. "You can't blame me for losing my temper, can you? Maybe I was a bit too harsh. At any rate, he left and never came back."

The air in the room became stifling to Webb. He felt he could not spend another minute in Barrie's presence. Taking his drink, he moved abruptly toward the cool twilight on the terrace.

When he reached the bannister, he looked down on the road, which was winding its way to the village below, and he imagined how Crispian had walked away from the barred door, losing himself in the night, after he had been driven from the warmth of the lights in the house.

Webb traced the road to the square in the center of the town, wondering in which of the little stone cubes Crispian had lived. The quiet evening had descended on the glowing houses; and there was a promise of peace in the air, which dissipated Webb's irritation at Barrie. In the ensuing stillness, he had the inexplicable sensation of being watched, of someone standing beside him, of not being alone. Turning sharply, he saw, with the terror of sudden shock, the mountain giant which had dominated their ascent to Santa Rosa. Until this moment, it had been lost from sight, both at the mine and at Barrie's house. But now from this terrace, he was facing the giant again; and this time the colossal slopes were incredibly near, looming up directly ahead of him, their enormous mass wedged into the triangular opening of a side valley.

There was a fascination in the overwhelming stature which drew Webb's attention away from everything else, absorbing him as if he had been pulled into the orbit of a powerful magnet. After the first shock, his fear gave way to a stunned admiration. His eyes searched the gigantic stillness, rising along immobile contours to the towering peak. He was trying to define the mystery of its impact and realized that it was composed of as many changing aspects as were contained in its shifting colors and shadows during the course of a day and a night.

Nevertheless, at that moment, he grew aware of one unalterable emanation which had an unexpected effect on him. Instead of disturbing him, this overpowering greatness quieted his anguish. The massive, sublime weight, so far exceeding the measurements of human concepts, gave him a strange assurance. It's very nature was such that it could not be touched or attacked, and therefore it knew no fear, not even of death, not even of time and the day's passing, for it would endure forever.

He clasped the bannister in a surge of confidence more absolute than any he had ever known, surrendering to that which could not be anything but good because it was so truly great and firm and strong.

"I was wondering what kept you out here," Barrie said, standing directly behind. Webb moved to the side, angry that the spell had been broken by the engineer's unnoticed approach. "El Soledad," Barrie said, pointing in the direction of Webb's fixed glance. "Highest mountain around here." The geographical information seemed to have exhausted his interest in the subject. Though after a moment, he added: "Something strange about the name. Should really be 'La Soledad' instead of El. Never could find out why the Indians make that mistake. But that's the way they are. No logic."

Turning, Webb saw that Barrie was looking at the lofty peak with unseeing eyes. There was something frightening in their blank stare. Slowly, the eyes shifted to the village below, and a concrete thought formed in their vacant gaze. "See that old house down there? Just off the plaza? That's where Crispian rented his room."

"I'll have to go there," Webb said, anxious to get away from Barrie. But before he could leave the bannister, the sun glowed up in a cleft between two peaks. Swiftly passing across the opening, like a stranger peeking through the slit in a curtain, it soon disappeared again. But during that short period, it had trailed a net of light over the town. And before the yellowish houses sank back into the pool of darkness, they seemed to flare up, one by one, burning like matches, until they were extinguished by the lapping tongues of the thirsty dusk. The last to flicker out was the little church, where at this moment, Webb surmised, Padre Paolo was celebrating mass, after having bandaged the wounds of the injured.

Webb cast a last glance at the immense spectacle spread out

before his eyes. Somewhere in this mountain kettle he would find a treasure left behind by Crispian.

Crispian's painting.

Perhaps, Mona could lead him to it. While he was walking down to the village, Webb recalled the strange plea in her eyes, and he wondered how she had really felt about Crispian. If Webb could arrange to see her alone, away from her father, she might take him into her confidence. It would be difficult to arrange such a meeting; but somehow he felt sure that she would help to bring it about.

He had, however, not expected to see her so soon; when he turned a corner of the steep road, she detached herself from the shadows of a high rock, which leaned over the valley like a petrified sentinel. She did not want Webb to stop; instead, she fell in step beside him. And before long, she had explained why she had waited for him; as he had expected, she did not want him to be misled by what she had said in her father's presence.

It was true, she told Webb, that until Crispian had been driven from their house, she had not been attracted to him; like other women, she had been deterred by his unprepossessing appearance. And she might never have looked beyond the façade, if she had not rebelled against her father's brutality. But once she had broken through the shell, it no longer mattered that it was her pity which had first provided the key.

Her words were almost inaudible, rarely forming compact sentences; rather they were like birds fluttering in a strong wind, or like trembling leaves swirling over a landscape of burning emotions.

She was shy; until she had met Crispian, she had never learned to confide in anyone. Her mother had died when she was a mere child—a year or two after they had moved to Santa Rosa; she hardly remembered her. And since then, she had lived behind high walls built around her by coarse and insensitive men—until Crispian, a fellow prisoner, had suddenly joined her isolation.

At this point, she stopped; it was all she had meant to tell Webb. She remained distrustful, even after Webb assured her that he was as devoted to Crispian as any friend could be. "He never had a friend," she said bitterly. "Nobody ever bothered to notice all the warmth and beauty in him. There was so much of it—it was nearly bursting his heart. But it was all locked up in him, because it had gone begging for so long. It'd been refused so often that it didn't even bother to come out anymore. In a way, he was like a hurt child that's given up trying."

Webb stared to the ground, walking in self-effacing silence, as if he were hopelessly striving to separate himself from her accusations.

"Just because he didn't fit into any pattern was no reason to refuse him a place at the common table. He wasn't trying to be different—he couldn't help it. And he didn't ask for much. I know how little he asked. There wasn't much I could give him; but to him, it was like a whole new world opening up." She faltered. "You see, he had never been loved before."

She withdrew into silence, and Webb realized that he could not get her to say anything more. The whole relationship between the two, so lasting in its magic that she was still in the grip of its spell, might well remain a mystery to him. In a way, he felt locked out at the threshold of an enchanted garden, the inside of which he would never know.

But one thing was clear to him, though it might not be to her. Unknowingly, she had achieved the opposite of what she intended; she had handed Crispian to the very destiny from which she had wanted to save him. Her compassionate love had dissolved the armor with which he had guarded himself. No longer able to clutch at the holds of bitterness, resentment, or accusation, he was drawn into the whirlpool of his talent.

"Do you know what brought him back to painting?"

She shook her head, suddenly frightened. They had reached the outskirts of the town, and she stepped back into the shadows, refusing to go further.

For a moment, she stood, undecided; then she told him of the day when she had taken Crispian to the ruins of the old mission. Though she could not be sure, she suspected that there flew the spark which set fire to his imagination. They had climbed up the steep hill, and while she was strolling among the crumbling old beams, she noticed that he was staring at the full view of El Soledad. When she approached, he pointed out to her how the tumbled cross before them seemed to be leaning against the mountain. It was a simple cross, really no more than two withered sticks nailed together, but somehow it had caught his fancy, and he told her how it should be painted. Later, when they descended, he seemed to have forgotten all about it; at any rate, he did not mention it again.

But the next day he was strangely absent-minded; and soon he grew more and more silent; in the end, he would not leave his room at all. She would find him lying on his bed; and the old widow from whom he rented his room told her that she could hear him pacing all through the night. "He would not tell me what troubled him," Mona concluded. "Just said it would pass. But it didn't. And suddenly, one afternoon while I was at church, he came rushing in, with a list of supplies he needed, expecting me to get them for him before evening. He was so wrought-up, he could not understand when I told him how long it might take."

Webb, whose aid had been enlisted at the other end, now understood Crispian's frenzy. He thought of Crispian's increasing silence, preceding the outburst. Visualizing him lying quietly in his room, paralyzed by the storm that was gathering inside of him, Webb could almost palpably feel the uncanny tension building up, a sultry pressure which could no longer be released except by an eruption of elemental fury.

"What was the subject of his painting?" Webb asked.

"Christ on Golgotha."

A flurry of excitement spread through Webb's nerves. "What became of the canvas?"

She looked at him, as if she were weighing her answer. Then she drew back, her former distrust flaring up in her eyes. "It was destroyed," she said. And before he could overcome his sharp disappointment, she had fled into the night.

Disturbed and puzzled by her abrupt escape, Webb walked toward the plaza. It was obvious that Mona knew more than she had told; but her refusal to talk about the destruction of the canvas had been so blunt that Webb saw no way to overcome her resistance.

Preoccupied with the riddle of the painting's disappearance, he approached the house where Crispian had lived. He knocked at the door, without great expectations of learning anything of importance from the Indian woman who owned the house.

The fat, old widow was greatly impressed when he told her the purpose of his visit. Awed by the fact that the government of the Estados Unidos was sufficiently interested in Crispian to send a special representative, she now saw her former boarder in an entirely different light. Defending herself against any possible accusation of neglect, she assured Webb most vigorously that she had taken excellent care of Crispian. And by the time she was leading the consul toward the painter's room, she had convinced herself that she had always suspected what an important person she had sheltered; and she denied, with an agitated fluttering of her skirts which nearly extinguished the candle, that her boarder had left anything behind.

The room, in its emptiness, seemed to confirm her claim; it looked as bare as if it had never been lived in. Searching for clues, Webb gazed from the cot in the corner to the table and the two rough chairs in the center; there was nothing else; the rest was ascetically bare. While the widow was showering him with an unending stream of words, he wondered how Crispian could have spread out the enormous canvas, which Webb remembered to have been larger than the entire wall. Near the ceiling, he saw three small blotches of yellow paint, the only vestiges of Crispian's labors. Strangely alive amidst the shadows creeping over the white chalk wall, these tiny remnants were like outcroppings of a vast, lost treasure.

He hardly listened to the widow, who was now telling him about the days when Crispian did not get up from his cot. She admitted that she had seen nothing unusual in that, because her poor, deceased husband had done the same for years, being a lazy good-for-nothing who had shrewdly and happily refused to get up and work.

Confirmed in his original assumption that the widow could contribute nothing of interest, Webb turned to leave. But the woman stepped into his way, clutching at his sleeve, for the first time without speech as she was struggling to reach a decision. Then she broke down and confessed that she had retained some of Crispian's belongings, not because she had intended to steal them, of course not, but simply because they had seemed of no use to anybody.

A minute later, she returned with a shabby bundle, which

Webb untied, growing increasingly impatient as the knot refused to submit to his feverish haste. Finally unwinding the strings, he found on top the ill-fitting suit, which Crispian had evidently cherished and preserved in the futile hope of returning some day to civilization. Beneath the dead man's jacket, Webb found the two white shirts which had been a size too large, hanging loosely, as Webb well remembered, beneath Crispian's prominent Adam's apple. But those were the only items which could have stimulated the widow's greed. The rest was really quite worthless, even in this barren region; and Webb was about to return the bundle to her, when he saw, at the bottom, what appeared to be notes, scribbled on torn, loose pages.

Webb's hands trembled as he examined them in the dim light of the candle. Here, at last, was a glimpse directly into the painter's mind, a personal record, thoughts unguarded in their privacy. Now Webb was no longer dealing with his own impressions, nor would he be viewing Crispian through the filter of other people's eyes; here he had found a window across which to peer into the artist's inner world, a window of Crispian's own making.

Disturbed by the widow's unceasing explanations of her attempted theft, he begged her to leave the room. And when the door had closed, he sank on the chair, engrossed in deciphering the hasty scribbling.

He soon realized that these pages contained notes on the concept of the painting. Apparently, Crispian, while waiting for the supplies to arrive, had been so consumed by impatience that he wrote down the ideas which were shaping in his feverish mind, sketching in words what he was prevented from bringing to life on canvas.

On the second page, Webb found a vague entry which confirmed the truth of Mona's belief; the simple, withered cross was indeed the spark that had inflamed some remote, unguarded spot in the artist's soul, smoldering at first in a restricted area until the incandescent heat ignited adjoining portions. Day after day, additions and changes in concept revealed that the flames had spread with the searing fury of a forest fire, until all of his being was consumed in one blazing conflagration. And into this white heat of creation tumbled the cold blocks of past experiences, of sights etched into memory, of faces and persons met and forgotten, awaiting in hidden recesses of his soul this moment of sudden release.

Thus erupting, the whole realm of observed and lived events gave forth its contents, with the drafts of the rising flames drawing the pieces into the orbit of the fire. And there, the images were shaped and melted, cast and re-cast, purified of slack, appearing and re-appearing in different forms, moving from one part of the canvas to the other until they had found their most perfect place, their most ideal pose, their most true expression; and at that stage they would congeal of themselves, resisting further tests, refusing alterations, emerging instead with growing clarity, as they hardened toward their final form.

While Webb read on—slowly because the scribbling was at times so hectic and feverish as to become unintelligible—the concept of the vast canvas revealed to him meanings which he might have failed to recognize on the actual painting.

"The crucifixion," Crispian had written, "with the cross in the center. In the background, impersonal multitude watching a spectacle that signifies nothing to them; witnesses without testimony. Gray mouths. Perhaps some yellow eyes to merge with the foreground." For two pages then he forgot the crowd, and became preoccupied with the tints of the sky. Thereafter, he suddenly turned to the periphery on either side. "Screaming, tumultuous colors—the intoxicating beauty of the world—reds, browns, burnt sienna, streaking out toward the stillness of the blue around the cross."

Then followed descriptions of individual figures in the foreground; their concept, in some instances, revealed pathetic historical errors, though it could not be determined whether Crispian violated accepted tradition because of insufficient knowledge or artistic necessity. More startling, however, was the fact that he intended to use living people as his models for some of his figures; there were cryptic references to Padre Paolo, Barrie, Mona; and when Webb came across his own name, he wondered with deep apprehension what role Crispian had assigned to him.

But there was no further identification; it was not even clear whether he was among the main figures involved in the drama of the cross, or had been relegated to the bystanders, the guards, and Roman soldiers, of whom a trio was gambling at the right, their back turned to the cross. Yet even this callously indifferent group Crispian did not leave detached; successive changes kept drawing and fusing the flow of lines toward the center, steadily increasing the prominence of the cross, until the bleeding head of Christ became the focus to which all else was related, inextricably involved with it, by piety as much as by hatred, by faith as much as by irony, by devotion as much as by indifference, by compassion and by callousness, for—as Crispian wrote— "I have not seen any independent existence away from it."

And at a subsequent point, he referred to it once more in a cryptic, partly technical sentence: "Extend the lines of perspective not to the horizon but to a point in the Universe. Any view that does not encompass the stars, birth, and death is distorted, fragmentary. Revise groupings of Roman soldiers once more." Again, then, he returned to the Christ head, as he had done several times before, in each instance, however, falling back, ebbing away like a wave after its force has been spent on a rock.

His first vision of the face had been a terrifying concept of blood trickling down from the thorny crown, of excruciating pain, of pale, suffering lips, of forgiveness made all the more crushing by suppressing accusation. But this vision dissolved imperceptibly; and finally it had faded away altogether, leaving a strange vagueness in the very center of the canvas toward which all the other parts were straining for their dramatic fulfillment. In despair, he conceived a Roman soldier in front of the cross, who had been paid for his murderous work with some of the Roman coins that held the inscription: "To the unknown God."

But almost instantly, he rejected this make-shift device, castigating himself mercilessly, ashamed of having even considered a compromise. The next day, however, he seemed to have found a solution which, he believed, turned his failure into a victory; the very vagueness of the center was desirable, because it would permit the figures around the cross to project their meaning upon the inscrutable.

This, at any rate, appeared to satisfy him. He did not mention it again as a problem, turning instead to the important figures around the cross. For a while, he became preoccupied with the expression of their faces, which, he felt, had to mirror the pain and grief of the tragic event. But suddenly he rebelled against suffering, casting it out as the heaviest and the most strangling of all earthly chains. "I feel pity and compassion for others; I have no patience with pain in myself." And as if he had freed himself at last, he joyously rushed forward to embrace beauty, finding an exuberant release in beauty unburdened by meaning, undisturbed by emotion, pure and intoxicating in its sublime perfection.

Yet, beauty was not his highest aim. Though he did not deny that it was a vital tool in the artist's métier, he did not believe that it should ever be an end in itself. More startling, however, was the fact that he did not regard himself as a perfectionist; indeed, he insisted that he had never been concerned with perfection, since this was an aspiration that applied as much to the small accomplishment as to the great. "There are enough artisans," he had jotted down, "intent on demonstrating their ability; enough ambitious talents dedicated to proving that they can do something better than others; enough virtuosi who push their personality to the fore, subtly seeking admiration for themselves instead of enriching others by what they have to give." As for himself, he added in the next paragraph, he would rather express imperfectly an important truth than strive to give the most perfect form to something that was of no consequence.

That was about as close as he came to a statement of his artistic aims; except for a startlingly naive remark, two pages later, when he claimed that art should be functional. But by the time he had expressed what he meant by functional, the word seemed about as far removed from the practically useful, the objet d'art, the comfortable adornment, as a modern cosmology from the Farmer's Almanac. "It is the artist's duty," he had written, "to explore an ever-changing world, to re-discover and re-create it for each generation. His function in a nation's body is to experience life as it then exists and to communicate it to his contemporaries as the eyes, ears, the senses as well as the emotions, do for the individual."

Never before, he went on, had the need for a constant re-discovery of our lives been so great, because never before had the environment changed so rapidly. "The world tends to become a stranger to us with each passing hour, growing as it does, from day to day, in a million separate places. It keeps moving away from us in steps so small that we do not notice them. And yet, if we do not recapture it at intervals, we are bound to end up, before long, without a true sense of being, trapped by withered, petrified notions from previous world climates, leading phantom-lives in imagined surroundings that were true once, but no longer exist."

Reading this page, Webb asked himself how often he had made any attempt to revise views crystallized in earlier years. Perhaps, Crispian was right; perhaps, he had lived in a fictitious environment. At any rate, he had to agree with Crispian's subsequent statement that even the fundamental, the essentially unchanging truths of human experience, of man's relation to the eternal, the absolute, could only be seen in the mirror of one's own time, distorting as that might be; that, indeed, there was no better way to discover the unchanging than to become fully aware of the changing.

From that point on, the notes grew shorter; the creation stood before Crispian's mind as a vision completed and fully dreamed, now awaiting its birth. And at that stage, the doubts began: a cruel uncertainty while he measured himself against the enormous task, despairing at times of his capacity to live up to his vision. Afraid that he might fall short, but no longer able to extricate himself from the hypnotic demands of his creation, he was facing the ultimate struggle with the apprehension of one who has to risk all in a desperate gamble. He was, of necessity, forced into a crisis, involving his whole existence.

For there was more at stake than the challenge of artistic ambition, petulantly desiring success. He knew that it was to be his last work; and his final achievement would have to be great enough to compensate for all his past suffering. On one side of the balance was the heavy weight of tormented years, of bruising struggles, the whole question of a happier life, lived differently, lived without the sacrifices demanded by dedication; on the other side, the ultimate achievement, still an unknown substance on the scale. There was indeed much at stake; for his past, with fierce reproaches, demanded justification from his accomplishment, bitterly weighing and doubting its potential merit. And the outcome of his creation would decide whether his life had been spent in the morass of futility, or had found its triumphant vindication.

It was with this solemn awareness that he approached his task; and once he had accepted the challenge, the conflict disappeared, as if a ship, grating over hampering sandbanks, had reached the clear waters of the ocean. At this stage, there reappeared briefly the sense of doom, as he looked toward the dark horizon toward which he had set out, not knowing what he would find, nor yet what it would hold for him; but somehow aware that he would not return.

What caused this sense of doom did not become clear; in fact, Webb came to suspect that Crispian himself had not entirely understood the nature of the demoniac power that threatened him. In the notes, it had not yet manifested itself; nevertheless, it seemed to be present in every sentence, lurking behind and between words, still biding its time, while preparing to attack. And indeed, on one of the last pages, Webb ran into a deeply disturbing item; at first glance, it appeared to be no more than a brief, almost hurried entry, stating simply that Crispian had decided, on a sudden impulse, to cut away a few feet of the canvas on each side of the painting in order to enhance the intensity of the whole. Apparently, Crispian himself had not noticed the uncanny significance of this elimination. Considering it merely a technical improvement, he had disposed of it in a couple of lines.

But to Webb there were frightening implications in this minor decision. It seemed like the first manifestation of a rising need for intensification, as slight and yet as ominous a signal as the rustling of a leaf in the vanguard of a storm. The deceptive harmlessness of its initial appearance was utterly misleading; there could be little doubt that it foreshadowed a culmination of elemental fury. Indeed, Webb felt sure that, here, he was observing the beginning of that irresistible trend which gathered momentum in its ascendancy, doubling and redoubling its energies, until its contracted and compacted power threatened to exceed Crispian's will, to sweep him helplessly beyond his conscious aims, pushing and lashing him toward the limits of his endurance.

Since he was unable to control, subdue, or check its rising dominance, Crispian could only break its hold by interrupting the trend, by escaping, by turning to flight as he had done more than once in the past, the last time in Irozco, when he had destroyed the pottery tools. But so far Webb had found no hint in the notes that Crispian intended to draw back while he could still save himself. It was a significant omission; and Webb felt increasingly tormented by Crispian's oppressive silence on so vital, and perhaps fatal an issue. It could mean, on one hand, that Crispian had failed to guard himself against his growing absorption in the painting, ignoring the possibility that he might be drawn past the point of no return without noticing it; on the other hand, that he had decided to proceed this time beyond the borders of possible withdrawal, no matter where it might lead him.

Gripped by a deep anxiety, Webb read on, but he could find no evidence, not even a veiled inference, which could have revealed Crispian's attitude toward this crucial question. And when Webb turned the page, he was startled to see that the notes had come to an abrupt end. The final paragraph broke off in the middle of a sentence.

The canvas had arrived!

A disappearing streak of the pencil marked the end of another trail; once again, Crispian had vanished from sight. And the blank half of the last page left Webb standing before another locked door, this time shutting him out from the work room in which Crispian had struggled to bring his visions to life.

CHAPTER IV

Webb's glance turned from the notes to the three yellow blotches of paint under the ceiling; nothing else had remained of Crispian's masterpiece. The rest of the pale chalk wall was a tantalizing void.

He folded the notes and pushed them into his pocket. As immensely valuable as they had seemed to him, when he first found them, he now felt that they had merely increased his hopeless wish to see the finished painting which had superseded in its final fulfillment the groping, sometimes chaotic, but always gigantic concepts.

It was, perhaps, this desperate need which did not quite allow him to believe that the canvas had been destroyed. On his way out, Webb questioned the widow. But the moment he spoke of the painting, she burst into tears, denying that she had kept it, vociferously protesting her innocence. While it was true that she had appropriated the bundle with the clothes, she definitely had no reason to clutter up her house with an enormous and obviously useless canvas. She implored lightning to strike her dead on the spot, if she were lying to the representative of the Estados Unidos.

Though Webb gave her every assurance that he did not suspect her of theft, he could not allay her fears. Her memory failed her; she could not recall when it had been taken away or by whom; she did not know whether it had been stolen or destroyed. Finally, in an obvious attempt to clear herself of suspicion by focusing it on others, she suggested that it might have been taken by an Indian storekeeper, who was a well known thief, or by Don Hernandez, a Spanish nobleman, who was unpredictable enough to be suspected of anything.

Realizing that she would not tell him the truth, Webb left her in the doorway and walked toward the plaza. Before turning the corner, he looked back at the house, scanning the shuttered façade

79

which shielded the room where Crispian's struggles with his work had taken place.

Attempting to visualize the painter's frail figure in front of the enormous canvas, Webb found to his surprise that his imagination refused to project the image. Since he knew from the notes the immense scope of Crispian's undertaking, his mind could not reconcile the memory of the painter's insignificant appearance with the stature of the man as an artist.

Nothing could have revealed to Webb more clearly the astonishing double life of the creative personality. A strange transformation took place the moment Crispian entered his work room. Leaving his beggar's clothes at the threshold, he entered a realm where he rose far above anyone's pity, condescension, or charity. For then he was no longer the inconsequential registrant at the consulate, nor the hounded traveler seeking acceptance; indeed, he was no longer dependent on the world, but shaping and creating it; no longer subjected to life, but giving it; at that point, the emaciated, lonely painter turned into a king, holding in his hands an inexplicable power over life and reality, an unlimited authority greater than any ever possessed by an absolute monarch.

A cold gust of wind wafted a breath of distant snow toward Webb, as he rounded the corner. Crossing the dark pool of the plaza, he felt as though he were trailing his gesticulating shadow over the gutted ground to the amusement of a mock jury; and when he looked around, he noticed the strangely shaped houses surrounding the increasingly vast square like masked faces in a dream, some grotesquely serious, some sadly grinning, some twisted beyond recognition.

He stood, momentarily paralyzed, suddenly realizing that he no longer remembered in which direction he would find the street leading back to Barrie's house. Yet, he sensed keenly that above all he must move; but not knowing where to go, he could not advance until he saw at the other end of the plaza three dark, agile men strolling toward a house which was marked as a public drinking place by the sign: Cerveceria. When they passed the lane to their right, they turned their heads away in unison, without apparent reason; and, continuing their lively conversation, they soon disappeared in the tavern.

Anxious to know why they had avoided the sight of that lane, which at this distance looked none too different from the others, Webb crossed the plaza. And when he reached the lane, he responded with almost the same automatic movement of turning away, for he had seen the towering shadow of El Soledad, not all of it, only the compact foundation wedged into the side-valley. He did not admit to himself that there had been any particular reason for averting his eyes; all he allowed himself to acknowledge was a spontaneous need for human companionship. And so he followed the men to the cerveceria, explaining to himself at the same time that he might pick up some information about the painting in a public place where the villagers gathered to drink.

When he passed through the clattering pearl bead curtain, which fingered him greedily while gliding over his shoulders, his eyes could not immediately get used to the diffuse light inside. Emanating from no single source, as far as he could detect, a warm glow glimmered in the cavernous room like a banked fire which might, at any moment, spring into flames. Silhouetted against it, the drinkers remained strangely indistinct, though now and then a face was fleetingly illuminated when turning toward the light.

No one seemed to pay any attention to him, until he heard someone step up behind him. "The Padre was here, looking for you," a voice said. Wheeling around, Webb recognized Barrie's foreman, and felt vastly relieved on seeing a familiar face in this shadowy crowd.

"Where did he go?"

"Don't know. He said he'd be back. Maybe you'd better wait right here." The foreman drew Webb toward the center plank which served as a bar. "Have a drink." He waved to an old crippled Indian, who came scurrying from a corner with a large jug, pouring a colorless liquid into two bowls, his toothless mouth gaping in a meaningless grin; and without pausing, he scurried away, eagerly filling other cups that were held out to him from all sides.

Webb took a sip from his bowl and felt the fiery liquid burn on his tongue.

"You'll get used to it," the foreman chuckled. "The only liquor we can get up here." He emptied his bowl in one long draft.

"They brew it themselves. Indian recipe. Has some mescalin in it." He wiped his mouth. "Powerful stuff. Makes you see things."

Webb felt a spreading lassitude in his muscles, but no discomfort. Looking around, he noticed for the first time that the irregular, labyrinthian appearance of the place was caused by the slanted beams shoring up the ceiling wherever the many cracks and fissures indicated weak spots; but, oddly enough, none of the men underneath seemed much concerned, ignoring the threat of a cave-in, though an occasional trickle of plaster was bound to call their attention to the perilous situation.

Astonished by their indifference to this evident danger, Webb expressed his apprehension to the foreman who merely shrugged, no more disturbed than the others. And after a few more sips from his bowl, Webb himself accepted the constant threat as an unavoidable dilemma; his crumbling reasoning powers, shored up by weird arguments, convinced him that any sort of shelter was preferable to whatever dangers might be lurking outside.

This common need of refuge seemed to be the bond uniting the shifty men in this tavern; Webb sensed it in that easy camaraderie found more frequently among the sick than among the healthy; in that instinctive cohesion which can only exist after the recognition or confession of similar weakness and deficiencies. And after he finished his bowl, he came to wonder why he suddenly felt that they no longer regarded him as an intruder, but had admitted him to their group as a satisfactory member. This casual acceptance was offensive to Webb; and he turned away, as though to impress upon them that he was merely a passing stranger.

Meanwhile, the foreman was explaining that most of these men were workers in Barrie's mine, a tough, hard-bitten crew, potentially dangerous. The majority, the foreman said, had come from far away and from many countries; a polyglot crowd, they babbled away in different tongues, though occasionally Webb heard some English words which stood out with painful familiarity.

There was something disquieting about all this foreign conversation, and Webb demanded a second bowl. He was glad to be protected by the foreman, whose handsome, simple, clean-cut face was wonderfully reassuring in the midst of this nameless throng. The foreman, it turned out, was from San Francisco. He had been a prospector in many Western states, and also in South America, until he had ended up, for some reason which he pointedly failed to explain, in Santa Rosa.

At the end of his third drink, Webb lowered his voice so that it would be lost in the general murmur, and asked the foreman about the painting.

The foreman smiled, casually spinning the bowl on the plank. "Ah, yes, the painting. I wondered when you'd get around to asking about it."

Webb waited, but when the foreman gave no indication that he would add anything, Webb sensed that he had broached a dangerous subject. Nevertheless, he decided to go further. "I don't believe it has been destroyed."

"You're right," the foreman nodded. He waved to the toothless Indian, indicating that he wanted his bowl refilled. "Personally, I think somebody is hiding it."

"Who?"

"I don't know. I've got my own theory, of course. Everybody else has one. That's all we were talking about for weeks. But as usual nobody did anything about it—I mean, like trying to find out where it is." He chuckled. "The fact is nobody wants to find it. They're glad it has disappeared."

"Why?"

"Can't you guess?" the foreman grinned, winking his eye at Webb, as if he meant to assure him that there was no need to act innocently.

Webb turned away, resenting this sly attempt both to establish an intimacy he had not invited, and to cast doubt on his integrity.

"Since you insist," the foreman said, highly amused, "I'll spell it out. It's simple enough. Nobody knows who's been portrayed on that canvas. That's why everybody's afraid of it."

"Afraid?" Webb asked, incredulously. Looking up to the foreman, he wondered whether the man was more intoxicated than he had realized.

"Yes—afraid. Afraid of the truth." The foreman's features grew tense. "Suppose you'd been portrayed honestly—I mean, the way you really are—would you want to see your likeness?"

Webb stared into his bowl. He had meant to answer affirmatively, but found it more difficult than he could have expected. He struggled against his reluctance, but his tongue remained tied. He felt limp and weak, the more so when it occurred to him that the foreman might have been entitled to regard him previously with that conspiratorial look.

"Whether I'd like to see it or not," he finally brought out, "is beside the point. It may be an important work of art," he added pedantically, "and I'm determined to find it." Forgetting himself, he had raised his voice; and the foreman gripped his arm, warning him. But it was too late; a hushed silence had spread in the room, and several faces were turned toward Webb. After a few moments, the general murmur was resumed, but it now had an ominous quality. The air was heavily charged with tension, and the camaraderie had given way to a general alertness, a readiness to join ranks against the intruder who threatened exposure.

"You might as well know," the foreman whispered after a while, "there isn't a man in the crowd who is not on bad terms with the truth."

"What truth?"

"Any kind. They wouldn't be here, if they had the courage to face it, would they?"

The foreman's grin had that same confidential quality; and Webb was about to agree, when his brain, clouded by the colorless drink, signaled frantically that it no longer had the power to examine and reject conclusions of questionable logic.

"You don't think," the foreman went on, "that anybody in his right mind would come up to Santa Rosa, trading the comforts of city life for the hardships of this wilderness, unless they were pushed or driven?"

"I don't know," Webb said desperately. "I don't know why they're here."

"You do know," the foreman insisted. "You know well enough that nobody would settle in this no-man's-land, halfway between the plains and the mountains, altitude ten thousand feet, if he didn't have a very good reason."

"Like what?"

"Like having to get away."

"From whom?"

"From something. It doesn't matter what, does it?" Again the foreman winked his eye, and Webb felt the blood rise to his cheeks. By now it had become a matter of grave urgency to cling to rational thought patterns. "Are you trying to say," he asked sternly, "that these men are fugitives from justice?"

At this the foreman burst into laughter. "They're fugitives all right," he roared, "but from justice—well, that's quite another matter."

Surveying the room with a suitably severe expression, Webb was keenly aware that his instinctive fear had at last found its concrete motivation. He had stumbled into a colony of escaped criminals, and if they discovered that he was a representative of law and order, his life would be in jeopardy.

The foreman had read his thought. "Relax, consul," he cried, slapping him on the shoulder. "They're not afraid of you. They know you won't report them to the authorities."

"I shall have to do my duty," Webb said crisply.

"You can't," the foreman laughed, hugely amused, "because you're one of them, and they know it."

"How dare you—?" Webb exploded, rebelling against the attempt to strip him of his respectability. Not until this moment, when the loss of his dignity was threatened, had he realized how desperately he needed this automatic and long-cherished attribute of his consular rank.

The foreman blithely ignored his protest. "You're here, aren't you? That's all the proof we need. Nobody hacks his way through the jungle unless he has to."

Webb strained to refute the argument, but somehow it turned out to be incontrovertible. "I had certain reasons," he said weakly.

"We all have," the foreman nodded, eyeing Webb with earnest sympathy; and Webb turned away, squirming nakedly under the knowing glance.

"We all had reasons to leave our homes," the foreman said, his voice grating under increasing strain. "At least, we assume we had. More or less valid reasons, we hope—but we can't even be sure of that." He smiled bitterly. "The trouble is, it happened so long ago, we have forgotten the reasons." Swept up by sudden anger, he pounded the bar plank. "That's why we can't ever go back."

Webb noticed that the man's face had turned gray; he now looked tired, worn out. Apparently, the foreman had not merely been taunting him. Grotesquely distorted as his reasoning was, it nevertheless reflected an inner suffering that was undeniably real.

And perhaps the reasoning was not so distorted. Webb thought of a day in his childhood, when his father had punished him rigorously. As often as that memory had returned to him over the years, he had never been able to recall what he had done to arouse his father's anger.

"Take another look at those fugitives," the foreman muttered, turning Webb around. "There isn't a man in this crowd who would plead innocent to whatever crime you might charge him with. He couldn't deny anything. We know we're guilty, but we can't remember what we've done." His powerful body shook with a silent, mirthless laughter which could hardly be distinguished from convulsive sobbing. "That's the worst part of it. I defy you to think up anything more cruel than to leave a man his guilt without the remembrance of his crime."

He waved to the toothless Indian, who came at once to fill the bowl; and when the busy cripple, before scurrying away, observed the foreman's despair, his gaping grin seemed no longer due to his lack of teeth.

After gulping down the drink, the foreman nudged the consul, pointing to a wiry, little man in the corner. "See that pock-marked Irishman over there. Nice fellow until he gets drunk. Then he drives us to distraction with this tall tale of how he murdered his brother-in-law. Details and everything. Gets the rest of us wild with envy, because he's the only one who remembers his crime. But if you ask me, he's just bragging." He wiped his mouth, momentarily insecure. "Can't be sure, though. Sometimes he sounds so convincing, you've got to believe him. But it makes no difference. Even if it were true, it's not the murder that's bothering him. Might be some irrelevant thing long before that. So he's still not better off than any of us."

The Irishman had looked up. Sensing that they were talking about him, he approached swaggeringly, followed by his friend, a fat man with tattooes on both arms.

"Has 'e been blatherin' about me?" the Irishman asked Webb.

"Go away," the foreman growled.

"No use denyin' me misdeed. Murder it was, so help me," the scar-faced Irishman gloated, ignoring the foreman. "Killed me man with an ax. Surely ye remember readin' about it—'twas in all the papers."

Webb racked his brain, but could not recall reading any reports on this particular murder.

"Front page every day. With me picture and all," the Irishman went on, undismayed. "Cut me step-father's head clean off the shoulders."

"Last time, it was his uncle," the foreman sneered.

Stung, the Irishman turned on him, and they engaged in a bitter argument.

Meanwhile, the fat man seized the opportunity to step closer to Webb, shyly trying to get his attention. He was most eager to talk to the consul; he had many questions to ask regarding the manner in which the government preserved its records. Specifically, he wanted to know whether the filing system was kept by name, by the type of crime, or by case number. After some hedging, he admitted that he was trying to evaluate his chances of tracking down the file containing the charges against him. "By jiminy, if I could get hold of the evidence," he finally confessed with an apologetic and embarrassed grin, "I'd rush to the nearest Judge and request punishment. So I would, and no doubt about it. It'd be by far the best solution, don't you think?"

Caught up by the fat man's pathetic conviction, Webb nodded assent, before it occurred to him that the Judge might hand down a very stiff sentence; and he mentioned that possibility without meaning to crush the fat man's happy expectations.

"Naturally, I'm not counting on leniency," the fat man smiled. "But the way I figure it, no matter how stiff a sentence they slap on me, it's still better than self-punishment, don't you think?"

While Webb was still exploring this alternative, the fat man answered his own question. "Sure you agree. You've got to. After all, what could be worse than self-punishment? Nothing, nothing at all. Because, from oneself, one can't ever expect justice. Each case—a life sentence. You're guilty, until you die. That, of course, can't be helped, because you just don't remember what you're guilty of. There's a certain amount of logic in it, so at least you can accept it. But what has me stumped," he went on, still apologetic, still afraid to express his disapproval of authority, "is the need for all that secrecy. Why, we're not even permitted to know whether we punish ourselves for crimes which we have committed, or whether those crimes were perpetrated on us—by others."

He wrinkled his forehead to accompany his grave accusation with a sufficiently serious expression, but all he achieved was that his fat face appeared even more comical. "Please don't misunderstand," he went on, poking his stubby finger into Webb's chest for additional emphasis, "I'm not talking about any guilt they might have taught us as kids—when we were too young even to understand why some of the things we did were wrong and forbidden. All I mean is the aggression of others, which makes us angry and teaches us to hate; and since those are emotions not permitted to the weak, whether they be children or adults, we become the more guilty, the worse others have treated us." He shook his head, smiling submissively, as though he were.begging the consul's pardon for criticizing the strange ways of authority. "By jiminy, it doesn't seem fair! However, that's still not what I really object to."

Webb looked away, unable to disagree, and rather ashamed, when he remembered that he had referred to these men as fugitives from justice. During the many years of his loyal and dedicated labors as a civil servant, he had questioned, on more than one occasion, the fairness of a government directive, which he was forced to execute without daring to protest. To soothe his conscience, he used to tell himself that his superiors were guided by some inscrutable logic, which necessitated certain injustices. But, at this moment, Webb did not attempt to state his convenient excuses to the fat man whose round cheeks were trembling with an indignation which was held in check only by the fear of reprisal.

"Suppose we'd be willing to forget everything else," the fat man went on, "how could we understand the worst injustice? I mean, how are we to accept the fact that the more decent and sensitive a guy happens to be, the more vulnerable he becomes to the crimes of others. The finer type characters are obliged to burden themselves with the guilt of others, and must punish themselves, while those who go around doing wrong are usually hardened individuals quite incapable of feeling any guilt. Perhaps you don't believe it but it's true."

Webb shook his head, attempting denial, though he inwardly agreed with the fat man. It was true that the sensitive, good child suffered more at the hands of culpable parents than the callous youngster; that the reformer striving to better the world was hounded by self-reproach, while the ruthless bully was not; that the saint was weighed down by a guilt unknown to the tyrant.

Webb was aware that the fat man kept on talking, but he could not bear to hear anymore. His vision had become as blurred as his hearing; he sensed rather than discerned that he was surrounded by angry faces floating toward him on waves of implacable hatred. His intoxicated mind, panicked by the general breakdown of authority, rotated around the illusion that he was being pushed toward an abyss where the condemned waited for their long delayed revenge. The deadly danger re-awakened his will power; and with a supreme effort, he attempted to pull himself from the swirling eddies of his intoxication by forcing his impaired perceptions to contact and recapture the reality around him.

Gradually succeeding in focusing his eyes, he grew even more confused; for the swaying room crystallized into an ordinary tavern, none too different from those he had seen in the poor quarters of Puerto Carribas. And the men drinking at the tables revealed themselves, in this brief moment of lucidity, as an ordinary group of miners, their hard faces weary rather than menacing, their shoulders limp after the day's strenuous labor.

But even more startling was the fact that the pock-marked Irishman and the overgrown fat boy were not at Webb's side, but at a distant table, listening quietly to a mulatto who was singing a spiritual in a rich mellifluous baritone. Their distance was as shocking as it was inexplicable; for it presented to Webb the further possibility that he had imagined everything that had taken place.

Wheeling around, he stared at the foreman, trying to deduce from the man's wholesome appearance what had actually occurred; but the foreman's handsome, clean-cut face, other than registering some astonishment at Webb's distorted expression, offered no clue; and Webb was too perplexed to enlist the man's aid in determining to what extent he had heard inner rather than outer voices.

Helplessly floundering between two levels of experience, between two worlds so inextricably superimposed upon each other that he could not even distinguish which of the two was more valid, Webb relapsed into the treacherous lassitude of his intoxication. And at the same time, the foreman's features became diffused, disintegrating into a ghostly, writhing mass of torment. This eerie transformation had a more crushing effect on Webb than anything he had experienced so far. His last stronghold within these bewitched surroundings was dissolving before his eyes—the symbol of normalcy, this handsome, simple, uncomplicated face so often reproduced in the national magazines; the face chosen to advertise shirts, ties, and cigarette lighters; the regular guy, trustworthy and reliable; the airplane pilot, fearless and dependable; good Joe, sincere, straightforward, without any hidden depths, untroubled in his simplicity.

Since adolescence Webb had tried to pattern himself after this prototype. Never doubting the attainability of such unburdened plainness, which was not only his ideal but that of a whole nation, Webb had felt guilty whenever his own complexities had come to the fore. Considering them his personal deficiencies, to be ignored, or, at least, to be hidden in shame, he remained envious of those whose seemingly depthless surface kept alive his illusion that they were free of the inner complications which troubled him more frequently than he had dared to admit.

If he had clung to the fallacy, it was because the pain of his personal deficiency had been outweighed by the comforting thought that so many others had succeeded where he had failed. Together with millions of others, he had preferred to suffer the awareness of shortcomings in secret, while publicly acclaiming the common ideal, never admitting that it could not possibly exist. And even now, when he could no longer sustain his illusion, he felt no relief; instead, he was seized by an irrational anger which directed itself against the foreman. He suddenly hated the man's handsome, simple face, which had presented a picture of such admirable cleanliness, if not purity, before revealing itself as an artificial structure floating on a chaotic, obscure, and bottom-less underworld.

Venting his impotent rage on the colorless drink, Webb pushed the bowl from the plank, in a gesture that was intended to push the clay god, bearing the foreman's features, from its pedestal. The bowl clattered to the ground and broke; but mocking him still, the many fragments of the wreckage turned into empty smiles, grinning at Webb from every shattered piece.

The sweat was rolling down his cheeks in thick streams, salting his lips. His breath came in short gasps, and he knew that he had to escape from the suffocating air. Staggering toward the exit, he ran into the fat boy, who, miraculously back at his side, chuckled: "Wrong way." Bewildered, Webb looked in all directions, but found that the room was spinning with him. Wherever he groped, someone was saying: "No exit," until, finally, in one direction there was silence. But at that moment, the foreman gripped his arm and pulled him back to the bar.

"You can't leave until I've told you about the painting," the foreman laughed. "You want to know all about it, don't you?"

Webb nodded, swaying irresolutely, longing for the clear cool air outside.

"I've seen the painting," the foreman whispered. "At least part of it." And as Webb raised his eyes to him, the foreman grinned: "The part on which you are portrayed."

Webb leaned against the bar, steadying himself against the fear, which gently as a cobweb, yet firmly as a mesh of steel, descended on him, precluding any chance of escape. He knew that he was expected to ask what his portrait revealed, but he could not; indeed, it rapidly became more and more urgent to avoid the truth, even if his life were at stake.

The foreman was watching him. "You still want to find the painting?" When Webb did not answer, the foreman's sneer turned into a grimace of contempt. "I thought so. You're like the rest of us. That's why you'll never get out of here. So you might as well settle down and prepare yourself to live in this tavern. You'll learn to pity yourself, to complain about the injustice of being hounded by unproven guilt. Yet all along you'll know that all we'd have to do to escape is to track down the truth." He smiled bitterly. "But that means facing yourself; all of yourself.

What courage that takes, you can't know until you've tried it. More courage than you need to face a raging monster. The kind of courage a little man like Crispian had in his thin body. And that's why you don't find him here any longer."

Webb looked up, surprised and confused; he could not believe that Crispian had also passed through this tavern. But the foreman was pointing at an empty table, the only one unoccupied, because it was situated directly beneath the weakest sector of the crumbling ceiling. "That's where he used to sit," the foreman muttered. "Almost every evening after work; slumped on his chair, exhausted after painting all day. Sometimes, he couldn't even talk, because he had no strength left—except in his eyes. His face kept getting thinner; he was losing weight all the time. But he wouldn't give up. He was going to have it out with himself; and he didn't care if it broke him."

The foreman's fist clenched on the plank. His voice sounded hollow and hoarse as he went on to describe Crispian's last evening in the tavern. Though Crispian usually sat alone, that night he had joined some of the miners; humble and quiet as always, he drank with his friends, seeking companionship after the harrowing solitude of the day's effort. But he was unable to join in the conversation; he was still too preoccupied to detach his thoughts from his work; his penetrating glance was still turned inward, his mind still in ferment. Close to the brink of exhaustion, he was nevertheless unable to rest or pacify his aroused nerves. And when one of the miners asked him, half-jokingly, how lifting a paint brush could be so tiring, he answered quite earnestly that this was the least strenuous part of the work. And suddenly speaking with such feverish intensity that their smiles soon vanished, he said it was the digging into one's soul that was so hard. It was the getting at the truth; the pushing away of rubble, the hacking, clawing, scratching at the surface; the breaking through, and the bringing up of things which were soiled from lying in stagnant pools of lies, but could be recovered and transformed into sparkling treasures.

"He used words that they could understand," the foreman said. "And we knew what he was talking about. But we didn't think he'd get very far; we were sure he wouldn't make it. I tried to warn him. I told him to give up. But he wouldn't listen. He looked at me with those tired, piercing, burning eyes, and he asked me why I didn't try it myself, since it was the only way out. So I told him—I had tried."

At that moment, the foreman's fist suddenly shot out at the toothless Indian, who, in passing, had swiftly filled the bowl; missing the elusive cripple, his hand slapped heavily on the bar plank; and after a while he picked up the bowl as though he had no choice but to go on drinking.

"I think, maybe, I was afraid he might prove that he was stronger than any of us. I kept urging him to drink, hoping that he'd learn to resign himself. But his will couldn't be broken, though in the end his body gave out; his shoulders slumped and his eyes closed; he had passed out. There was nothing to do but to take him home; I carried him all the way on my arms like a child. And when I entered his room, there was Mona. She turned white when she saw him unconscious in my arms. I put him down on his cot; and she bent over his lean face, forgetting all about me."

For a long while the foreman hesitated. "Maybe I shouldn't tell you this," he finally said, his voice rasping like a blade drawn over a whirling whet-stone, "but until Crispian came along, I'd had certain hopes regarding Mona. Not that I was alone in this. There isn't a man in Santa Rosa who is not in love with her. When you first meet her, it's hard to imagine what an effect this girl has on men. There is no more wonderful woman in the whole world. You might say, she's the only woman we can admire. The only one—and the same one for all of us."

Again he broke off, this time losing himself in a long silence. "I hadn't seen her for weeks; and when I met her in that room, I wanted to ask her point-blank why she preferred Crispian to me. But I never got to say anything. It was no use; she would not have heard me. She was holding that thin, emaciated figure in her arms, the body of a child; and there I stood, with my broad shoulders, and she didn't even know I was there."

He laughed, a hoarse, almost silent laughter, as if it were choked by the convulsive tremors sporadically surging up from his chest. "I looked around, and there, against the wall, was the canvas, rolled up like an ancient scroll on which truth was written from one end to the other. I started to pull back the roll, but it was heavy; and it grew heavier, until I couldn't move it another inch. There it was, right in front of me; all I had to do was unfold it, and I would see everything I should know, everything I'd always wanted to know. But my arms were locked in a vise so tight I couldn't budge. The more I strained to lift my hand, the less I could move it."

The foreman's voice had trailed off in a stifled sob, and Webb did not dare to look at him for fear of seeing the humiliating spectacle of a strong man overcome by tears.

"When a man who has always been proud of his strength has to face that he is a coward, it's worse than death. Maybe that's why so many strong men die rather than admit their fear. I don't know how long I stood there. I was sure that Mona was watching me, waiting to see what I would do; and that made it worse. So I tried again. I told myself that Crispian might not have discovered anything too bad in me; I didn't even know whether he had painted me at all. And I desperately wanted to see everything else on that canvas. But I had not turned the roll more than a foot, when a hand emerged from behind the bend, slowly reaching out on the unfolding canvas. It might have been my own; I never found out; I stopped pulling and dropped back. That was the end of it. I didn't get to see more than this narrow strip, right in front of my eyes, just as I've never been able to take a good, clear look at the world, because I was always afraid of running into myself if I took off my blinders."

He shook his head, clutching the bowl so hard that the knuckles of his massive hands turned a pallid gray. "After that, I didn't have to ask Mona why she preferred Crispian to me. I stepped back from the painting; I just didn't have it in me to look at all the truths this little man had dared to face. I walked to the door, and when I turned back, there she was, holding his small shoulders on her lap; his gaunt head with the sunken cheeks was raised up, and the limp arms were hanging over her knees. He was lying like a child in her embrace—but to me he looked like a giant. So I said nothing to her; I walked out, and I've never seen her again. Because I have to spend my evenings in this tavern, and after that night I know I'll never get out."

The murmuring chorus of the amorphous, nameless throng behind Webb swelled up in angry menace. He was swept by terror, when he sensed that he was being blamed in some way for the foreman's defeat, and for that reason was about to be attacked. Once again, he tried desperately to reach the exit, but his strength failed him after a few steps, and he tumbled against the bar plank.

Yet, before he could fall, someone was holding him up. Hovering over him was the face of a stranger, a man of remarkably distinguished appearance, whom he had not noticed before. The gentleman whispered that he had come to his rescue; speaking rapidly, he gave Webb instructions, detailing the method of escape; and although Webb did not understand the reasoning, he was impressed by its incisive logic. It was as helpful as the stranger's arm around his shoulders, which steadied him on the way to the exit. And Webb, at first resisting, then surrendering to the secure hold, sobbed helplessly, when he reached, at long last, the gently parting bead curtain.

CHAPTER V

OUTSIDE, Webb leaned against the wall, closing his eyes to avoid seeing the rapidly revolving plaza. The crisp mountain air, drying the sweat on his face, was beginning to clear his thoughts. Indeed, Webb was surprised how swiftly the effects of the colorless drink wore off. The second time he looked at the circling plaza, its speed had diminished; and soon, as though the brakes had been applied to a merry-go-round, the houses came to a halt, each in its former place, watching him silently and somehow defiantly, as though challenging him to doubt that they had actually performed their grotesquely exuberant dance.

"Permit me to introduce myself," the distinguished stranger said, after waiting politely until Webb had recovered. Flourishing his hat, he bowed courteously. "I'm Don Hernandez." When he saw that his name had failed to make an impression on Webb, he added, somewhat piqued: "Though we have never met, my dear Consul, you may remember that we've exchanged some letters."

Webb looked up, studying his savior with new interest. He did indeed recall the Hernandez correspondence, eccentric letters reaching him originally from Madrid, on stationery adorned by the emblems of several branches of an aristocratic family which traced its ancestry back to the medieval ages. The file, highly legalistic in content, involved the inheritance of a lost mine in the mountains above Santa Rosa, to which the Spanish nobleman claimed title, though he had neither any information regarding its location, nor even proof that it actually existed. The entire matter had appeared too much like the hopeless scheme of a crank to be taken seriously; and it had certainly not occurred to Webb that the Spaniard might be persistent enough to pursue his alleged inheritance to this wilderness; nor could he have imagined the writer of the bizarre and at times ludicrous letters to be a man of such distinguished appearance. There might be more to this lost mine than Webb had assumed; for the man certainly did not look like a fool; his eyes glimmered with an extraordinary, even dangerous intelligence.

When Webb inquired whether he had located the mine, the Spaniard sighed, his eyes momentarily losing their sparkle, clouded by a dark hunger. "My dear Consul, this is too serious a matter to be discussed in the streets. If you will follow me to my home, I shall be happy to submit all the proof to your judgment."

Without waiting for Webb's consent, he bowed, clicked his heels, and led the way, crossing the plaza with an alacrity which somehow stirred Webb's suspicion. He felt quite sure that the Spaniard was drawing him to his home for some undisclosed purpose, and he grew increasingly distrustful. When he saw that Don Hernandez was heading directly toward the dark lane, previously avoided not only by Webb but by the three villagers as well, he slowed down, falling behind, and finally stopping altogether. The Spaniard turned and faced him across an empty distance, his eyes glittering beneath the high, pallid dome of his forehead which was fringed by silvery hair of a shade much like Webb's own.

For a while, they studied each other. Don Hernandez did not repeat his invitation, nor did he attempt to persuade Webb. Instead he offered a deal. "My dear Mr. Webb," he said coldly, "before you decide to refuse my hospitality, may I point out that I have some information of considerable value to you. The fact is, I might help you find the painting."

He turned and walked ahead, not once looking back at Webb, as though he knew that the consul could not resist. And, indeed, Webb felt himself irresistibly drawn toward the opaque lane, which opened like a yawning gullet waiting to swallow him. To dodge it, to avoid it became increasingly important; but there was nothing to hold on to; everything was gliding with Webb, the very air was streaming toward that dark channel; and in the end he yielded to a vast surrender which made even death appear preferable to any further resistance.

But at the last moment, an unexpected sound came to meet them from the depth of the lane; approaching footsteps reverberated in the darkness, as though within the walls of a tunnel, unhurried and yet steadily coming closer with an inevitable, almost fateful beat. Webb stood frozen to the ground, waiting tensely at Don Hernandez' side, scanning the black void, until a silhouette emerged, detaching itself, growing, starting to cast a shadow and following it; and finally condensing, not into a spectre of terror, but into the vastly reassuring, black-robed figure of Padre Paolo.

The Padre seemed almost as relieved as Webb, when at last they met again. "I was searching for you everywhere," he said, after greeting Don Hernandez. "My heart was troubled, for you might have come to harm, a stranger in a strange town." He hesitated, looking from Webb to Don Hernandez, as if he were trying to judge how well they had come to know each other. "It is late," he said to Webb. "I shall show you the way back to Senor Barrie's house."

"Just a moment," Don Hernandez said. "Mr. Webb has expressed a wish to visit my humble abode."

Padre Paolo held the consul with his dark, questioning eyes. Standing between the two men, Webb grew flustered. He sensed that there was a deep-seated antagonism between them; he had never seen the Padre so restrained in his manner, nor so disturbed and uncomfortable as in the presence of the Spaniard.

"You haven't changed your mind, have you?" Don Hernandez smiled.

"I apologize," Webb stuttered, "but I might not find my way back. Perhaps, I could visit you—some other time."

"As you like," the Spaniard said, gracefully covering his defeat with a nonchalant smile. "But in case you should change your mind, permit me to show you where I live." Drawing Webb to the edge of the lane, he forced him to look at the dark rim of the hills, behind which the base of El Soledad was hidden. "Right there. Almost in the center of the pass." He was pointing to the triangular wedge, where a light glimmered in utter loneliness.

Then he bowed, clicked his heels, flourished his hat, and walked briskly down the lane, his agile figure wading bravely into the rising flood of darkness, until he was submerged, the sound of his footsteps surviving him a while longer like a lingering memory.

Padre Paolo led Webb in the opposite direction, guiding him toward a steep street which plunged into the plaza with the arrested speed of a dry creek. Having turned his back to the dark lane, Webb felt a sudden decrease of its overpowering magnetism; and before long, it began to seem unlikely, if not incomprehensible, that he had ever felt its hypnotic influence.

At this point, he could not even understand his fear of Don Hernandez. The man, after all, was no menacing phantom stalking the dark streets of Santa Rosa; Webb knew his entire background, all the data were in the file at the consulate. And yet, Webb had been deeply affected; for unknown reasons, something inside of him had strongly responded to the Spaniard. It would be important to uncover the cause; and Webb began to regret that he had left the man so abruptly. He now felt that he had to know more about him, and he questioned the Padre.

"I have known him for more than a year," the Padre replied. "Yet, I cannot say that I know him well." He broke off; and when Webb prodded him by explaining that Don Hernandez had claimed to possess valuable information concerning the lost painting, the Padre listened attentively and in the end agreed: "He would not lie to you. Whatever else may be said against him, one cannot question his sincerity. A most dedicated man. Truly he is. The more is the pity."

The Padre fell silent; his reluctance to discuss Don Hernandez hinted at some sort of personal involvement which rendered a fair judgment either too difficult or too painful. Yet, perhaps for the same reason, he was unable to dismiss him from his thoughts without attempting to justify himself. "I have often prayed for him. He is much in my thoughts. It may be, senor, that among the many human errors the one most disturbing to us is to see a good man pursue the right aim in the wrong way." Again he paused. "It is so with Don Hernandez. He means well. He is a brilliant scholar in many fields; also somewhat of a theologian. And surely he cannot be blamed for wanting to take possession of the rich mine he has inherited. But he will not succeed."

"Has he, at least, managed to locate it?"

"Indeed, senor. He has obtained irrefutable proof that it is at Zapar, a lost village, situated so high up on the mountain that it cannot be reached, for it almost touches the peak of El Soledad."

Webb remembered the dark hunger in Don Hernandez's eyes, and now understood its cause. In all likelihood, the Spaniard had made his home on the pass, so that he could watch the mountain; hopelessly pinned down, he was both dreaming of his inaccessible wealth and seeking ways to take hold of it.

"It is truly a tragic promise," the Padre continued, "as it would be to any man. To inherit such wealth and yet to find it withheld. Quite naturally, he seeks means to appropriate what already belongs to him. But all his legal documents do not suffice; for there is a clause in the testament requiring that he must personally take possession. And he will never reach Zapar by building a ladder with his proofs, no more than the kings of Babylon could penetrate the sky with their tower."

The Padre shook his head. "I have tried to reason with him. But it is no use. He does not dare to climb to Zapar; and he refuses to leave Santa Rosa. When I question the wisdom of his legal maneuvers, he gets angry and retaliates by questioning my faith, my right to believe without proof. His arguments are so clever that, each time I leave him, I am shaken. For he is an educated, well-read man, and I am only a mountain priest with no schooling and a slow mind. So he never fails to defeat me with his brilliant logic, and I go away with doubts in my heart, until, in the course of my lonely travels, I hear the truth speaking to me in words so plain, so simple that even a child could understand. And then I know that he is wrong. But I cannot tell him why, for I know not how to prove it."

Troubled by his insufficiency, the Padre lapsed into silence. The strain of climbing the steep street taxed their lungs, making speech more difficult. On two occasions, the descending torrent of stone was broken by stairs, which slowed their ascent. The houses, rearing up like cliffs on each side of the street's narrow crevasse, were mostly still, their inhabitants having retired for the night, though now and then the Padre was greeted by a tardy villager closing some shutters, or lugging a last load of firewood to his kitchen.

"About Senor Crispian," the Padre said, when they stopped at the end of a long flight of stairs, "what have you found?"

Looking down on the plaza, now a small square far below them, Webb told the Padre all he had learned from Barrie and Mona; from the widow, the notes, and the foreman. The bits and pieces of information seemed to fall into place while he spoke; and their conglomeration began shaping a continuous whole, tracing Crispian's course from his arrival in Santa Rosa to the last evening spent in the tavern with his friends, the miners. But there the thread snapped; beyond that day, he had no hint, no clue, not the slightest indication of Crispian's fate. This total lack of further information was too surprising to be accidental; and Webb suddenly realized that the fault was his own; unconsciously, he had refrained from asking questions which might have revealed to him how much further Crispian would draw him.

"And then?" the Padre asked, watching him unobtrusively.

Webb looked away. "That's all I know."

"You didn't hear where he went after he left Santa Rosa?"

"No." Webb started to walk ahead, as if he could outrun the knowledge that was coming toward him. "I wasn't even aware that he had left. No one told me."

"And you didn't ask," the Padre said, falling in step beside him. "This is strange, senor, for you must have known that he could not have remained here." When Webb did not attempt to defend himself, the Padre, scrutinizing him with a sidelong glance, continued: "In truth, senor, to have climbed so high and not to go further is difficult. It is better then to be in the plains; better even in the jungle. For there is no peace in Santa Rosa. No peace and no rest."

For a moment, Webb wondered whether the Padre was hinting that Crispian had returned to the jungle; but he did not dare to make sure. Even doubt was preferable to the certainty that Crispian had gone higher still, and that Webb would have to follow him. "He could not have left Santa Rosa before he finished the painting," he said hastily, in an attempt to stall the Padre.

"I don't know," the Priest said, thoughtfully. "He was interrupted, senor. It is certain that he had not yet accomplished his work, when he was driven from the widow's home."

"Driven?"

The Padre nodded. "By Senor Barrie." He went on to report what he had heard from one of his parishioners, a girl who had stayed behind in church after mass. A friend of Mona's, she had been instrumental in helping Crispian escape from Barrie's wrath. When Barrie had found out that his daughter continued to see the painter, even visiting him secretly in the widow's house, he had been seized by a murderous rage. As the boss of the mine, he dominated the town; and Crispian, warned just in time, had to seek refuge on Don Hernandez' hacienda. The Spaniard had kept him hidden in his distant and isolated place, where Crispian continued to work on his painting in a converted barn, while Barrie assumed, as did the rest of the town, that he had fled back to the jungle.

"How long did he stay on the hacienda?"

"Two or three weeks," the Padre replied. "Until suddenly—one morning—he was gone."

"Did he take the painting along?"

"I don't know, senor."

"It seems impossible that he would have left it behind," Webb concluded hopefully, almost triumphantly. "And if he took it along, he must have returned to the plains."

"He did not return, senor." The Padre, emphasizing each word, dropped the short, compact sentence like a rock in the path of further evasions. "Surely you must have suspected that he could not resist El Soledad. By now, you have been long enough in Santa Rosa to have experienced the pull of the mountain."

A chill ran down Webb's spine; he felt small and naked, stripped of all subterfuge. They had reached a high platform, where a side-lane veered off at sharp angle. The Padre was gazing at a distant spot to his right, and when Webb followed his glance, the majestic silhouette of El Soledad came to meet him halfway, an indistinct substance, visible only as a dense dark within darkness.

"How high did he go?" Webb asked, no longer pretending.

"Zapar."

The word fell like a hammer blow. Webb shrank from the harsh and forbidding sounds in the name of the village just below the peak, where Don Hernandez' lost mine was located. His eyes followed the mountain's rising contours, but could not trace them all the way to the summit, which, merging with the night, was shrouded in darkness. While staring at the distant height, he felt himself seized by the indescribable fascination of the soaring lines, lured on imperceptibly, gently, and yet irresistibly—until he succumbed, all of a sudden, to an attack of vertigo so turbulent that he had to hold on to the Priest.

Regaining his balance, he noticed that the Padre was watching him with a fixed stare. In no way surprised by Webb's vertigo, indeed referring to it, the Padre asked quietly: "Do you still wish to follow Senor Crispian to the end of his journey?"

The question which Webb had feared so much had finally overtaken him. And he was not ready for it; he could not reach a decision; it was too soon after the ordeal in the tavern. He still felt hollow and weak, all wound inside; and he knew his surface composure to be so brittle that it could not withstand any test; it was bound to collapse under pressure. "I haven't thought about it," he said curtly and turned away, hoping that the finality of the gesture, if not the meaning of the words, would ward off the Priest.

But Padre Paolo either failed to detect the intent of Webb's evasion, or he chose to ignore it. Determined to force the issue, he said: "If you choose to return, senor, I shall guide you back to the coast."

For a long while, they walked along in silence. The Padre, after pressing the choice, could do nothing further to hasten Webb's decision. They were climbing up a curved stairway, when Webb asked: "Do you consider it at all possible that I could reach Zapar?"

"I cannot say, senor." Evidently, the Padre did not want to influence Webb one way or another; but in spite of his desire to avoid any responsibility, he could not refrain from conveying a warning. "The road is hard, senor; as harsh as the mountain. Perhaps too harsh for all but the few." His shoulders sank. "It was too harsh for me."

"For you?" Webb looked at him, startled. "You have attempted it?"

The Padre nodded. "Once. Some years ago. Never since." His eyes closed as though to blot out the remembrance of inhuman struggle and defeat. In halting speech, he related how he had been called to Zapar by the Indians living in the small mountain village, a strange tribe quite unlike any other in the entire territory. They were short, sturdy men, with powerful lungs, as enlarged as those of some Indian tribes who had adapted themselves to the highest regions of the Western Andes; indeed, the inhabitants of Zapar might be an offshoot of those tribes, though it was inexplicable how they could have drifted so far afield. Since they rarely descended to Santa Rosa, very little was known of them, not even how many of them had survived. They were uncommunicative, jealously defending their isolation; proud and silent, they clung to their mountain fortress, enduring its hardships without complaint or surrender.

"I had never expected to hear from them," the Padre said. "But one day, a messenger tracked me down in the jungle. Their chief's brother had lost both arms in a rock slide. I was summoned to bind up his wounds, and I had to obey; for this was a duty I could not refuse." A harrowed expression dilated his eyes as he described the ascent; a strong wind, finally turning into a storm, had opposed him at every step; and by the time it let up, his spirit was broken. He barely managed to drag himself to the shelter above the glacier, the only refuge in the entire region, about halfway up. "I could not climb beyond the waist of the mountain, senor. My strength was shattered. And they did not help me. In truth, senor, they are a strange people; for they would not support me the rest of the way, so that I could reach Zapar. Instead, they carried down the wounded man on a stretcher. And by the time they reached the shelter, he had died."

The Padre's voice was almost inaudible, while he described how the Indians were sitting around, speaking in a strange language. In the end they had departed without paying any attention to him, as if he were not worth being noticed, because he had lacked strength to make his way to Zapar. And they had left the dead man behind, discarding the lifeless body as if its disposition were of no further concern to them. And the man's dead eyes kept staring at the Padre until he could no longer endure it. He ran from the refuge, preferring the awesome descent, staggering downward, falling, tumbling, his legs cut and his hands bleeding. "I shall never know," the Padre stammered, "how I found my way back to Santa Rosa. It was late at night, when I dragged myself into the church; and I prayed until dawn, seeking the help and the guidance which the Indians had refused me. And in the end my heart opened to tell me that my strength had failed, because the wish to cure the sick was not enough to challenge the mountain. And I knew then that I would be called again and must try once more."

The mountain priest's breath came in short gasps; and all of a sudden Webb understood why Padre Paolo had pressed him so mercilessly for a decision. Afraid that the summons he expected might come through Webb, he had tried to turn him back, but without openly dissuading him. And indeed, at that moment, the Padre was saying: "It is possible to reach Zapar. And if you decide to risk it, I cannot refuse to guide you." He looked down to conceal the plea in his eyes, adding humbly: "The choice, senor, is yours."

The Padre's anxiety was so intense that Webb was impelled to reassure him at once; but at the same time, he was reluctant to commit himself. He had grown increasingly aware that he was facing one of the most important decisions of his life; for to interrupt the journey short of his goal, to run from the challenge without even submitting himself to the test, would be more humiliating than any failure or defeat. Indeed, the prospect of future doubts and remorse made the withdrawal to Puerto Carribas appear as difficult as the ascent to Zapar. It almost seemed that he had run into a trap which was rapidly closing.

The Padre slowed down at a high crossroad near the end of the town. Pointing to the left, he said: "This is the road which will lead you back to Senor Barrie's house."

Webb looked at the angry building which had appeared at the distant end of the sidestreet like a cork bottling up a narrow outlet. The Padre's glance turned to a lonely house clinging to the hill above them. "I shall spend the night away from you. There is illness in the home of the Senora Rivaz. Her father—he is old and will not live to see the dawn." His massive shoulders bulged under the black cloth, unconsciously responding to his acceptance of the heavy loads placed on him by other people's sorrow. "They want me to wait for his death."

Webb passed the crossroads, climbing a few steps higher, and then looking down on the glittering lights of the village.

"Where are you going, senor?" the Padre asked.

"I don't know," Webb said. In every direction, he saw hills softly billowing toward the sky. There was no level ground in Santa Rosa; one could not walk evenly along horizontal streets as in Puerto Carribas. In this mountain village, one either ascended or descended; one always had to choose.

The Padre approached. "You will need some rest, if you decide to climb to Zapar. El Soledad is a proud mountain, and does not admit those who are tired." Waiting in vain for Webb's answer, he prodded: "We shall have to leave at dawn—if it is still your wish to follow Senor Crispian to the end of his journey."

Webb felt the Padre's glance resting on him as heavily as at the crossroads to Irozco, when the Priest had stopped him, showing him the opaque trail vanishing in the jungle. At that time, Webb had found the courage to proceed. But now, as he looked up to the crest, which divided the dirt road from the sky, a nameless terror, impalpable, distantly present, a black dust of fear, came rushing toward him from all sides, blown up by the night until it stood before him as a shapeless phantom, contemptuously eyeing his weakness.

In that instant, Webb knew that he could not force his way past this mocking apparition; but his cowardice was too humiliating to be confessed. "I'd follow Crispian," he blurted out, "if it'd serve any purpose. But you said yourself those Indians at Zapar don't speak our language. They would not tell us anything about him."

"I did not say that, senor." The Padre was looking at him sadly. "They might."

A strange contest had developed between the two men; each was compelled to push the burden of refusal upon the other.

"Even so," Webb stuttered, clutching at straws, "they could not tell us as much as Crispian has told us in his painting. If we could find the painting—"

The Padre interrupted. "The painting, senor, may be at Zapar."

"Impossible," Webb cried out, triumphantly. "The canvas was too heavy. He could not have taken it along."

The Padre's dark eyes did not let go of Webb. "Senor," he said quietly, "what did you set out to discover? What is more important to you? Crispian, the man—or his work?"

The trap had closed, demanding of Webb, as a price for his release, the surrender of all his pride. "The man," he whispered. Having thus confessed his weakness, he now flung himself into extremes of self-contempt. Suddenly carried away by a fierce desire to prostrate and humiliate and debase himself, he screamed: "I can't go on. I can't! I don't have the strength!" He listened to the silence, as though he were waiting to be reproached or forgiven, condemned or absolved, at any rate expecting an answer. But the silence grew, spread, flowing freely and irretrievably toward borderless expanses of time, until Webb shouted: "One cannot ask more of a man than there is in him. I know my limitations—I should never have allowed myself to be drawn from Puerto Carribas."

Finding no other objective than himself for his churning anger, he forcibly diverted it to Padre Paolo. "You were waiting to hear me say that I'm running away. All right—I'm saying it! I want to get away as fast as I can. I'm going back to the coast in the morning!"

The Padre had left him at the crossroads. His black robe flowing in the wind, he had disappeared and reappeared around the bends of the serpentine path, until he arrived at the solitary house where he would wait for a life to end and for a death to begin, the death of an old man, the father of the Senora Rivaz.

For a long while, Webb did not move. His outburst, after draining him of all energy, had given way to an oppressive calm singularly devoid of any aims. The abrupt change in his plans had left an emptiness which had to be filled. But after the brief and almost exultantly tragic moment of his renunciation, he had to look forward to flat years of grinding resignation; to a shameful retreat and a humiliating return to Puerto Carribas; to the unendurable yet enduring despair of his self-inflicted defeat.

The prospect was too harrowing to be faced so soon after the unmerciful annihilation of his pride; and his thoughts, weary of straying about in scattered panic, soon focused on his sole remaining objective: to find Crispian's painting.

As a result, he decided to return to the plaza, and from there to proceed to Don Hernandez' hacienda. But he had not gone very far, when one of the streets he had chosen at an intersection, though at first plunging downward at a steep angle, unexpectedly arched upward again, carrying him to the crest of another hill. Somewhat confused, he went down another road, which promised to descend farther; but again the same thing happened, and he was swept up to the rim of another hill.

Time and again, he was hurtled from one crest to another like a small boat in a choppy sea. Descending, he had the sinking feeling of one shooting down an endless decline; and when he climbed upward, he was lifted by the hope of reaching a vantage point from which he could see far enough to orient himself. But the hills were never sufficiently high, never quite gave him a chance to look beyond the repetition of other small elevations. And it occurred to him that, if he were trapped in Santa Rosa, this was how his days would be spent; indeed, it might be compared to what his life had been in Puerto Carribas; a life of small victories and small frustrations, the victories losing their value as soon as they were achieved, the frustrations too petty to permit a sense of tragedy, since they turned too rapidly from pain to boredom to have any meaning.

Yet, one could not stand still, neither on the crest nor in the trough. For as one sank down, the hills inevitably rose up, becoming more alluring with a promise which was not fulfilled when one had climbed them, because then they were no longer high, but had levelled out under one's feet. What made it worse was the knowledge that somewhere behind all those little mounds was the soaring peak of El Soledad, the single majestic slope that offered to unify the separate starts and futile little achievements into one steady ascent, promising a cumulative result to one's efforts, instead of the merely repetitive movement which left its events like stones on a road traveled, instead of piling them unto a pyramid as a monument to own or to contemplate toward the end of one's life.

Looking around, Webb noticed that the shutters on all the houses he passed were tightly drawn over the windows; apparently, he was not the only one affected by the mountain's obtrusive presence. In the plains, the questions it raised could be ignored; but here, in the immediate vicinity, the conflict could not be pushed from one's mind. It was inevitable that the people of Santa Rosa vacillated between yearning for all the mountain promised, and shrinking from all it demanded; every hour of the day, they would wonder, doubt, measuring their courage against their weak points, longing and refraining, much like the inhabitants of a gambling town who are under the constant strain of deciding whether or not to test their luck.

It gradually became apparent that the last street Webb had chosen was leading him beyond the confines of the town. Rising less steeply than the others, it soon turned into a dirt road, then into a narrow trail winding along the watershed of the promontory which hugged the town like an arm holding a sleeping child.

Striding along briskly, Webb often stumbled over rocks, and occasionally over dead branches which snapped at his legs as they broke. At one point, coming dangerously near to the edge of a cliff, he obtained a full view of the valley; and there he could see, for the first time, that the promontory was curving gently toward the lonely light in Don Hernandez' house.

Relieved that he could reach the hacienda without passing through the dark lane at the plaza, he accelerated his steps. For a half hour or more, he forged ahead between trees, twisted into tortuous shapes by the storms thundering down from El Soledad. The path was smooth enough to permit rapid progress, until suddenly the ground gave way under his feet, and he fell against the broken remnants of a brick wall. Scrambling up, despite a fierce pain in his left leg, he saw that he had tumbled into the shattered foundations of a building, perhaps the ruins of the old mission which Mona had mentioned. And indeed, crowning the slope to his right, was the simple cross, the two withered sticks nailed together, which Crispian had described in his notes.

Haunted, Webb tried to escape from the abandoned mission; but he could not easily find his way out of the sprawling ruin. For some time, he erred about in a graveyard of lost prayers and devout offerings accepted and unaccepted, of solemn questions answered and unanswered, of humble dedication by men long since vanished. The eroded belfry had tumbled on the chapel, crushing it, shattering its roof and breaking its cross-beams which stuck from the mangled body like splintered ribs. Finally, after passing across the empty refectory, Webb managed to regain the road; but as he hurried away, shaken and trembling, his foot loosened a stone which rolled back, striking a half-buried bell, so that its eery reverberations pursued him, following him down the path, until the stirred-up ghosts came to rest in an uncertain silence.

It took longer than he had expected to reach the pass; and when the path ceased to curve toward the right, gradually disappearing from sight, he wondered where he had lost his way. But since he could not be far from Don Hernandez' house, he nevertheless went ahead, directing his steps toward a clearing where the moonlight, which was now beginning to filter through the trees, formed a triangular pool of unobstructed radiance. When he reached the outermost edge of the plateau, his breath caught, and he stood rooted to the ground, unable to absorb all at once the splendor of the spectacular view before him.

He saw not only the pass to his right; he saw, beyond it, the side-valley to which it led, a mile-wide traverse, slightly tilted as it rose toward the base of El Soledad. The immense cone of the mountain's foundation, a rilled, furrowed, rubble-strewn surface, ancient and withered, covered an incredibly vast area, as if it were gathering strength from far and wide to support the colossal summit. Yet here, at its roots, there was no hint of the precipitous walls near the peak; the lines mounted casually, almost lazily, as if the giant were not yet flexing its muscles, preserving its energies for the heavier tasks to come, when the struggle to lift the stony ramparts higher and higher began in earnest.

Though Webb strained his eyes, he could not penetrate those upper levels. The moonlight was moving along the ground in a semi-circular area, reproducing the shape of the break in the clouds. As it glided upward along the lower slopes, they came to life, glittering, sparkling, the rills and rocks shifting, scurrying about, while rearranging their shadows. Everywhere the rising flood of light touched off intense, almost hurried activity; the impenetrable darkness receded rapidly, disclosing more and more of its cloaked possessions in a splendorous unveiling. Webb held his breath, hardly able to wait until the full height of the distant peak would be revealed; but suddenly the light paled, struggling a moment longer as the clouds narrowed the circle, and finally fading, vanishing as though extinguished; and soon the magnificent vision had expired in total darkness, as if it had never existed. And when Webb's eyes tried to recapture the lost splendor, there was nothing left but the pinpoint of light flickering in Don Hernandez' house.

The wind kept whistling past him, while he stood at the edge of the cliff, waiting for the moon to break through once more. But the clouds did not part, and the giant remained hidden, watching Webb rather than being watched by him. Looking at the dark valley, Webb thought of Crispian, who had once honored him by calling him his brother. In retrospect, Webb's rejection of the poor painter seemed impossible; for now he had to consider this humbly offered kinship as a precious gift too generously bestowed. Their positions had been so far reversed that Webb now found his sole comfort in the reflected glory of his pride in Crispian, who had ventured forth into the unexplored darkness; an anonymous hero, stepping forth from the ranks of timid souls, daring the ascent of the mountain, setting out, with the simple dignity of true courage, toward the distant heights of the human spirit.

Though Webb could not follow him, he nevertheless had a share in Crispian's glory and sacrifice, as anyone has whenever man's proud spirit rushes beyond the barriers of human weakness and debility, undaunted by his infinitely low station, or by the foregone conclusion of his inevitable defeat. And despite the painful realization of his personal inadequacy, Webb could no longer feel entirely discouraged or contemptuous of himself, because Crispian was truly his brother, as were all the other men throughout history who had pitted their souls against the impossible.

Embraced by this larger brotherhood of men, Webb no longer found it so difficult to accept his limitations which had never before intruded upon his consciousness with such clarity. He was a small man, a man of modest gifts and modest ambitions, and he had tried all along to regard his inadequacy as an asset, defending it with a smug vanity. But, strangely enough, at this point he no longer suffered from the blow that had swept away the array of his prides, small and large, which even the most modest person must accumulate and preserve as protection against the unbearable truth of everyone's innermost insufficiency. Instead, he found that the hidden shame, which is the inevitable counterpart of any pride, had melted away in the collapse of all barriers.

What was left was an unexpected wish to be more than he knew himself to be, so that he could approach the greater goals he had come to recognize; an unexpected longing to rise above the mediocre satisfactions which had once seemed so full of promise, but now lay as far behind him as the flatlands of Puerto Carríbas. Here he stood, halfway between what he had been and what he now yearned to be, his honest self-appraisal no longer content with his past competence, yet warning him to stay within the limits of his strength. Indeed, he keenly sensed the danger in his recognition of the beauty above him; he might yet succumb to the fascination of the rich rewards promised to anyone exploring his being to the limits of his potential.

In spite of his vehement decision to escape from the mountain, the contest, he suddenly realized, was not yet at an end. His rejection had not been accepted; and he would have to be on guard, prepared to meet any swift and unforeseen onslaught of the fateful attraction.

CHAPTER VI

A THIN, lean, old, shrewish housekeeper sent Webb to the stable where he found Don Hernandez behind three merry, prancing goats; surrendering none of his aristocratic bearing to the manual occupation, he was milking the liveliest of the three animals as ceremoniously as if he were engaged in some important ritual.

"Welcome, Mr. Webb," he said, in no way embarrassed, nor showing any surprise that his reluctant guest had arrived after all. When the udder ceased to respond to the delicate touch of his sensitive, long, tapering fingers, he picked up the bucket, invited Webb to follow him, opened the stable door with a stiff bow, and crossed toward the main building; on the way, he vaguely indicated the various barn-like shacks with the brief explanation: "Self-supporting!"

They passed through heavy entrance doors into the house, where the eccentric nobleman handed the bucket to the housekeeper with as graceful a gesture as if he were presenting to her a precious gift. The shrew, however, did not accept it in that spirit; taking it from him rather gruffly, she asked whether he had cleaned out the stable. Webb did not hear the answer, for his attention had been drawn to the many works of art adorning the lofty hall, which reminded him in design and construction of an old Spanish castle. The candles burning in four candelabra could not dispel the brooding gloom gathered under the arched ceiling; yet, they cast enough light on the paintings and statuettes to permit Webb to evaluate their rare and precious beauty. Apparently, the Spaniard, in moving to Santa Rosa, had taken along all or a portion of his possessions; he had come prepared for a protracted sojourn.

It was not the first time that Webb had stumbled into an island of civilization and luxury where he least expected it. Some years ago, while traveling across Mexico on official business, he had stopped at the house of a wealthy American, an insurance broker

113

from New York, who had retired at the age of forty. Webb hardly believed his eyes, when he saw, in the midst of a jungle, the fabulous home which this man had built for himself. Enjoying his solitude in extravagant comfort, he never ventured beyond the few villages in the immediate vicinity; not even to visit another American whose house, equally isolated and luxurious, was only a hundred miles away. Indeed, the only communication between them was shortly before Christmas, when they sent each other some cases of scotch, sometimes receiving the same brand they had dispatched.

"I want you to meet my wife," Don Hernandez said, leading Webb into the drawing room.

Webb studied the little, plump woman who nodded a friendly reply to his greeting, without interrupting her busy knitting. She sat, rather uncomfortably, in an ornate, straight-backed chair, which did not fit her figure; indeed, she did not seem to fit either into the Gothic surroundings or to Don Hernandez. In every respect, she appeared to be his opposite, not too bright, but sturdy, down-to-earth, sensible, a Sancho Panza to his Don Quixote.

"Mr. Webb is the American Consul in Puerto Carribas," Don Hernandez explained. "He came to find the painting."

When she looked up, gazing at the beautifully framed picture on the wall opposite her, he smiled indulgently. "Not the Goya, my dear. Mr. Webb is not generally interested in art. He was forced to travel so far to conduct an official investigation, on behalf of his government." He smiled at Webb. "At least, such is the rumor around town."

When she looked at him questioningly, the Spaniard went on: "However, it might be safe to assume that Mr. Webb has far more important reasons—of a personal nature. As a matter of fact, I'm inclined to believe that we owe the honor of his visit to the fact that he could not resist the overpowering wish to see what our friend Crispian had to say to him in the last will and testament. I'm referring, of course, to his painting."

Webb ignored the ironically phrased truth. He had noticed that a shadow had crossed the woman's face when Crispian's name was mentioned. Meeting Webb's glance, she quickly turned back to her knitting.

"Unfortunately, Mr. Webb," Don Hernandez continued, "the painting is not my property. I'm not allowed to show it to you without authorization from Mona. However, if you wish, I shall send a message to her; let us hope she'll consent."

With a courteous gesture he invited Webb to follow him; they crossed to the adjoining study, where the Spaniard sat down at a cluttered desk and wrote a brief note.

"Suppose Mona refuses to grant her permission?" Webb asked.

"In that case, my dear sir, I should be placed in a very difficult position." He looked up with a thin smile. "Aggravated by the fact that I'm as eager to show you the painting as you are to see it. However, I'm a man of honor; and I'd find it most painful to prove myself unworthy of her confidence. Except under certain conditions."

"Are you suggesting a bargain?"

Don Hernandez studied Webb as cooly as if he were measuring an opponent. "Before we discuss an arrangement, I suggest we wait until we have Mona's reply."

"Why do you want me to see the painting?"

The Spaniard's pen scratched as he signed the message with a flourish. "For one thing, because it is apt to affect you most powerfully." His smile became even more enigmatic, when he added: "For another, I should be willing to wager that it will force you—to climb to Zapar."

"How?" Everything in Webb froze in guarded tension.

Don Hernandez shrugged, giving no answer. He blotted the ink, got up, and left the room to give the message to the house-keeper.

Webb, swiftly exploring the Spaniard's hidden motives, came to suspect that his host would attempt to send him to Zapar; it was the most likely conclusion considering Don Hernandez's need to obtain more precise information in regard to his mine. As a result, Webb prepared himself to reject any attempt at persuasion, to turn back any maneuver, to refuse any deal. This did not seem to present any difficulty; he felt assured that nothing the Spaniard could say or do would weaken, much less break his resistance. But the cryptic reference to the painting was far more troubling; no matter how much Webb racked his brain, he could not guess or foresee what unpredictable element that canvas might contain, what surprise he might run into, what shock might throw him off guard.

He heard the voices of Don Hernandez and the housekeeper in the hallway, at first in hushed conversation, then clashing in heated altercation; but he could not understand what the quarrel was about. Looking around the small, cluttered study, he became intrigued by the vast number of books, nearly bursting the shelves which lined all four walls up to the ceiling, the overflow being stacked in high piles on the floor. The collection, as Webb soon discovered, was priceless, containing row upon row of rare volumes, first editions, old printings, precious medieval scrolls; yet value alone had not governed their acquisition. The selection of titles revealed a guiding motif, a central subject of study. There were, as Webb saw at a quick glance, not only the Latin and Greek philosophers, but Persian mystics, the Koran and the Bhagavad-Gita with several commentaries; gnostics and agnostics; Talmudic literature together with the Cabala; Egyptian hiero-glyphics, Sanskrit and Arabic writing, translated and expounded; all the early church fathers, some obscure monks, and many mys-terious alchemists; the ecstatic writing of Western and Oriental visionaries. An entire section was reserved to the books of the Bible, not only of the old and the new testament, but also of the excluded apocryphal works. On a bottom shelf Webb found com-prehensive compilations of primitive myths, sagas, fairy tales gath-ered from all parts of the earth, from all races, peoples, and tribes. These, in turn, alternated with volumes of anthropological, cul-tural, and psychoanalytical studies, all attempting to reduce the poetry of myth formation to scientific fact, and perhaps not quite succeeding.

The same incongruous juxtaposition was repeated on other shelves. Everywhere Webb found well-thumbed and well-studied scientific works, not of a general nature, but selected to serve the specific aim of contradicting the holy scriptures, to correct, ana-lyze, explain, and by explaining to refute them. The clashing combination was too pointed to be without meaning; and Webb wondered whether it indicated a desire on the part of Don Her-nandez to disprove, or by denying to prove more surely; to obtain, after filtering all the miraculous testimony through the sieve of rational arguments, the pure substance, indisputably true. This, indeed, was more likely; for Webb remembered that the Spaniard had applied, in his bizarre correspondence, the same method of matching proof against counterproof, until in the end he produced, as magically as by a sleight-of-hand, a conclusion, which, in consequence of much testing, appeared to be irrefutable.

"Ah, my dear friend," Don Hernandez exclaimed, as he came through the door, "I see you are interested in my library. A priceless collection. My hobby, sir, and my passion."

There could be no doubt that it was a passion when he began to tell Webb, with the fierce pride of the collector, how, where, and under what difficulties he had acquired some of the rarer volumes. They were, he explained, vitally important to his work, absolutely necessary to carry on his research. Having started on the subject he could not stop. His eagerness to discuss his work with someone intelligent enough to understand it was almost pathetic; Webb's visit obviously presented to him a rare, if not unique, opportunity. At length he explained his method and approach, but neglected to mention the subject matter of his monumental work, being so immersed in detail that he forgot to outline the overall content. As far as Webb could gather, Don Hernandez had undertaken to compile an immense encyclopedia of comparative religion for the express purpose of proving that certain beliefs were undeniable facts, facts as concrete and indisputably true as any established by the natural sciences.

"Let me show you," Don Hernandez said, a proud and yet uncertain smile flickering on his pale lips, as he bent down to pick up a medieval scroll. "Thirteenth century. Alsatian visionary." After handing the parchment to Webb, he selected a small book from a nearby shelf. "Sixth century. A Chinese poet. Compare the similarity of detail in the description of their visions. Notice the words they use in expressing their joy at the wealth they found. Most remarkable, the way they both agree on all essential points." With a sweeping gesture, he encompassed the entire wall. "In fact, up and down the centuries, there is a conspiracy of agreement, a perplexing amount of individual testimony, each so similar to the other, though the witnesses were invariably alone at the decisive moments, that we cannot assume it to be perjured. Indeed, if we attempted to doubt their veracity, we could not possibly explain their miraculous agreement; and we would have to solve a far more incredible situation than any they claim to have experienced."

He broke off, watching Webb both triumphantly and anxiously, like a virtuoso waiting for applause. "As a rational and highly intelligent man, my dear Mr. Webb, I'm sure you will agree?"

Webb nodded, not so much because he agreed, but because he did not have the heart to express any doubts as to the merit of the Spaniard's heroic efforts. He had noticed a long row of bound manuscripts already written by Don Hernandez. Choosing a volume at random, he glanced at the pages, which were filled with footnotes, references to indices, to tables of content, to files and cross-files.

Delighted by Webb's interest, Don Hernandez explained the necessity of a meticulously scientific approach. "You must understand, sir," he said, with almost fanatic intensity, "that in our time research is more important than search. Suppose you search and you find what you are looking for—what good is it? You cannot keep it, unless you can prove it. Today, we must prove, prove, prove."

He interrupted himself, passed his hand over his forehead, and smiled. "I forgot. Undoubtedly, our mutual friend, Padre Paolo, has told you that I am obsessed by the problem of proof; that I attribute too much importance to it, not only in the matter of my inheritance, but generally." Waving Webb's protest aside, he started to pace silently, gradually growing more nervous. He had lost his assurance; indeed, Webb was reminded of a tight-rope walker who, having slipped, struggles to regain his equilibrium. The crisis, though passing swiftly, had been so acute that Webb felt it could not have been a rare occurrence. There was every indication that the Spaniard's zeal was constantly threatened by persistent doubts; that he continued his exacting work against the mounting resistance of a haunted, inner denial.

"Personally, I'm very fond of the Padre," Don Hernandez said without real warmth, "though we often clash on that issue. I'm afraid his simplicity is archaic; I respect him as I would admire a museum piece. He is a relic from the past surviving in our modern time, historically interesting, but quite out of place." He turned to Webb, smiling wanly. "I don't mean to involve you in our quarrel as a judge. But, perhaps, you would like to hear my side of the argument. It may be of some importance to you. In fact, it may influence your decision—whether or not to proceed to Zapar."

"I've already reached my decision."

"You have?" Don Hernandez looked at him with tense expectation.

"I'm returning to Puerto Carribas."

The Spaniard's shoulders, hopefully raised, dropped in broken disappointment. "Too bad," he said after a while. "I'd hoped you might bring back some valuable information. It is quite impossible for me to get any reliable facts from the Indian messengers who pass my house once in a while." He shook his head. "However, I might have known; it was to be expected that you could not proceed. You are an intelligent man, reasonable and sophisticated, a perfect specimen of twentieth century education. You wouldn't have it in you to storm a mountain."

A hot flush of anger rose into Webb's cheeks. "If you're insinuating that I was afraid of the hardships—" He broke off, flustered. "I'm neither a weakling nor a coward. My decision was based on perfectly sound reasons."

"Naturally. There's the rub, my dear Mr. Webb. The reasons. By the time an intelligent man has thoroughly considered a heroic deed or an act of faith, his strength has been sapped, his vitality drained. To achieve anything daring one must be a fool or inspired by the holy madness. And our civilization, though it still has its abundance of fools, provides such strangling straight-jackets for the latter that even the best of us are helplessly paralyzed."

"I hardly consider myself in need of a straight-jacket," Webb said dryly.

"How could you, my dear sir—when it is already wrapped around you so tightly by modern thought that you can't even stir. You're not a coward, Mr. Webb; you are a prisoner. You may long to regain the freedom of your soul, but to no avail. The barbed-wire enclosures of the concentration camps so popular in our age are nothing compared to the impregnable barriers imposed on us by the scientific insistence on proof."

He looked at Webb, as though expecting him to agree or disagree, his posture not unlike that of a fencer who stands ready to parry any lunge of his opponent. And when Webb, who was beginning to feel as incompetent as Padre Paolo to cope with the rapier-like thrusts of the man's brilliant mind, said nothing, Don Hernandez turned away, almost disappointed.

"Please understand," he said after a while, "I don't quarrel with the facts; I bow to them as any intelligent man must in our time; we have no choice but to accept the tyrannical demand for proof. It is the cornerstone of science, the key to its success. An excellent method for technological progress—but a tragedy, perhaps the most tragic event in the history of mankind, when it was transferred from the laboratory to life in general. There has never come into being a more devastating prohibition than the precept to believe only that which can be proven; nothing else. The consequences are incalculable; with one stroke it wiped out philosophy, faith, imagination; it destroyed the whole rich life of the soul, stifled its poetry and zest, cut off its intuitive projections, inhibiting our outlook, shrinking our view of the world; and in this manner it limits, narrows, shortens us. Whether you realize it or not, you and I, Mr. Webb, are victims of stunted growth, unable to fulfill our potentialities. Because we were born in a century which, by placing its trust in test tubes, precision instruments, and glistening laboratories, has produced a generation of spiritual dwarfs."

Webb moved away, casually approaching the book shelves. The Spaniard's reasoning was less bizarre than he had assumed. Having listened to it at first with fascinated, but abstract, interest, he now felt that it was coming uncomfortably close. He recalled, somewhat disturbed, the supercilious satisfaction with which he used to mock, in his student days, anything that lacked the scientific seal of approval. It also occurred to him that his youthful arrogance had steadily lost its appeal, leaving him, in his maturity, perturbed by the vague uneasiness that he actually knew very little, permitted himself to believe even less; and, as a result, did not have enough, all in all, to live either wisely or well. But despite his growing awareness that the powers of his spirit were withering away, he had continued to wear the ever more confining armor of a faintly ironic agnosticism, though in the end not so much because of inner conviction, but because he could think of no way to cast it off. He certainly could not return to the richer life of his childhood, with its irrational but stimulating, instinctive, and therefore natural wealth of belief.

"Make no mistake about it," Don Hernandez was saying, "we are trapped. On one hand, it is impossible for us to rebel against the tyranny of rational judgment; we can't quarrel with the principle of evidence presented and tested. On the other hand, there comes a harsh awakening when we realize that the outposts of science also serve as roadblocks limiting the expansion of our minds. And the boundaries staked out by them form a far more narrow circle than we had assumed in the first flush of victory. Indeed, when you consider how little can be proven, compared to how much we need to know, you'll realize how small a territory has been left to us. A fraction of the total, a mere pinpoint in the universe of the soul."

He stopped at the window, looking out into the night. "The fact is, my dear Mr. Webb, we have become separated from the larger part of ourselves. We know that we've inherited a fortune. But, since we lack proof, we must exist on the pittance that is doled out to us; we remain paupers dreaming of our inaccessible wealth."

He lapsed into silence, his eyes scanning the darkness in the general direction of El Soledad. Webb wondered whether the Spaniard, at this moment, was thinking of his lost mine at Zapar. Strangely embarrassed, as though his thoughts had intruded upon the privacy of the solitary figure at the window, Webb turned away. His attention was drawn to a simple prayer book on the shelf; he pulled it out and leafed through the faded pages. A slip of paper, inserted between the covers, revealed that it was a precious old volume, one of the first books ever printed in Massachusetts; and that Don Hernandez had found it in the ruins of the old mission. As Webb gazed at the familiar prayers, memories of childhood Sundays mingled with the desolate image of the mission's shattered belfry tumbled on the broken chapel. He tried to recall at what stage in his development the structure of faith had collapsed inside of him; but he could not trace it to any single event.

"It's no use, Mr. Webb," the Spaniard said directly behind him.

Looking back, Webb saw that Don Hernandez was watching him with a sad smile; and he returned the book to the shelf in some haste.

"I've tried it myself, more than once," the Spaniard said. "But it's impossible—we can't go back. A mind familiar with the accumulated knowledge of the last centuries can't sing those hymns without being plagued by doubt. We lack the rough-hewn simplicity, the convictions, the strength of the spirit in which those prayers were written."

He frowned; the sharp glitter of his eyes turned on Webb, held him a moment, then passed on. "However, my dear sir, when I referred to their strength, I didn't mean that we are weak. Far from it. The truth is that we are not living in a decaying culture, as so many historians and scholars have claimed. Don't let anyone tell you that we are decadent, that our civilization is tired. There has never been an epoch more hungry for belief, nor one more bursting with vitality. But that only makes it worse. For there is the tragedy. We attempt to break out; we must. But we can't overcome the barriers of scientific thought; no matter how hard we try, we can't pass the barriers of proof."

He left Webb and started to pace restlessly. "The brain, sir, can defeat anything except itself," he said, rubbing his forehead in that same unconscious gesture which Webb had observed several times before, but which he understood only now as the instinctive reaction of a man crucified by his despotic reasoning powers. "We have elevated our intellect to a dominant position above all else," the Spaniard went on. "Now there's no help for it; we must submit our beliefs to its approval; and nothing can pass unless we can supply evidence."

The fanatic expression returned to his face, lighting a strange, dancing fire in his eyes. "For that reason my work is so vitally important. I have invaded the field of faith; I'm building a rational road, step by step. A tremendous task, I assure you; I've spent years on it, and as yet there's no end in sight." Momentarily, he faltered. "Of course, you may object that my proofs are tenuous; that my progress is slow. But—" He waved the doubt aside almost angrily. "At least I've recognized the problem, and I'm doing something about it."

He picked up a sheaf of his manuscript, glanced at a page or two, at first critically, but then becoming more and more absorbed. He sat down behind the desk and read to Webb a passage in which he dealt with a vision of St. Francis of Assisi, analyzing it, investigating and eliminating the psychological factors, comparing the residue to similar truths distilled from the meditations of older prophets and mystics. The patient, but futile labor, the overwhelming, undaunted effort illustrated to Webb, more clearly than anything the Spaniard had said about the dilemma of modern man, the difficulties which he himself had encountered. He was sitting on a hand-carved, medieval bench which faced the window. The darkness outside was impenetrable; he saw nothing but the flames of the candles, reflected in the opaque rectangle as in a mirror. Only once did the mountain loom up; for a brief moment, it poured into the window, a silvery spectre in the incandescent light of the moon, framed, but not caged, surrounded but not encompassed, its peak hidden behind the blinds, its foundation concealed by a row of books.

Then it disappeared; and Webb, who had leaned forward, encountered the reflection of his face in the place where the mountain had been. Quickly he moved aside, withdrawing from his own features which, though unchanged, no longer seemed familiar; he had felt as if facing a stranger, whom he had known a long time, but of whom he actually knew very little.

"What do you think of the last paragraph?"

Webb came to with a start. Don Hernandez was watching him. "Very interesting," Webb stuttered.

"You haven't been listening," the Spaniard said coldly. "Your thoughts were far away. My humble efforts could not hold your attention. Or else you feel that the subject matter is of no concern to you."

"Not at all," Webb protested. "I wish you'd read on."

The Spaniard shook his head. "You needn't be polite." His hands trembled as he shuffled the pages of the manuscript. "Perhaps, you think that my work has no value; that I delude myself; that my efforts are wasted." He waved Webb's objection aside. "You have a right to your opinion."

He got up and paced the floor, shaken by Webb's refusal to share his delusion. "However, my dear sir, to ridicule my efforts is not enough. The problem exists; it can't be denied. And mockery alone will not abolish it. I must ask you, then, if you've found a better solution?"

Webb shrank from the bitterness in the voice. A glare of incipient hostility had seeped into the Spaniard's eyes, as if the deluded brain sought to revenge itself on Webb, who had torn the merciful cloak from its self-deception.

"I'm not ridiculing your efforts," Webb muttered.

"Let us be honest, Mr. Webb. You've never held me in high esteem. I remember distinctly the polite irony of your letters when I first brought the mine at Zapar to your attention. It was perfectly obvious that you considered me a fool." He gave a short laugh. "And yet, my dear Consul—here you are, in Santa Rosa. For different reasons, naturally; different starting point, different direction. Nevertheless, we've met in the identical place. Which was, of course, inevitable, since we both had to find a way out from an intolerable situation."

For a while, he paced, irritated, restless, at times like some noble animal intent upon breaking from its cage, but shrinking from the bars which had defeated it too often. Gradually slowing down, he stared at his manuscripts, then turned away abruptly. "You may be right, Mr. Webb—perhaps, my work is futile. But do you know of a better answer to the problem? What are we to do? We live in an epoch which some day may become known as the age of ignorance, a century in which the machine flowered and men wilted; it may well be that future generations will refer to it as the Dark Ages of the soul. I have no doubt that ultimately we shall be able to prove what our souls already know. Some day—perhaps a thousand years from now. In the meantime, you and I, Mr. Webb, are caught in a desolate interim period, extending from the unfulfilled promises of science to the premature grave of a strangled faith. We must try to adjust ourselves. But how?"

His shoulders sagged; the fire in his eyes died out, no longer casting a glow on his pale face which suddenly looked unspeakably tired, the skin sallow, the lips limp. "How? What are we to do? I'm speaking of men like you, like myself; rational, educated men, men of integrity. We can't imitate Padre Paolo's peasant faith; we should laugh at ourselves; we are not naive enough. We have no choice, then, but to resort to subterfuges, as so many others do. But we are too honest; we can't join those who cheat their intellect by permitting a vast number of undetected and irrational assumptions to slip into their outlook; or those who seek compensation in the hollow pride of a sterile agnosticism, or in angry nihilism; while yet others find refuge in crass superstitions, ashamed, but nevertheless addicted."

He stopped and looked at Webb. "I'm sure you've tried all those patent-medicines; you've worked your way through the whole assortment of make-shift devices; and you've found that none of them is a solution. Again and again, when one after another disintegrated, you would see the same bleak landscape, and you would ask yourself the same question I've asked just now: What are we to do?"

Webb quickly shifted his glance from the dark window to the wall, as if his thoughts had been read. He recalled, perhaps irrelevantly, the solemn and important ritual of fixing and sipping his drink; the many minute details of custom and habit which had counteracted the blue haze of the mountain range in the distance. In those days, he had not been aware of the anxiety underlying his preoccupation with the strict discipline of his routine; but now, in retrospect, it seemed hard to understand how he could have guarded himself so effectively for so long a time.

At that moment, the Spaniard's wife entered. She had come to remind her husband that he had failed in his duties as a host. "He has the most wonderful wines in his cellar," she told Webb. "But he's so absent-minded, he never thinks of drink or food."

Don Hernandez apologized. For a while, he spoke to her in a Catalan dialect, which Webb did not understand; then he bowed, excused himself, and went to the cellar.

As soon as he had left, the plump, little woman's attitude changed; she frankly admitted that she had sent her husband on an errand, because she wanted an opportunity to talk with Webb. Without delay or subtlety, she told Webb that she was desperately unhappy in Santa Rosa. Perhaps Webb could help her persuade her husband to return to Spain, where they had the means to live sensibly and pleasurably—if only he could be freed of his fatal obsession. How or when it had taken hold of him, she could not say. At the time of their marriage, he had been considered one of the most brilliant minds at the university in Madrid. Rich, young, and diligent, he had earned for himself a reputation not only as an inspiring teacher, but as the country's foremost authority on comparative religion. Yet, some years later, unaccountably, and refusing any explanation, he had resigned his professorship. Withdrawing to his country estate, he had spent years on his monumental work, until, one day, he was notified by an obscure Barcelona attorney, whom she had not trusted at all, that he had inherited a lost mine far away. Instead of disregarding this whole shady business, he instantly prepared to leave Spain. During the voyage he had seemed exceedingly exhilarated; and it was only after they had lived for some time in Santa Rosa that his elation evaporated. In fact, she had almost succeeded in convincing him to return to Madrid, when this ragged, homeless painter, Senor Crispian, came along. The two men had spent hours and hours in this study, sometimes talking until dawn. There had been some violent arguments; she had heard her husband's angry voice, hammering at Crispian, who would say very little. Nevertheless, whenever she saw them come out, she could judge from her husband's flushed face that it was the little painter who had won all the arguments. And after Crispian had set out for Zapar, her husband had said nothing further about returning to Spain. By now, she had just about given up hope; she was afraid that nothing could pry him loose anymore.

Webb's curiosity was aroused by her report of the arguments between the two men. He would have given anything to learn what had been said; but the woman had heard little and had understood even less. It all hadn't made sense to her, she said. And just then, Don Hernandez returned with a flask of Madeira. Pouring the golden liquid into three glasses, he first served his wife, who scurried from the room, holding the glass in a tight grip and eyeing it so greedily that her excessive interest betrayed, in a flash, the only solution she had found for her boredom.

"I suppose my wife has complained to you," Don Hernandez smiled, not as ironically as Webb had expected, but rather sadly.

"She would like you to return to Spain," Webb said, fulfilling his promise to the woman, whose bewilderment in the face of her incomprehensible exile had touched his heart.

"I know." Don Hernandez held the long-stemmed glass against the candle light, studying the rich, warm glow of the Madeira. "I don't blame her."

"Perhaps, she is right. Perhaps, you should leave Santa Rosa."

"Perhaps," Don Hernandez agreed, but his tone of voice contradicted any hope held out by his vague statement.

"She also mentioned that you had long arguments with Crispian," Webb said, closely watching the Spaniard's reaction.

For a while, Don Hernandez did not stir; only his pale complexion turned a shade more pallid. "Quite true," he said. His eyes wavered to the clock in the corner, as if to determine how much longer they would have to wait for Mona's reply.

The pendulum clicked out the seconds, relentlessly punctuating and thereby accentuating the silence.

"I never saw Crispian during the day," Don Hernandez began. "He was working and I did not disturb him. But at night, no matter how tired he was, he would come here." He paused, smiling ironically. "At first, I assumed that he was captivated by my brilliant conversation, and I paraded my knowledge before him. It was not until much later that I understood the extent of his kindness; he sacrificed hours of badly needed sleep, in an effort to help me."

His glance strayed to the candelabra on his desk, so that his face was averted; he wanted to give the impression that he was studying the beautifully curved lines of the bronze base, but actually he was trying to hide the remorse which had come to him too late. Standing there, in the flickering candle light, he looked more than ever like an El Greco figure, pale, haunted in semi-darkness by apparitions from above and below, his ascetic face reflecting a torment which only the most fiendishly cruel of all torture instruments, the human mind, can produce; he could have been, Webb felt, a model for the Great Inquisitor or for one of the martyred saints, with equal justification.

"It was not that he deprecated or ridiculed the value of my work as so many others do," Don Hernandez said. "He was too kind for that. But he did question its necessity. And that was the point on which we clashed."

The Spaniard pointed at the medieval bench which Webb had occupied a little while ago. "He used to sit there for hours, listening to my arguments; though, sometimes, I could not be too certain whether he was concentrating on what I said, or looking at that part of the mountain which can be seen from here. And in the end, he would say to me: 'I need no proof that El Soledad exists. I know it is there.' I would look out the window, and if it happened to be so cloudy a night that nothing could be seen, I would say: 'You're wrong. You believe you know. And mere guesswork without proof is too hazardous to be acceptable.' But he shook off my objections. 'To believe is to create. And to create is to believe,' he said. And then he would describe what he saw; the man had the power of a magician; his words could conjure up images, shapes; entire worlds came into being. I have looked at his painting, and it meant nothing to me, because I have no sense of color. But when he spoke, I saw. I saw valleys and crests and peaks, and I saw Zapar, though neither of us had ever been there, and of course I have no proof it is really like he described it. But it could be, my dear Mr. Webb, it could be exactly like that."

He stood, momentarily insecure, lost in thought; then he shook his head. "But I don't know," he said, emphasizing the word know, and looking at Webb with a sad, defensive smile. "You see, Mr. Webb, he was right—for himself. I've since realized that he, as an artist, does not have to wait for proof. He creates his own world, and therefore he need not measure, weigh, or test; he has created it with his own mind, and so it cannot be anything but true. We have no right to demand proof of the artist; all we may ask is that he be honest and true to himself. And for that reason a man like Crispian lives fully; he harvests the wealth of the soul, while the rest of us exist, as it were, in abeyance. Not even in doubt, sir; in abeyance, waiting until more evidence is gathered, confined, hemmed-in, barren."

His back turned to Webb, he stood gazing at a magnificent Rembrandt etching of a Dutch landscape; for a while, he seemed to be losing himself in the mysterious world of the small fishing town. "What makes it worse, Mr. Webb," he said after a while, "is the fact that even the most rational among us are constantly disturbed by the unknown, the unproven, the uncertain; we try to ignore it because we're so afraid of both error and ridicule. But it can't be banished; it returns to plague us; it keeps intruding; indeed, we are reminded of it every time we contemplate a work of art."

Webb looked away as he felt the Spaniard's eyes turning on him. "In our time, Mr. Webb, only the artist can escape; art is our sole link to the world outside our prison. Perhaps, you have invented as many sound reasons for wanting to see Crispian's painting as you have discovered not to climb to Zapar; you may forget them all. The fact is that we can't follow Crispian because we're not creative; but we can decipher the messages he sends back. The artist can still reach us through the single breach left in the wall civilized man has built around himself; only the artist —no preacher, no lecturer, no philosopher or prophet. From the cave drawings to the skyscraper museum, art has survived as the only magic in our lives. It is the only bridge, our last means of communication with the lost continents. We still allow ourselves to be affected by it; it is permissible to be stirred; and so we reach out, stealthily like thieves; we cross the borders, we sense, suspect, and sometimes yield to the reverberations returning from the distant shores of our soul. Indeed, on those rare occasions, we can still fathom our depth, even today; but it is only in the concert hall, the theatre, the art gallery that modern man can still experience the ecstasy of his greatness; he is bound to feel small in a city street, in the class room, or in the laboratory—"

He interrupted himself, standing still, listening to sounds drifting up from the courtyard. A moment later, Webb, too, could hear the voice of the housekeeper. But she was not alone; instead of sending a message, Mona had come herself.

CHAPTER VII

She was out of breath; her hands trembled as she twisted the riding whip, bending and releasing it with quick, angry movements.

"You've stirred up the whole village," she told Webb, accusingly. "Until you came along, people were content to believe that the painting had been destroyed. But when you went around asking questions, you aroused their suspicions again! Now they'll resume searching for it!"

"Suppose they do? Are you afraid they could find it?"

"They might."

"Then it wasn't destroyed?"

She bit her lips. "What do you want? Why can't you leave it alone?"

"I've got to see it."

"I'm not going to show it to you!"

Don Hernandez moved the table lamp slightly; its luminous orb trembled past Mona, briefly illuminating her flushed, angry face before drawing new shadows over it.

"I'm as anxious as you," Webb said, "to preserve it."

"You're not. All you want is to satisfy your curiosity."

"I want more people to see it. We can't leave it here. It has to be taken to a safe place."

"It was safe enough where it is." She hesitated, on the verge of elaborating; but then, aware that she might betray some clue to its hiding place, she broke off, and turned to the door.

"If the canvas is not protected against the mountain climate," Webb said, following her, "it will be destroyed by humidity and extremes of temperature as surely as by the villagers—or by your father."

She stopped. "I've done the best I could." An incipient doubt seeped into her voice. "But if you know a better way to protect it—?"

"You can't. Not here."

Her glance wavered helplessly from Webb to Don Hernandez. "What do you want me to do?"

Webb sensed that he had chosen the right point of attack. "The painting has to be shipped to the States."

"To whom?"

"He may have heirs."

She stared at him. Then, abruptly, she left the room, walking so hurriedly that Webb could not overtake her, until they had reached the hall.

"Why should it go to someone who never did anything for him?" she asked, while they passed through the high portals into the courtyard.

"There are laws."

She shook her head, and he realized that he had made a mistake. "Legalities!" she said contemptuously. "It can't be claimed under any law. It must remain as free as it was when it was created."

Webb's ingrained sense of duty fought with his desire to see the painting. "I promise to do all I can to safeguard your interests."

"You don't understand. It doesn't belong to me either. To no single person. He once said that even he did not own it; that it belonged to itself."

"Perhaps he meant that he wanted it to belong to everyone." He sensed that she was weakening. "At any rate, he could not have wanted it to remain hidden."

The argument had struck home. For a moment, she stood irresolutely, then moved away from him as if she needed some time to herself in order to make up her mind. He thought it best not to disturb her, but when she started to leave the courtyard, he followed her, determined to give her no chance to escape. She was walking uphill, at first rather aimlessly, by-passing the road; but soon she accelerated her steps. He noticed that she was heading toward the pass; and suddenly, as though he had known it all along, the thought flashed through his mind that the painting could not be far from there.

He hurried to her side, assuming that her resistance had been overcome. However, she was still not entirely convinced. She stopped abruptly, studying him in a new flare-up of suspicion. "If I show you the painting, will you promise to leave Santa Rosa?" When he nodded, she looked at him, still undecided, still in the grip of conflicting emotions. "I wouldn't show it to you," she whispered, "if I hadn't been told that you found his notes. It's strange that you should have been the one to discover them." She closed her eyes, listening to the wind. "Perhaps, it means that he wanted you to see the painting."

Webb did not stir, realizing that at last the scale had tipped in his favor. A moment later, she broke away; now that she had made up her mind, she was in a feverish haste to carry out her decision. She hurried ahead, climbing up to the pass; and without pausing to catch her breath, she descended on the other side.

Webb could not keep up with her; before long he had lost her from his sight. He was standing alone in a field of boulders. Above him was the dark borderline of the pass, which he had crossed, perhaps too recklessly. For as he looked down, he saw that there were no more obstacles between him and the gently rising plains which passed imperceptibly into the mountain.

He drew back, but stepped on a loose stone and slipped, sliding downhill. Stumbling, gliding down the steep slope, he saw Mona again, at some distance below him; she was approaching a dilapidated shack, which was half-hidden behind a clump of trees. By the time he had reached her, she had pushed a rusty key into the lock; turning it with some difficulty, she pushed back the worm-eaten, squeaking door and entered the dark hut.

Inside, she lighted a candle, and Webb saw that they were in some sort of storage room. Looking around the dismal interior, with its haphazard array of tools, dusty bags, and debris of all kind, Webb realized that this was indeed a secure hiding place; no more unlikely environment for a work of art could have been found.

When Mona started to lift the canvas from behind a pyramid of stacked barrels, Webb rushed to assist her. Together they raised the heavy roll, stirring up clouds of dust which nearly choked Webb, forcing him to draw away from the gray pall in which torn spider webs floated, fingering the void for a new hold. Once the canvas stood vertically, Mona took the flapping edge and pulled it alongside the wall so that the roll unwound with a creaking noise.

As the canvas unfolded, Webb lost sight of Mona. He stepped back, the blood pounding in his temples. It suddenly seemed that the candle was no longer illuminating the room; that, on the contrary, its dim flame had disappeared in the flood of light which splashed from the painting, radiating of its own luminosity, as it rushed against his eyes in a torrent of tumultuous and almost blinding colors.

It was an intoxicating sight, which did not diminish in splendor as the tempestuous flow began to reveal its frozen nature in the passage of time, and the figures, in their growing stillness, offered themselves to recognition. While Mona continued to pull back the roll, Webb identified in the sector already unfolded, many of the elements Crispian had described in his notes; and yet, the reality so far surpassed his expectations that he realized how small were the powers of his imagination which had been unable to visualize the beauty projected in the painter's descriptions.

There was so much to see that Webb's eyes strayed erratically from the fascinating details of the landscape in the background to the mysterious mood of the sky above; from the cruel glitter of the soldier's armor to the impersonal crowd held in check by the guards; these spectators were indeed, as Crispian had conceived them, witnesses without testimony; but although their gray mouths failed to give voice, their yellow eyes reflected the excitement of the spectacle so dramatically that their expression alone would have sufficed to reveal the tremendous event they were watching.

Standing only a few feet away from them, Webb felt as if he had wandered into this throng of curious onlookers who had streamed from the city to see the crucifixion; and not unlike them he was looking here and there, trying to gain a better view; but he could not step back far enough to survey the whole panorama; the room was too small; he was inextricably involved with the figures on the canvas.

But though he could not obtain an impression of the overall composition, he gradually grew aware that his attention kept being drawn from left to right, from the periphery toward the center, guided by the inobtrusive magic of the lines, so masterfully conceived that they carried the observer along as they streamed and flowed in the direction of the cross. Following them, Webb's glance was suddenly arrested by the tattered figure of a beggar holding out his bowl to him; at his side was an old man, who in turn supported a woman on crutches; all three were watching Webb as if they expected him to recognize them. But his memory could not identify them; and so he passed them, his glance searching for a familiar face, when he was stopped by the inexplicable sensation that he had noticed and yet overlooked someone in this crowd. Glancing back, he discovered a child, a small boy, about ten years old, peering at him from behind the taller and more dramatic figures, so inconspicuously placed that he would have eluded Webb's notice once more had it not been for the pathetic call of the dark, deep-set eyes.

The child was lost, more utterly lost than Webb had ever seen anyone before; there was an aloneness as it can only be felt by a child. The crowd was passing the boy without paying any attention to him; no one even stopped to inquire to whom he belonged; no one showed any concern or interest, nor offered to help him find the parents from whom he had been separated.

If indeed there were any parents. The boy's loneliness was etched too deeply into his features; they did not express a momentary panic, but rather an enduring, almost quiet despair. The longer Webb looked at the boy the more convinced he became that this youngster had no one in the world; there was a darkness in his eyes which showed that the sun of affection had failed to rise in his toy-sized universe; and though he was still waiting, it was somehow hopelessly evident that he alone among children would never be cared for, would never be protected and loved.

Once before Webb had suspected the loneliness of Crispian's childhood. But evaluating it in terms of his own occasional solitude as a grown-up, he had failed to consider the far more crushing effect on a defenseless child; and he had not been affected as deeply as he was now when the suffering was shown to him through the child's own eyes. Indeed, the pervading sadness which streamed from the boy's portrait was of such penetrating power that Webb felt it had not been artistically conceived; it was more likely that an inner force greater than Crispian's conscious will had guided his brush, subjugating his hand, using it as a tool to express a submerged, but not forgotten, anguish. Webb knew that there had been no mention of this boy in the notes; apparently, it had come as an after-thought, breaking through in the course of work, forcing Crispian to give life to a pain which, evidently, had lost none of its virulence over the years.

Nothing could have been more tragic to Webb than to see that Crispian, even in his maturity, even at the height of his powers as an artist, had been unable to resolve the sorrows inflicted upon his unprotected childhood. In fact, Webb felt that this small, unobtrusive space of canvas might well be the key to the far more important sections; and he was confirmed in his conviction when he saw, only a few feet away, the towering, massive, almost colossal figure of Padre Paolo, overshadowing the child, looming so tall and large in the foreground that Webb had to step back to encompass it all.

The contrast was staggering. Still enhancing the mountain priest's stature, Crispian had created a magnificent portrait of heroic proportions. He had intensified all the characteristics, had enlarged all the facets of his personality, stressing the extraordinary nobility of the features, a nobility made even more remarkable because it did not have its roots in a gentle refinement, but in a robust, almost aching vitality. There was something truly awe-inspiring about the vigor emanating from the bare head, from the grizzled, iron hair which stabbed at the broad shoulders, the gnarled hand clenched around a high staff. And suddenly Webb understood the cryptic references in the notes; Crispian had used Padre Paolo as his model for Saint Peter, the apostle who had both loved and denied his master.

It seemed impossible that the frail child behind the Padre could have lived to produce so powerful a statement of faith; though, on the other hand, it was perhaps inevitable. The boy's very helplessness and insecurity had given birth to his faith; if he had not succeeded in building for himself a stronghold of indestructible hope, impregnable enough to keep away both bitterness and despair, he would have been crushed. Having thus survived, he had here created a monument to that which had saved him; indeed, Webb was beginning to realize that only a man who had often battled his weakness could have forged so overwhelming an image—an apotheosis of faith, faith sublimated by doubt, faith opposed, resisted and yet indefeasibly triumphant.

To achieve this effect Crispian had stressed rather than minimized the Padre's dispute with his God; instead of showing only his devotion, he had emphasized the conflict. This was evident not only in his expression, but in his posture; his head was raised questioningly, the strong eyes averted from the cross, penetrating the sky, perhaps accusing God, perhaps demanding an explanation of the tragedy taking place at this moment.

Whether Webb derived this impression from the portrait itself or from the notes, he could not determine. He did indeed recall that the whole question of the nature of faith had involved Crispian very deeply; time and again, he had grappled with the problem, probing, questioning, refusing any pat answer, as indeed he never allowed himself any easy solution. But Webb had not expected that Crispian would arrive at the conviction projected by this portrait. For here Crispian was showing him that belief could never be more than a sham unless it had come to grips with doubt; that untroubled proclamations of faith were never more than a howling in an inner desert of unbelief; that blind acceptance was a house of cards, vulnerable to the slightest gust of misfortune, all too easily collapsed into that barren cynicism which had flattened the spirits of recent generations.

It was a truth well known in the past, as evidenced by the wisdom of including Job's angry accusations in the Bible. The moment of despair, rebellion, even of violent denunciation, had been significantly recorded in the lives of the greatest believers, of Moses, of many saints, as if to note that doubt was as essential to true faith as ashes might be to the rise of the phenix. But it was also a truth forgotten by the young idealists of the present day, who took the first intrusion of doubt as a signal to shed their convictions and to scurry to the more convenient opposite of a facile pessimism. And in that, Webb found the portrait's deepest meaning to himself; if it had stirred him so profoundly, it was because he recognized himself guilty, as a young man, of that same swift surrender.

He could not be sure whether his interpretations would be equally evident to other observers; perhaps, he had read into the painter's work meanings that welled up from inside himself. His personal relation to the artist and to the people portrayed had set up a magic current; there was a flow and a counter-flow, an intermingling, a shaping of his individuality and a losing of his separateness. He could not contemplate the canvas as a detached spectator; he was part of the painting and it was a part of him.

He did not know how much time had passed; probably less than a minute, for Mona had not even finished the unrolling of the canvas. He now heard the creaking noise behind him. Wheeling around, he saw that she was pulling the painting toward the closing of a full circle, the length of all four walls being necessary to its complete unfolding. As a result, Webb was surrounded on all sides by the flaming colors, transported to a distant land, moved back in time to the actuality of an event occurring not long ago, but here and now.

So vivid was his impression of the people who came crowding toward him that he shrank back; for he found himself standing in the midst of a group of slaves, half-naked, their backs welted from old sores, their wild faces pushed threateningly close to Webb, as if they were clamoring for his help. And as they stretched out their contorted hands, he could almost hear the clattering of the chains.

Withdrawing still further, he suddenly came face to face with Bradley, on whose back, at that moment, the whiplash of an overseer descended. A flash of pain streaked across Bradley's face and was trapped in the corners of his mouth where it twitched in an erratic dance of shifting highlights. The twitch reminded Webb of Bradley's nervousness during the formal dinner party to which Crispian had not been invited because of his ill-fitting clothes. The overseer's whip on the millionaire's back illuminated the full irony of Webb's error. It was not Crispian who had needed his friendship; it was the man to whom he had extended the hospitality of his home without offering him the hospitality of his heart; the man in the impeccable tuxedo, whose restless boasting of his far-flung business enterprises had annoyed Webb so much that he had ignored the bewildered plea of the twitching mouth, silently begging for an explanation of a pain, which Bradley himself could not comprehend.

Webb passed the tattered, bleeding slave whose chained hands, raised in a gesture of supplication, were so dangerously close. And into his field of vision moved the three Roman soldiers, whom he remembered so well from the notes. Gambling on an oddly shaped rock in the corner, they seemed set apart from their surroundings; indeed, there was something appalling in the frozen stillness of their concentration. Even Webb's approach evoked no response; they were so absorbed in the vicarious symbols of their game, which they had substituted for the reality around them, that Webb felt himself stopped as by a wall.

Watching them, he came to sense that Crispian had captured more than their indifference to the tragedy of the cross, which was their main function in the overall concept. Not satisfied with the mere assertion of their callousness, Crispian had penetrated deeper and deeper, until he pierced through to a core of meaning, which, unexpectedly, gave forth its contents in a shower of illuminating insights.

Nothing could have been more startling to Webb than to recognize some of his own attitudes in the three immobile gamblers. He had never been interested in cards, nor in any game of chance. But the truth revealed by these players was not the sick passion of testing luck. They had withdrawn from reality because of their inability to respond directly to life's bewildering variety of stimuli and challenges. Since they could not deal spontaneously with the countless number of forever-changing situations, they had exchanged living facts for dead symbols. Reducing life's indomitable freedom to the arbitrary rules of a game, they led a synthetic existence in which the actual emotions of triumph and defeat, of frustration and fulfillment, of self-assertion, pride, fear, and joy were reproduced by the turn of a card or the roll of a dice.

And in a larger sense Webb had done the same. Rather than seeking his own answers, he had withdrawn to live like a participant in a polite game, exchanging cards with fixed values. There could be no other explanation for his strict adherence to convention, his humble acceptance of fashionable ideas, his eager submission to social rule and custom; it had facilitated his conduct, providing ready solutions for every contingency. It did not matter whether the established rules suited him or not, whether he believed in them—one did not question the rules of a game, for without them there would be disorder; there would be no team to which one could belong. He had chosen to comply, so that he would be sheltered against the world's unmanageable complexity, protected against life's tumultuous demands.

Any sort of regulation had appeared preferable to disorder. Indeed, if he had so strongly believed in an orderly universe, it was because a galaxy, spiraling according to strict celestial laws, was less to be feared than one which would travel as whim or mood might dictate; perhaps, for that reason, he had taken an inordinate pleasure in every new discovery which proved that nature was not free, but bound. And though he had no longer believed with the primitive tribes that the forces around him could be manipulated by magic, he had extracted from the mechanistic-mathematical world systems an almost equally satisfactory concept: nature was imprisoned by laws. And the Lord of Hosts, if such a supreme power existed, could not be a Creator, to be admired; nor yet a willful master, to be feared; Webb had been inclined to see in Him, whenever his mind attempted to form an image, the attributes of a super policeman watchfully patrolling the vast spaces to see that there was no chaotic disturbance of the mathematical peace.

But now, facing the freely created beauty before him, Webb no longer felt the need to guard himself against the wild, the uncontrollable, the unpredictable. Instead he yielded to an unaccustomed recklessness. Longing to take part in the unfolding drama, he looked further.

There was, not far from the gambling soldiers, a strange face, mask-like and yet vibrantly alive, the features exuding a pent-up, sultry, perverted sensuality which parted the naked lips in a smile half-pained and half-cruel. Webb noticed that the man's fixed gaze was directed to a reddish streak on the ground, a trace of blood gleaming on the road over which Christ had passed. The sight of the blood sent a chill down Webb's spine, not only by its intimation of blows struck and wounds inflicted; but also by its relation to the mask-like face. It illuminated the lust for pain underlying the sensual smile, a lust which gratified its perverted instincts by suffering vicariously the pain inflicted on others.

The rust-colored slur had struck an ominous chord; it was a superbly integrated part of the composition, foreshadowing the culmination of the tragedy. Webb knew that by turning to the center of the fourth wall he would see the cross; but he refrained from rushing to the summation of the painting, to its ultimate fulfillment. It would be premature; he felt he had to follow Crispian through all the preceding stages. He knew from the notes that Crispian himself had considered it necessary to work from both sides toward the center, gradually finding his way, probing, searching, recognizing perspectives and correlations; he had to pass through all the preparatory experiences, perfecting and freeing himself, in order to rise to the supreme climactic achievement.

This progression was evident in everything Webb had seen so far. There had been, at first, an unsettled exuberance reflected in joyous splashes of color, a wavering uncertainty at times, too much tension at others. But gradually the geysers and cataracts of emotions flowed into a broad stream. After a certain point, Crispian swept ahead with masterful assurance, never again groping, never uncertain, guided almost somnambulistically by the unerringly true impulses of his talent. His style, always original, developed without formal schooling, imitating no one, reached an ever greater individuality, until in its very uniqueness, it became most generally true. His remarkable technique, however, though quite noticeable in the beginning, gradually seemed to disappear, not so much by accident, but rather as if he had been striving to push it aside so that it could no longer stand in the way of directly communicated emotions. Indeed, it was as if his psychic energies had become so intensely powerful that they no longer had to rely on aesthetically controlled or calculated effects. By some miraculous process they had transferred themselves to the canvas, and from there they leaped at the observer, affecting him with such stunning vigor, with such glaring, almost blinding radiance that they seemed to have reached him directly from the electrifying visions in Crispian's mind, without passing through the intermediary of the painting. And finally, as one approached the focal center, the searing effect of naked, quivering, incandescent emotions became so strong that Webb shrank back as if he had been touched by the flame of a torch.

He turned to the other wall and started again at the beginning, realizing before long that on this side, too, Crispian had accomplished the same crescendo. As Webb passed, at first gently, through realms of beauty, he caught glimpses of meaning, some of which he understood and others he did not; but even when encountering elements which he could not grasp, he did not doubt their validity. There had been enough evidence to convince him that the artist would make no mistakes, would not let him down, would not try to deceive or trick him. And each passing figure, each conquered and mastered square of the canvas lessened his recurring apprehension that Crispian, after having achieved so much, might yet lose, if not the campaign, at least a skirmish or a battle.

He was looking at a rider whose horse was rearing up into the flaming sky, when he felt that his vision became blurred. He closed his eyes, realizing that he needed a respite. There had been too much to absorb all at once; his thoughts were swamped by too many impressions. He tried to take hold of himself, but the painting had produced a state of mind which he could not control; it was an experience unlike any he had ever known. He sensed that the beauty had swept away all heaviness, irresistibly drawing him out of himself, stirring up undefinable vibrations which set his soul dancing, clumsily at first, then freely in tune with the intoxicating rhythms. He felt unburdened and adrift, no longer on firm ground, but gathered up, rising exuberantly to a realm where beauty mingled with poetry to sing out in lyric rapture, where reason was guided to truth by easy and effortless flashes of intuition.

Even the acceptance of personal truths was made possible by the assuring presence of beauty, which had stilled his fears. When it occurred to him that he had not yet encountered his own portrait, a shock of momentary panic shot through his nerves; but it passed without disrupting the sweep of his exhilaration. No matter how damning Crispian's final judgment of him might be, he had no desire to avoid it. Indeed, he looked forward almost impatiently to the verdict, which, though it might pronounce his guilt or failure, would settle any doubt.

He opened his eyes again, but before going far in search of himself, his glance was arrested by the large figure of Don Hernandez. Clad in a black, shiny, silk-like material, the Spaniard was standing alone, elevated on a boulder, his ascetic, pallid features sharply outlined against a dark sky in which heavily charged clouds flickered with a barely contained threat of lightning.

He was, as Webb recognized at once, the Pharisee described

in Crispian's notes; he also saw that the figure had been transformed considerably since the original concept, having grown,
above all, in importance. This was evident not only in its size,
but also in the fact that it halted the flow of the crowd streaming up from the side. He stood there, rigid and isolated, the only
disruptive element in the interwoven continuity of the painting,
somehow like a dam blocking a flood. It almost seemed that Crispian had run into unexpected resistance which he had to overcome before he could proceed; and rather than hiding the obstruction, he had recorded it in its full significance.

After his talk with the Spaniard, Webb knew why his first impression of the man had been so deeply disturbing to him; but he
was astonished to see that Crispian had been equally affected,
though for entirely different reasons. The paralyzing power of the
intransigent brain had held no terror for Crispian; nor had he
been forced to struggle with the tragic error in the Pharisee's
basic approach; he had merely recorded it, almost impartially,
or rather with a compassion fully deserved by someone so fervently, even heroically dedicated as Don Hernandez.

It was this dedication, however, which had touched off in Crispian, by its very similarity to his own consecration, a burst of
anguish, perhaps long suppressed, perhaps often resisted. With
incredible expressiveness, he had captured in the man's glittering
eyes that fierce, hard glint characteristic of the fanatic, a perpetual
fire which had turned into a frozen flame, artificially nourished
and compulsively renewed from a store of restlessly churning passion.

There was no doubt in Webb's mind that here, much more
than anywhere else, the painter had fought out a deeply personal
conflict; but he could not relate the fear of fanaticism to Crispian
until he realized that no one who strayed from the ordinary could
know along the way whether he was following a delusion or the
command of genius; in either case, the uncompromising sacrifice,
the solitary quest, the rebellion against accepted patterns were
not only similar, but identical in nature. Only the end result could
proclaim, in retrospect, the distinction. For Galileo might have
been wrong, as thousands of other brilliant pioneers were; and
in that case he would have been considered a crank, stupid and
stubborn enough to go to prison for the sake of a fallacious assumption.

Yet, the daring endeavor, the quest, the effort and sacrifice had to precede the accomplishment; and in those long, grinding years there was no tangible way of obtaining assurance either from oneself or from others. There was only gnawing doubt, relentless, tormenting enough to drive even an adventurous mind back to the banal, but safe community of thought, as Webb himself had been driven back time and again. Though he had never ventured far enough to lose contact with the group, he now recognized in the caricature before him what he himself might have been, had he dared to break from the rank and file and become more truly himself. And for the first time he fully understood the hidden tragedy of Crispian's loneliness, terrifying enough in itself, but made even more tormenting because it was haunted by this spectre which had mimicked his efforts with the frightening distortion of its inverted features, until he had found the strength to free himself by banishing it into the shape of this ghastly image.

Having passed the obstacle, Crispian rushed on, impelled by an increasing urgency. The tempo of the lines, the rhythm of the colors seemed to oscillate in a more rapid flow as he was building toward the climax. Time and again, he preferred to interrupt or forego a deeper probing, permitting echoes of meaning to ebb away in mysterious side-valleys rather than allowing them to impede the inexorable acceleration.

Aroused by this urgency, Webb moved on more rapidly until his glance was stopped by an arm reaching out from behind a rock. He assumed that this was the spot which had caused the foreman's panic; and he was struck by the irony of the fact that the foreman could have looked farther without seeing himself. For the arm ended in a heaving shoulder belonging to someone who was trying to lift himself up, but was still invisible, having not yet emerged from behind the rock.

For a long while, Webb's eyes remained fixed on this arm. He had realized that, if the foreman's description was correct, his own portrait could not be too far away. His apprehensions returned, paralyzing him; he had to gather all his courage to shift his glance. A moment later—he saw himself.

His breath caught; he moved a step closer, incredulous at first, refusing to believe his eyes, then almost shyly seeking to avert the unexpected praise expressed by Crispian. With infinite kindness and an understanding of greater sympathy and charity than Webb, in his own estimation, would have ever granted himself, Crispian had chosen him to represent an entire group for which the painter had felt the greatest loyalty and affection. Standing in the vanguard of a procession, endlessly crowding up from the horizon, Webb was the only one whose features were distinct; indeed, he had been painted with such loving care that his face, though in no way losing its ordinary, commonplace qualities, had become surrounded by an aura, a strange glow. It was evident that Crispian had poured into this single portrait all the love and devotion he had felt for the group as a whole.

To have been placed in this prominent position was an honor which Webb felt he did not deserve. He knew well enough from the extensive descriptions in the notes that he was not to be considered the leader or even the spokesman for this group; his features had been selected to personify the millions of people, whom Crispian, in a bold stroke of invention, had symbolized as the "Thirteenth Apostles," comprising all those "who were called, but not chosen," the anonymous men of goodwill from whom the future drew its strength of survival; the inexhaustible supply of decent human beings issuing forth from the womb of time, always reduced, decimated, but always replenished so that their number never varied; in short, the simple people in whose innate goodness Crispian believed with such fervent conviction that this single faith was the unshakable axis around which his entire world revolved.

The patient and enduring procession with Webb at the head ran squarely into the powerful, almost Herculean figure of Barrie, who, as the Roman Centurion in charge of the crucifixion, blocked the way with his raised sword. When Webb saw the fierce, coarse, terrifying face, he no longer had to ask why Barrie would destroy the painting, if he ever discovered it. Because even Barrie, no matter how blind and imperceptive he was, would have been terrified by the stark horror of this portrait.

The muscular body, the glistening helmet, the sword and shield reflected in a hard glitter all the brute force in this world which ruthlessly crushes, indeed seeks to annihilate without mercy anything which is defenseless, paradoxically reacting to weakness not with pity, but with anger, hating those who lack the power which the bully, insecure in himself, most admires.

However, this was not all, as Webb realized after the first shock had worn off. Crispian had endeavored, in this portrait, to tear off the mask from the face of ancient, timeless evil; and he had achieved a singularly frightening effect by permitting its hatefulness to shine through selfrighteous protestations of innocence, making each more loathsome by its contradiction of the other. But in other ways he had failed here as in no other part of the canvas. Possibly because he had not been content to condemn evil; he had tried to understand it. He had shown the thick layers of stupidity which must be an integral part of evil; he had penetrated the twisted subterranean shafts and had turned up the components of defectiveness as well as the deeply hidden fires of an inner hell in which self-punishment was more surely accomplished than outer justice was to be feared.

But, in the end, either because he had failed in his efforts, or possibly because he had withdrawn from the conclusion that evil was a demoniac force which could not be explained, he had left the portrait incomplete, somehow unfinished. A monstrous fragment, Barrie stood there in the frozen pose of a terrified aggressor, his fist clenched around the hilt of his raised sword, stubbornly waiting for an attack that would never come.

Webb noticed the deep blue which glowed up behind Barrie, streaming from the fourth wall where Webb would at last see the gigantic center panel. His pulse quickened. The first cross with the dying thief had loomed up; it broke into the composition like the first deep chords of a fugue. The colors, now applied in heavy, almost wild strokes, resounded like the blaring of trumpets; at times, the paint had been squeezed directly from the tube, so that it protruded coarsely, curling from the canvas as if it were seeking yet another dimension. But, at a distance, the rough texture lost its effect of uncontrollable ferocity; on the contrary, the colors were so superbly attuned to one another that they merged like individual instruments to produce the harmonious and majestic orchestration of a symphony rushing to its triumphant conclusion.

At that moment, Webb heard Mona's voice calling him. But he could not detach his eyes; almost helplessly he raised his hand to silence her. His glance had passed from the first cross to the woman directly in the shadow of Christ, a mysterious figure mentioned several times in the notes, though Crispian had failed to make it clear whether he intended to depict Magdalena or Mary, the woman or the mother. Webb was not too surprised when he saw that Crispian had given her Mona's features; but what bewildered, even shocked him, was the break in style, the strange unreality of the portrait. Compared to the flaming vitality of the other figures, her face seemed faded, desiccated and flat.

A split-second later, the painted figure detached herself from the dark background and came toward him. Bewildered, still immersed in the imaginary world of the painting, he was too confused to recognize his mistake until she stood at his side, saying something about Barrie which he did not understand. Turning back to the spot she had just left—he stifled a scream of terror.

The painting was slashed. The dark background against which he had seen Mona was a harrowing void. The entire panel with Christ in the center was missing; it had been ripped out, a murderous crime that had left the rest of the canvas like a bleeding body from which the heart had been torn.

Mona was pulling at his sleeve, trying to attract his attention. He sensed the urgency of her words; he noticed that she was trembling with fear. And when he heard Barrie's voice in the distance, barking at Don Hernandez, he understood why she wanted to drag him from the hut; but he could not tear his eyes from the slashed, empty rectangle.

"Who slashed the painting?" he cried. The brutality of the crime had aroused in him an insane fury which nearly strangled his voice. "Who did it?"

"Crispian."

Her answer spun him around. He stared at her, still carried along by the momentum of his anger which could not be suppressed as quickly as it had been deprived of its cause. "Crispian? I don't believe it. It's impossible."

Tears flooded her large, dark eyes. "It's true."

"How could he?" Webb cried. "Why? Why?"

"Because he was not satisfied with it."

"Not satisfied?" Webb's hand swept the ocean of colors around them. "Not satisfied—with this?"

"With the part he cut out."

Webb stared at the sprawling void. He could not conceive that Crispian had failed to such an extent that, in order to wipe out the only part where he fell short, he had to destroy the entire masterpiece. "It couldn't have been that bad," Webb whispered.

"It was magnificent!" she exclaimed, her eyes flaring.

"And yet—?"

Her shoulders sank. "I tried to stop him. But he said it was not good enough. It had to be better."

At that moment, Barrie's voice roared up, nearer this time. A deathly pallor spread over her face. Quickly, she blew out the candle. And as the splendorous colors, the heroic figures, the strange and foreign land expired in darkness, she drew him to the door. Outside, in the cold, clear night, she hastily shut and barred the door, forgetting the key in the lock. When she started to run off, Webb held her back.

"Did he destroy the missing panel?"

"No. He continued to work on it."

"Did he finish?"

"Not here. He said it couldn't be done in Santa Rosa. So he took it along." She looked away. "He didn't care if anyone ever saw it. All that mattered to him was that it should be right."

"Where is it now?"

"At Zapar!"

PART THREE

EL SOLEDAD

CHAPTER VIII

An ALL-KNOWING dawn arose and seeped into the night's dream, scouting the obscure landscape in advance of the sun. For a while, the mountain kettle's fate hung in a twilight balance; but before long there swept over the horizon a new day, still untried and therefore undaunted, buoyantly confident that all things were possible to its young power.

Here and there a peak was ignited, its glimmering luminosity fed by the descending fire-line which ate inexorably into the substance of the dark. And El Soledad's far-flung shadow, cast over the side-valley, was gradually rolled back. Majestically gliding over the tilted plain, it withdrew into itself, exposing to the light, as it passed over them, three small human forms bravely approaching the stony bastions.

Dwarfed without being conscious of it, Padre Paolo and Webb rode side by side. Behind them, sauntering on bare little feet, followed an Indian boy whom they had taken along to let him lead back their burros once they had reached the base of El Soledad.

At the end of the long traverse, their animals began treading cautiously among the jagged outcroppings, their advance impeded, slowed and finally stopped; they could not pass across the graveyard of boulders at the foot of the cone.

The Padre dismounted and handed the reins to the boy who leaped into the saddle, happy to show off his prowess. A fleeting smile softened Webb's haggard features; but when he had to surrender his own burro, his hand momentarily clutched at the reins. He thought of the car in which he had started his journey; he recalled how the burro had carried him past the glistening, useless machine lying helplessly amid the exuberant, entangled jungle growth. Now he also had to relinquish his burro. He was forced to proceed unaided, stripped of all support; henceforth he would have to rely on himself alone.

151

For an hour or so, they were walking upward on a barely visible trail which rose like a thin, straight pencil line drawn diagonally across the rubble-strewn cone. They could not see the mountain's body which was still hidden behind the ramparts above; but they frequently heard a distant thunder when a rock, breaking loose from remote heights, came rolling, tumbling downward, sometimes exploding in a fierce crash, sometimes clattering to a slow, grating halt. Yet even if they had not heard this sporadic activity, they would have known from the desolate rubble delta over which they passed that the mountain was engaged in an unceasing cleansing process, continually casting off, discarding all surface elements which could not withstand the tenacious boring of erosion.

"Beware of the mountain sun, senor," the Padre said, stopping at his side and opening the bundle with their provisions. "Among these shiny rocks, it has a power quite unknown in the lowlands." He took out a small ball of fat and started to rub the rich, creamy substance on Webb's hand. When Webb instinctively withdrew his arm, the Padre held it fast. "It is necessary, senor," he said. "The sun will burn your skin without mercy."

After covering his own bronze, much eroded face with a slight film, he carefully knotted the bundle, and strode up the path.

For a while the trail's level space was just broad enough to permit them to walk side by side. The Padre, Webb noticed, kept his gaze fixed on a spot beyond the valley, where at that moment the house of the Senora Rivaz emerged on a slope sprouting up behind the pass.

"Last evening, senor," the Padre mused, "when we were standing at the foot of that slope, you told me you were returning to Puerto Carribas. Is it permitted to ask what happened to change your mind?"

Webb stiffened, edging as far to the side of the path as he could without sliding down. "I told you," he said, watching the many-edged stones over which he had to pass.

"When you came to the house of the Senora Rivaz," the Padre said, "you told me that we had to go to Zapar, because the Christ painting was there."

"I said more," Webb insisted, "much more."

"Indeed, senor," the Padre nodded, "much more, and all of it spoken in a haste of fever. You told of the woman by the cross, of the Roman soldiers, of Crispian, Mona, and Don Hernandez. You spoke of everyone but yourself. You did not mention a word of what had happened to you."

The mountain priest, Webb realized, was more perceptive than he appeared. Last night, at the house of the Senora Rivaz, the Padre seemed to have accepted Webb's explanations without question or doubt.

"If my reasons were not convincing to you," Webb said, "why didn't you question them before we left Santa Rosa?"

"It would have made no difference," the Padre said quietly, almost sadly. "For in any event, with or without valid reasons, you had to go to Zapar."

His head bowed, the Priest walked along in silence. "What matters, however," he added after a while, "indeed, what will prove most necessary and important to you, is that you should know what made you decide to climb El Soledad."

He waited, giving Webb an opportunity to protest that he knew well enough why and how he had arrived at so vital a decision, perhaps the most fateful election in his entire life. But when Webb, rather than attempt to communicate in clear and logical terms the diffuse inner processes that had led to his choice, preferred to say nothing, the Padre went on: "Sometimes, senor, a man thinks that he has acted on whim, in anger or haste, without reflection or even against his better judgment. Yet, senor, it is never so. Always there are reasons, chains of reasons running through all parts of a man's being, from past to future, so that, whether to strike a match or to scale a mountain, it is necessary that in every recess of his being a vote has been cast."

The Padre, striding ahead more rapidly, picked up a pebble from the slope above them and weighed it in his hand. For a moment it seemed that he would not press Webb any further; but then, with a slight tremor in his voice, he proceeded to add a warning that appeared to be directed as much to himself as to Webb. "Whether you know those reasons as yet or not, you must get your answers ready, senor. For the mountain will ask you questions. Do not believe that you will climb very far with clever arguments or cunning excuses, because they will not satisfy either yourself or El Soledad. Nor should you hope to last very long with a stubborn: 'I have made up my mind; so be it.' For you have not set out to perform a violent deed, which may be accomplished in a matter of minutes. You have chosen to place your soul on the grindstones of a thousand granite rocks which will keep wearing away your subterfuges, hour after hour."

The trail, narrowed at this point by a rubble heap which had slid down from above, forced them to walk in single file. For a few moments the Padre's black shoulders were swaying in front of Webb; then the tall figure was back at his side. "The mountain, senor, will give you no peace and no respite. It will ask why you risk your life to climb its slopes. It will demand to know why you exert yourself beyond the point of exhaustion to scale yet another wall. It will come to you as a persuasive, well-meaning friend and as an awesome enemy. And one way or another, you must be sure of your answers; for if you are not, your endurance and resolution will have to fight not only the cliffs but your own doubts." He dropped the pebble, which he had been polishing between his gnarled fingers, from one hand into the other. "Senor, the last time I battled El Soledad, I learned much of his ways. Though I surely did not get to know the whole arsenal of his weapons, I would not hesitate to say that of his many harsh demands, none is more harshly enforced than that a man must know all of himself, if he is to reach Zapar."

Again the path narrowed, forcing them apart. But though it widened before long, the Padre did not return to Webb's side. Instead, he started to walk ahead briskly, setting a faster pace as they were nearing the upper rim of the cone.

The Padre, Webb thought disconsolately, need not have exaggerated his image of the mountain's despotic nature in order to lend vigor to his warning. It was disturbing enough that Webb, in spite of his prior attempts to gain clarity, knew so little of the manner in which his will to escape had been broken.

Looking down on the pass and the little storage hut, in which Crispian's painting had unfolded its unforgettable splendor, he recalled how he had stood beneath the dark trees, listening to Mona's and Barrie's distant quarrel, to the hoofbeats as they rode away, and to the return of silence. He could still feel the cold, clammy touch of the sweat breaking out on his forehead while he had walked back to the shack—and was stopped at the thresh-

old, when his strong impulse to see the canvas once more became stalemated by an equally strong fear of the gaping hole in
the center.

For some undefinable reason, he could not bear to face again
the ruthless gash, the bleeding void in the painting's body. His
reluctance, as he now recognized, had been an irrational reaction
which should have given him pause; but since it manifested itself
as an angry aversion rather than any sort of fascination, he had
failed to foresee that the bleak, repugnant emptiness would eventually tempt and ultimately lure him to Zapar.

Expecting no more than a renewal of his previous impressions,
he had entered the dark hut—utterly unprepared to meet the
new experiences that were in store for him. At first, he had sensed
only an intangible potential of floating, as yet unattached sensations, still lying dormant in the dusty air, but ready to condense
on him at any moment. The insubstantial impression, however,
had dissolved almost as soon as it had been registered, without as
much as warning him that the notion might have been derived,
not from the outside, but from a deep inner pressure of buried
emotions, straining to heave and rock their way to the surface.

He had found the canvas exactly as he had left it; and yet, he
had reacted to it with a slight shock of surprise. In the darkness,
Crispian's painting had appeared to be nothing more than a flat
expanse of coarse, dead matter. Its brilliant colors, all its glow and
radiance had been extinguished, leaving only an inanimate, lack-
lustre, cadaverous substance, similar in appearance to the rags on
the floor, or to the worm-eaten, wooden boards behind it.

And yet, it was different from other dead matter, since it had
the capacity to restore to existence the latent life of its figures.
This inert mass of woven fabric, of rough thread and hardened
pigment could reproduce the magic world he had seen; the vibrant
faces, the varied people, the individual men and women could be
revived as soon and as often as they were reached by a beam of
light.

The realization had touched off in him a sense of the miraculous. There was indeed something extraordinary in the fact that
the painting could vanish and re-appear; that it could die, as it
were, and yet continue to exist. The timelessness of art had invited him to conclude to the even greater timelessness of the

human spirit. And he, a frail, lonely, frightened man, lost in a desolate wilderness, had eagerly responded to the possibility that the mind's innermost substance might have the same deathless attributes as its creations.

As an enlightened person, he had never before allowed himself to question the axiom of total extinction after death, disposing of any other view with the same faint and fashionable irony he had observed in other educated people. He had never even ventured so far as to explore for himself the grounds for such categorical rejection. And yet, when he stumbled unexpectedly over a tendril of immortality in that dark hut, he had avidly grasped, clasped, clutched at the long-withheld promise.

Even now, as he strode up the sun-lit mountain side, he could not deny or ignore the remarkable fact that an inanimate object like a house could only pass from existence to destruction while the melody of a song did not necessarily perish with the voice that sang it. The content of a book was invariably attached, but never tied, to the print of its dry pages; and so it could survive the annihilation of any single volume, just as the harmonies of a symphony, once they had been conceived in the composer's mind, were no longer dependent either upon the mute symbols in any separate, destructible score, nor upon the lifeless orchestra instruments which were nevertheless necessary to resuscitate the symphony on each individual occasion.

To assume, then, that the music did not exist when it was not heard, he told himself almost triumphantly, would be as absurd as to claim that Crispian's painting had ceased to be whenever no light fell on it. The invisible, the inaudible, and even the nonexistent, could return to existence, could become visible, audible, and again be as real, or perhaps as unreal, as it had ever been. Indeed, the creations of the human mind continued to live on in a strange twilight of immortality, untouched by the stream of time in which they slumbered without ceasing to endure.

He looked up, saw that Padre Paolo had gained on him, and accelerated his steps. While his shoes crunched over the rubble more hurriedly, he wondered what the mountain priest would say if he could read his present thoughts, if he knew that Webb's inner world, at that moment, was wildly gyrating around its axis; that the man who, in the plains of Irozco, had sarcastically referred to the Priest's belief in an "immortal soul," was now trying to explore the vast number of consequences which a possible reversal in his outlook might entail.

He felt a resurgence of the same aching, hammering, blindly groping excitement he had experienced during the night, when the black canvas leaped back into life. By striking a match, he had re-awakened the flaming world in Crispian's canvas from its slumber. And, in one miraculous moment, the wondrous shapes and radiant colors had been restored, had returned from non-existence, glowing up in their former dazzling, brilliant splendor.

Once again, he had stood in the center of a work of art, communicating with an illusion which was as true an experience as any actual event; an illusion so self-contained within its boundaries, so independent, so immune to its environment that it stood ready to reveal itself at any time, anywhere, as superbly indifferent to the ornamented halls of a museum as it was to the incongruous setting of a shack in the midst of a forlorn wilderness.

Almost jubilantly he had looked around, re-discovering everywhere the same groupings, the same perspectives and colors, all the figures so well remembered. Their impact, as they sprang toward him in the first flare-up of light, had been at least as thrilling as the first time; and perhaps even more so. But soon afterwards it had become clear that he was not going to simply revive his previous impressions. Here and there, he had encountered a new stillness, at first in patches, then gradually spreading, unobtrusively, but more and more chilling in its overall effect. And before long, though he still kept searching out faces and people like old acquaintances, he had been forced to acknowledge that something new had entered the picture, interposing itself, freezing the ardent colors and removing the figures from him. Though rationally he could still have pointed out what emotions and passions were expressed in certain blotches of paint, these feelings could no longer communicate themselves, at any rate not to him. And in the end he had felt as if all the vibrant life around him had become petrified in a glacial stillness.

The light that fell on the painting was the same; the canvas stood as before; the difference was in him, the observer. He had attempted to believe that the wearing off of the emotional impact was in itself nothing extraordinary; the effect of any work of art, he had told himself, was reduced by repeated contact. But the argument had not seemed convincing enough. And when it occurred to him that his failure to immerse himself in the painting's content might be due to his anxious avoidance of the gaping hole in the center, he had lashed himself, almost hauntedly, to re-establish his prior relationship to the canvas.

But again, he had been stopped by the flat surfaces as by a strong glass. He knew what was behind it, but had not been allowed to feel or live it. Try as he might, he had been unable to respond once more to Crispian's exultant affirmation of the earth's beauty and life's glory. He had not heard again his friend's last song of joy, faith, sadness, anger, pain; of hope and torment, of aloneness and friendship and love—a song both rhapsody and elegy, because it had flowed from the heart of one who was regretfully leaving all he had long praised and admired.

Instead, his glance had been drawn again and again to the awesome gash in the center. No matter how hard he had struggled to avoid it, his eyes kept returning to it. It had seemed inconceivable that this hollow, porous nothingness, idly traversed by torn spider webs, could exert a greater fascination than all the singing colors around it. And yet it was true; the bleakness, dismal and inexpressive, had drawn into itself all content from every part of the canvas; the absence had become more vital than the presence, the void more absorbing than its surroundings, the enigma more spell-binding than the clearly perceived.

And incredible as it seemed, the emptiness had been alive, gradually changing while it had held him with the hypnotizing stare of its empty eye. He could not remember every phase of his reactions, but he did recall that, at one point, he had surveyed the gash, somehow incredulous, swept by a horrified disbelief, unable to grasp how an artist could become so obsessed as to destroy his greatest achievement.

Only the torn, curled flaps had survived as silent and tragic clues to the painter's conflict, marking the crisis where he had been swept past the point of no return, beyond safety, toward the unknown, the ultimate. Whenever, in the course of his journey, Webb had encountered evidence of Crispian's struggle with his demon, he had asked himself what might happen if his friend, instead of interrupting the trend toward intensification, would surrender to it. That there was no way to hold it in check had become abundantly clear. While reading Crispian's notes, Webb had foreseen that the gathering energies would not stop at a first, minor reduction of the painting's size, but would further contract its overall dimensions, an agonizing expectation more than disastrously fulfilled by the enormous, starkly expressive elimination in the hut.

Watching the colors pour over the ragged edges, he had tried to put himself into Crispian's place; he had attempted to understand what forces had acted on Crispian, but had found it impossible to imagine how they could have seized his friend so powerfully. And while his attention was thus diverted, while he concentrated on Crispian's struggle, he did not notice how, during that time, he himself was seized by the very forces he was seeking to discover.

He did not know how long he had stood there. Time had passed him at a distance, without intruding. Entranced, captivated by the staring darkness inside the empty eye, he had followed the turbulent flow of lines rushing up to the rims and plunging into the darkness inside, disappearing as though swallowed up in a vortex.

From broken limbs and slashed patches of colors he had sought to derive the composition of the missing panel. He had imagined an extension of the stump, which was all that had remained of the cross—and the wooden beams had started to loom up in the vacuum. He had conjectured how large the martyred Christ would appear on the cross; he had imagined the tilted head, the bleeding cheeks, the tortured arms. And in this manner, by assuming and concluding, he had created forms; the darkness had become palpably alive, implicating him irrevocably in the desire to make sure, to see more, to know all.

It was during that period when his decision to climb to Zapar had come to the fore; by the time he had perceived it, it had outgrown the stage of questioning; it was fully shaped and already accepted.

Indeed, only now, from his present height, bathed in sunlight while he visualized his nightly silhouette in the hut's faintly iridescent gloom, was he able to recognize how he had tried and failed to resist the imponderable influence that emanated in a cold stream from the gash, as from a lightless whirlpool of swirling eternities.

Only now, as his lungs were beginning to feel the strain of the more rapid ascent, was he gripped by the fearful apprehension that the same demoniac drive, which had swept poor Crispian to his death, was also acting in him.

Padre Paolo was padding along in the monotonous gait of the mountaineer who has learned to preserve his strength; while Webb, unable to adjust himself to a steady rhythm, was alternately falling behind and catching up.

The path was beginning to rise more steeply. Webb's eyes, seeking rest from the sun-sparked rubble, strained to focus on the Padre's dark robe, where they soon produced the illusion of a black emptiness in an otherwise glittering world.

He thought that they were progressing at a snail's pace, but when he looked downhill to judge how high they had climbed, he saw that the valley now appeared almost level with the pass; Don Hernandez' hacienda had shrunk to a small enclosure; and the tall trees, their majestic crowns reduced to tiny immobile blossoms, were shrivelling away, step by step.

He found it hard to believe that he could have undergone the most fateful experiences of his life within this diminutive area, already so far removed that it looked as flat and unreal as a toy-landscape sketched by a child. Only part of a night had passed since he had marched up that Lilliput road to Don Hernandez's house. And now, no more than a few hours later, instead of returning to the coast as he had intended, he was heading in the opposite direction; he was ascending the mountain he had feared so much.

The Padre was waiting for him at the side of a huge boulder. "Perhaps, you would like a rest, senor," he said, unobtrusively scrutinizing Webb's expression.

"I'm not tired."

"As yet, senor, there is no need to rush ahead. A hurried start will not help you overcome your indecision, nor will it settle your doubts." His glance swept the white mist which came streaming up the foothills. "In fact, senor, it is better to examine them now, before the trail turns so steep as to press harshly on all your powers. The mountain is giving you another chance to know your will, before you are engaged beyond retreat, before El Soledad itself joins you in battle."

He indicated the broad, gently rising notch in the mountain side which circled the rim of the cone. "As we go up this ramp," he said, "we can still walk side by side. It will be possible to talk together, if you wish." The slight pause he left was just long enough to give Webb an opportunity to consent. "Or else, if you prefer, to think undisturbed by yourself."

Without awaiting the Consul's choice, he walked ahead; and Webb followed, purposely falling behind. Much as he would have liked to take the Padre into his confidence, he could not admit to his guide, whom he had implicated in the perilous ascent, that he did not know why he was climbing to Zapar; that some mysterious drive, stronger even than his fear of death, had overwhelmed his instinct of self-preservation.

The mere suspicion that this might be the same drive which had lashed Crispian beyond all hope of contentment was as alarming as to realize that the fire which one had watched consuming the neighbor's house, had also sparked one's own roof.

Instinctively pushing back the cuffs of his shirt in that neat and orderly gesture he had executed a thousand times in his office, when the cuffs had been neither as frayed nor as soiled as they were now, he sought out every detail that distinguished the impassioned, tempestuous, uncomproming artist from the sensible, disciplined man Webb knew himself to be.

On one of the crests before him was a rock, in which he believed to detect, for a moment, a semblance of Crispian's ascetic features. The wisp-like image held just long enough to point up the contrast between his own passing insignificance and the artist's titanic striving that sought to hammer its visions into the rock-like hardness of immortal substance. Then a thin spray of water trickled over the face of the solitary boulder, and the similarity to Crispian's gaunt head was lost.

Webb thought of his own work at the consulate, and their inequality became glaringly, sadly apparent. He had very little occasion for creative thinking; the more closely he conformed to regulations, the better did he satisfy his superiors; his decisions could only be correct or incorrect, never beautiful or ugly. But when Crispian stood before his easel, his creation was to be judged by its merits; if the composition was excellent, the coloring could be better; and from better—to better still—to best—there was no pause, no plateau and no rest; in unbroken succession, the soaring curve led to the unattainable ideal of perfection.

Webb's pulse beat faster; for the first time, he had found an almost visible interpretation, a plausible illustration that matched all the symptoms of Crispian's drive. Indeed, it explained the painter's relentless dissatisfaction with anything he had achieved; it made clear why his striving could never cease.

For his aim, in its ultimate extension, was to attain that which could not be attained. In the central panel, as Crispian had told Mona, he had sought to give form to that which could no longer be formed; he wanted to express that which could not be expressed; he was straining to shed light on the invisible. And, inevitably, since his yearning was not to be pacified, he could never find peace; because his goal, in the final and tragic analysis, was— the impossible.

Webb strode ahead more briskly. Again the suspicion that he, too, might be compelled by the same longing for the absolute, encircled him, touching him almost playfully, but drifting, skipping away before he could grasp it. It had occurred to him just then that the rising curve of excellence, which had so well described the artist's unavoidable embroilment with the impossible, was also applicable to any other human endeavor. Indeed, it did not matter whether the progression was by way of more, still more, and most; or richer, greater, higher, faster. In man's ability to conceive of a superlative, there operated an abstract propulsion which always seemed to be driving toward concrete goals, but always survived and exceeded their eventual attainment by the simple mechanism of transforming what had appeared as an end into a stepping stone for further demands.

A slight sting from just above the heel of his right foot groped tentatively toward Webb's attention, but he was too preoccupied to pay much attention to it. He thought of Don Hernandez's fanatic quest for absolute proof, of Barrie's zeal in mining and undermining the mountain, of Bradley's unceasing labors to acquire more wealth. He recalled an Alpine village he had once visited, where a small cemetery contained the bodies of all those who had died trying to climb a nearby peak, reputed for a long time to be too difficult to scale. Everywhere he seemed to be faced by the paradox that the impossible, instead of discouraging and frightening away otherwise rational people, exerted on them an unavoidable and often fatal attraction.

If his assumption were correct, Webb reflected, touched by a fleeting anguish, if the absolute were indeed the concealed goal of a drive which acted not only on Crispian, but on others, perhaps even on him, his present ascent, too, might be motivated by deep yearnings which were ultimately directed upon unattainable ends.

He rejected the notion with more vigor than it deserved; for on the face of it, it was too absurd to be taken seriously. He told himself that his goal, after all, was concretely and reasonably defined: he was climbing to Zapar. But then it occurred to him that at various stages during his journey—in the jungle, at Irozco, at Santa Rosa—he had resolved to go no farther than his next objective. And now, as he looked at the ridge before him, which Padre Paolo was just beginning to ascend, Webb realized that there would be still higher crests behind it. And even if he surmounted one after the other, there would be more to follow until finally there would rear up—the impossible.

He walked faster in order to close the gap between himself and the Padre. To be near another person, even without speaking, would help to quell some of his growing insecurity. Not only was it settling in the marrow of his bones, chilling him from inside out, but it was also beginning to separate him from himself; because the man who might be possessed by an irrational longing for the unattainable was certainly a stranger, not the known self of abstinent, truculently unambitious and supremely reasonable moderation.

As a realistic person, he had always appraised his objectives in terms of potential fulfillment and had certainly never embarked on any hopeless endeavors. With the exception of his present, unaccountably reckless ascent, he had no cause to suspect that his ordinarily temperate, even humdrum existence was actually interlaced by insensate dreams. He would, in fact, find it difficult to consider his own modest wishes and longings as the rudimentary beginnings of boundless desires, already focused, as far as they went, upon what could not be. Still it was conceivable that, precisely because he had never pursued any aim to its final goal, he had failed to detect the direction inherent in its earlier stages.

The sun flared up in a dent of the diagonal skyline, and Webb noticed his shadow following alongside, gliding over the rocks in grotesquely distorted shapes, breaking apart and reforming, forever changing, forever pouring itself over the ground and gathering itself up without ever losing its substance. For a while he watched it, wondering whether the busily gesticulating projection beside him resembled a demonic stranger in him, who might be reaching for the impossible in the same boundless manner as his shadow, just then, tumbled into the depths of a gully, where it suddenly grew tenfold in size.

Webb shrank from the sight; in every nerve sprang up a rebellion against the unlimited, the uncontrolled, the ill-considered, the bacchic sweep toward the unachievable.

There was something deeply disquieting about the drift of his thoughts. It seemed to be all in a dangerous direction, away from the secure beliefs he still hoped to keep, to hold, or else to restore and regain. His glance fixed on Padre Paolo's broad shoulders, as if he needed a firm hold to steady himself; as if the sight of their stability could help him counteract that recurring sensation of being adrift, which swept over him in waves like dizzy spells.

Accelerating his steps, he reached Padre Paolo by the time the trail left the ramp. The Padre, without asking what had prompted Webb to come up to him, moved quietly to the outer edge. For a while, they climbed in silence on the path which now coiled its way up the steep slope in a grand pattern of five serpentine turns.

"Last night," the Padre began at length, "when Mona showed you the painting, did she not tell you why Senor Crispian abandoned the larger part?"

A short section of the trail had crumbled off, forcing Webb to take a long, precarious stride over the gap. "He felt distracted by all that surrounded the central panel. He said it kept him from reaching the core."

"And yet," the Padre mused, "you mentioned that he had already signed the canvas, because he considered his work completed?"

"He did. For a while, after he had finished, he seemed content, even happy. Neither Mona nor Don Hernandez suspected that he was still questioning what he had accomplished. And then— suddenly!" He noticed that the strain of climbing made speaking more difficult than he had realized and waited a few seconds to catch his breath. "Suddenly, he was no longer satisfied. He felt he had to do more."

"What more, senor? What, do you suppose, was the cause of that unending dissatisfaction?"

For a moment, the expression: 'Man's devine discontent' flashed through Webb's mind, but he quickly refrained from using it. For it could also apply to him; indeed, he wondered whether Padre Paolo had already recognized the parallel to Webb's own need to go beyond Santa Rosa. But it was difficult to read the priest's weather-beaten features. There had been a tensing of attention; perhaps he suspected something, perhaps not; and perhaps even he had known all along what Webb was only beginning to discover.

"Was there no way," the Padre prodded, "that Mona could have saved the painting?"

"She tried," Webb answered. "She pleaded with him to be content with what he had achieved. Apparently, she had sensed, much sooner than Don Hernandez, sooner even than Crispian, the danger in his increasing unrest. She even drew his attention to other parts of the canvas, by finding faults here and there. And for a while, she actually succeeded in distracting him; he made some corrections; at any rate, he seemed to find peace."

Looking down on the descending valley floor, Webb brushed a tawny, coarse-textured stone over the ledge and listened to its thin clatter before turning back to the Padre. "But after a few days, she told me, Crispian grew restless again. He kept himself fever-ishly busy, even at night; and since he could not sleep in any event, he would get up before dawn and rush to the pass to watch the sunrise. When he returned, he would seem depressed to the point of despair."

Webb slowed down as they approached the second hairpin turn. Before heading in the other direction, he took a long look at the steadily widening panorama, his glance passing over the broad-backed foothills that floated on the fine white mist like a school of young whales. He felt he could understand, in the face of this scintillating, inimitably shaded color scheme, the despair of an artist who compared his work, not to that of any other man, but to the greater creation.

"Toward the end," Webb continued, "Mona came more and more frequently to the hacienda, as often as four or five times during a day and an evening. If she took such risks, it was because her concern for Crispian had become even greater than her fear of being discovered by her father. But even so, she could not prevent the inevitable."

The Padre remained silent, and Webb wondered how to explain to him what he meant by the inevitable. Don Hernandez would have easily understood the abstraction; but the mountain priest needed images, concepts that could be visualized, whether they were derived from reality or from fragments fused into poetic visions. Only then could his mind seize on them, this slow, primitive, wonderful mind that shied from abstractions and fell behind when confronted by facile deductions, though in the end it would unerringly find its way to the truth, sometimes laboriously, circuitously, but always as infallibly as a weight that sinks of itself to the deepest point.

"One afternoon," Webb went on, "she found Crispian in front of the canvas, hanging burlap strips over the sections adjoining the center, shifting them back and forth, as though he were measuring how much should be cut away. When he noticed her, he pulled her outside, locked the door and hid the key. That evening, he started to work once more on the central panel; for two days and nights, without interruption, he painted on the Christ figure; he neither slept nor ate anything in all that time. And when Mona arrived the following morning, she found him asleep or unconscious on the floor."

The trail became almost too narrow for both of them to walk side by side. "When Crispian awoke," Webb continued, "he seemed quite well. In fact, all during dinner, he was unusually gay and carefree. But, suddenly, he left the table. Mona rushed after him; however, by the time she reached his workroom, the first gash had been made, and it was too late to stop him."

"And after that evening?" the Padre asked, moving closer to the upper slope to give Webb more room.

"There was nothing more she could do," Webb said, indicating as much by his tone as by a gesture that his report was completed. "The following morning he had left for Zapar."

The Padre kept nodding or somehow rocking his head against the rhythm of his supple gait. It was impossible to determine whether he was mulling over what Webb had told him, whether he was waiting for further information, or simply concentrating on the exacting ascent. A couple of times he looked at Webb, but it was not until they had passed the fourth turn that he said: "Is there nothing else you wish to say about Mona?"

"That is all she told me."

"Then you do not know that Mona went along with Crispian, that she climbed with him to Zapar?"

Staggered, Webb reached for the mountain side, his hand tracing a line over the smooth rock before sinking back to his body. "I had no idea," he muttered. "Neither Mona nor Don Hernandez dropped as much as a hint."

"They would not, senor. It was to be a secret, and yet it is not. Everyone in the village knows it. But fearing Barrie's wrath, they do not speak of it. If I happen to know, it is because I was passing through Santa Rosa, when Mona came back from Zapar."

Webb held his breath, enduring the brief moment when the mountain priest seemed undecided whether or not to say more. "I was, perhaps, the first person to see her on her return," Padre Paolo continued, somewhat haltingly, edging forward along the threshold of his hesitation. But once he had crossed it, his voice, though always sonorous, became even more vibrant while rising to the task of conjuring up, for the first time in words, a deeply moving and often remembered vision. "I saw her from the church, senor, just as I was about to leave after evening mass. I was all alone—every one of my people had left. But I did not feel alone that evening. I thought I should return to the altar for another prayer, but there was in my heart a desire to ring out the bell, though it was hardly the time to do so. I walked toward the belfry, and as I passed the broken stained-glass window to the left, I looked out. And there was the mountain; there was El Soledad, holding the sun like a tired child in the bend of his arm, and then I knew why I had wanted to ring out the bell."

The Padre, unaware of Webb's impatience, paused as if the memory were so vivid that he was held anew in the spell of the mysterious dusk. "By the time I saw her," he went on, "the sun was all the way behind the crest. So I did not recognize at once that it was Mona; all I saw was a woman coming down from the mountain. And it was not until she was quite near that I could make out who it was. She must have discovered me at the same time, because she left the path and approached and entered the church."

"What did she tell you?" Webb asked, unable to subdue his impatience any longer.

"She said nothing, senor. Not one word."

"And you didn't question her?" Webb erupted, so disappointed as to sound almost vehement.

"I had no right. My robe, senor, obliges me to wait until someone wishes to speak to me. I am not a judge whose duty it is to question. No more than I could ever question you."

"But you could have asked her about Zapar! About Crispian's last days, about his death!"

"I did, indeed, ask her if Senor Crispian was still at Zapar. She nodded, saying nothing; and then she left. Only much later did I find out that she had not misled me. For, in truth, poor Senor Crispian was still alive at that time." Noticing Webb's reaction, he added: "Indeed, it is surprising. I often think, even stranger than that she had dared to go with him, is that she came back before he had died."

Webb waited, expecting the Padre to elaborate on his remark; but the mountain priest remained silent, until, sensing Webb's churning curiosity, he added: "I do not know, senor, what happened between them. For Mona did not tell anyone after her return to Santa Rosa. She never spoke of it, not to friend or stranger, and never once to me."

In slanted beams, the sun's blaze shot past the dark contours high above them, sometimes touching the Padre's head and sometimes fanning out in a gully. Once, when Webb felt the warm light on his face, he stood still, involuntarily raising his head in the direction of Zapar, toward the hidden peak, toward the point of no mystery, where in a wide panorama all could be known and seen. But the heavy stone masses above him protruded so far out that they eerily covered him without, however, giving him shelter. A moment later, a last bouquet of sharp rays lanced from the sun's outer edge stabbed at his eyes; then the blinding glare withdrew once more behind the diagonal line that separated the crest from the glimmering blue sky.

For some time now the Padre had been leading the way, while they traversed, more or less sideways, the many ribs which the mountain sent down from a bony promontory. And for some time Webb had been considering the possibility of turning back; indeed, he had wondered how many more obstacles he would yet overcome—before reaching the absolutely insuperable barrier.

That he would ultimately run into that final blockade he no longer doubted. For if it were true that he, like Crispian and others, was spurred by a desire for the impossible, he was actually seeking this decisive defeat; he could not stop short of that craggy ridge toward which the Padre was heading; he had to move on toward the insurmountable obstruction.

Indeed, he now understood why a man would not stop before he had reached that which, to him, was unfeasible; why his soul would drift on, would keep coursing in restless search, with feelers in all directions, forever passing what was fulfilled, never held fast until in its silent, undivulging, opaque manner it had wrapped its cloak around some unattainable hope.

A chill of which the source could have been outside or within him, ran down his spine, when he reviewed his past, wondering whether he had failed to see his life's chosen defeat. And when he thought of his friends and acquaintances, he recognized how many of them clutched at some hopeless quest, concealing their secret, inadmissible entanglement with that which rebuffed them, their illicit romance with the impossible.

Looking up to the ridge where the trail swam out into the blue, he noticed that the Padre was waiting for him beneath an overhanging bluff.

"You must remain in this shelter," the mountain priest said after Webb had approached, "until I have crossed the roof of the cliff." He studied Webb with a sidelong glance from underneath his bushy eyebrows, then approached the narrow passage which wound its way upward inside the base of the rock. "Do not move, senor," he said, "until I call you. There may be stones falling from above."

Wiping a sudden itch from his burning, fluttering eyelids, Webb felt tempted to tell the Padre that he could go no further, that he had reached his insuperable barrier. But then, while his guide disappeared in the perpendicular channel, he remained silent. It had occurred to him that the drive which kept pushing people toward the outer reaches of the possible did not become less vigorous after it was blocked. On the contrary, at that stage it would become most disastrously operative. Thrown back upon itself, finding no other outlet, swirling and fermenting in a man's heart, it would turn against him; it was then that it started to breed and foment the countless manifestations of incurable, inconquerable discontent, battering a person from within, while, on the outside, holding him pinned against the unattainable.

A trickle of sand came gliding over the roof of his shelter. Gazing beyond it, Webb realized that here he was facing in a direction which the mountain had not previously opened to him; and though he could not see anything below the ocean of white and gold mist, he knew that he was looking North. Beyond those blue cloud banks hovering over the horizon, was his country, were the vast plains and populated shores, were the proud cities in which people lived nearer the impossible than in any other part of the world.

While pebbles and stones rolled and tumbled over the rim above him, he recalled two of his friends who had died of heart attacks at too young an age. He thought of the exhausted businessmen opening yet another branch office; of the executives ruling the gigantic corporations, the jet pilots flying at supersonic speeds, the teachers in overcrowded schools, who were all nearing the limits of human endurance. He thought of the workers at the assembly line, of the secretaries, the department heads, the sales forces and shipping clerks, all trying either to meet the demands of increasing efficiency or to stem the tide of rapidly multiplying production. He thought of the heroic struggles, the breakdowns, the nervous disorders, as countless millions were forced, blindly or knowingly, voluntarily or helplessly, to obey the despotic spirit of the accelerated age that churned and swirled around the borders of the impossible.

"Senor, do you not hear me?" the Padre called from above.

"I'm coming," Webb shouted, torn from his thoughts.

At first, the narrow passage was not too difficult to climb. But soon it forced him to proceed on all fours, clasping at every hold he could find. In the end, climbing with his back pressed for support against the rocky wall behind him, he emerged on a slanted shield of rubble, which he had to traverse in order to reach the Padre.

Twice, he nearly slid down, loosening torrents of sand and stone which rolled out into space before plunging past the shelter below; but ultimately he managed to crawl unharmed to the flat spot where the Padre awaited him.

"We shall eat after we reach that crest," the Padre said, pointing at the steep ridge above them, and then walked ahead at once.

Gazing at the high dividing line where the trail leaped up as if to float out into the sky, Webb wondered what view to expect from the top. For a while, as he toiled up the sharply rising path, he struggled against a corrosive fatigue. But gradually he experienced a throbbing sense of exhilaration—which, he felt sure, could not yet be caused by the thinning air at this altitude.

Instead, he believed, his elation might be due to the fact that he seemed to have stumbled upon the answer to a question which had occupied him during many of those lonely evenings he had devoted to the voluminous history books in his library. Since the study of history was his favorite pastime, a hobby which had supplanted an earlier, and long since frustrated, ambition to enter politics, he had often wondered what forces were winding the hidden springs in mankind's evolution, what unknown and unknowing mechanisms drove the race to proceed, to advance at any rate if not always progress toward the better.

And now, at long last, he felt as if the mysterious propulsion had suddenly become illuminated from within, enabling him to trace the creeping progress of the drive toward 'better, greater, and more'—which, in prehistoric times, had wrought its changes so slowly as to render them almost unnoticeable in the course of millennia; which had moved at a barely quickened rate in the still sluggish dawn of history; which had gathered speed as civilization doubled and re-doubled its energies; which had multiplied its intensity as it rose to the present furious crescendo that over-powered all men, not only because of its rapidity, but also because they were nearing the impossible.

The Indians in Irozco, Webb reflected, rubbing his hurting eyelids, were not yet as flagrantly involved with the impossible as was the scientist in his daily contests at the boundaries of the known and feasible. With the human predisposition toward the superlative still largely dormant in the early stages of progress, the primitive was less likely than civilized man to ever reach that which he could not accomplish, and thus come to know his phys-ical, nervous, and mental limitations.

Paradoxically, the greater the achievement, the greater the dis-content. The more modern, the more aspiring, the more rapidly learning and developing a person, the harsher was his clash with the impossible apt to become. And so it was surely not without significance that at no other period had there been a more opti-mistic belief that all things were possible; indeed, it almost seemed that people wished to deny the existence of the impossible alto-gether, at a time when they were more intensely involved with it than ever before.

He was climbing the last and steepest section of the path, as he explored the featureless propulsion which, having no defined aims of its own, could infuse any human effort; which might present itself as praiseworthy aspiration, as the desire to excel, to acquire more power or fame, to drive faster, to fly further, to build greater and higher; to construct pyramids, then towers, and finally skyscrapers, to rise from the earth, to ride the air and ulti-mately to soar into outer space.

A few more hard-fought steps, and he stood on the ridge, breath-ing heavily, needing rest, fighting off the swift attack of a dizzy spell, when he saw that the trail ventured far out on a ledge be-fore swinging back in a soft curve to the promontory.

Once again, he was facing north. Beyond that swaying skyline was his country, with its teeming populations, the burgeoning cities, the crowded sidewalks, the haste and exhaustion. In the heart of that distant sky were the millions of individuals, whirling within an ever faster turning centrifuge, their pace quickened, their lives speeded up, as their civilization spiraled toward the impossible.

They left the ridge; the northern horizon dropped below the fiercely serrulated crest. And Webb, once again isolated behind the mountain wall, suddenly felt as if the full weight of his impersonal contemplations was gathering on him.

The Padre stopped in the trough of a gully and spread out some food on a cloth he took from his bundle. He sat down on a rounded rock, while Webb dropped to the ground, resting his aching limbs.

They ate silently, dividing a large piece of bread, some cheese, raisins and dried bananas. When he had finished, Webb leaned back, closing his eyes.

But before the growing lassitude had a chance to spread through his muscles, the Padre got up, tied the bundle, and resumed the ascent, waiting once or twice until Webb, after a slow start, had managed to reach him.

Before long, however, Webb fell back again. As the Padre moved steadily away from him, Webb looked down on the valley where he saw the uppermost houses of Santa Rosa, infinitely small, sprinkling the rim of the mountain kettle like arrested, hardened, unaccountably petrified foam. It occurred to him that they were the only human beings within miles; that, indeed, they were hours away from the nearest village. The thought made him feel his vast separation more keenly; it was as if sheets of gauze came fluttering down from the sky behind him, blurring the contours of the distant human habitations to make them appear still farther removed, gently enveloping him in an inextricable isolation. And as the glimmering air gave the impression that veil upon veil descended in a wide arc, wrapping itself around him almost tenderly, he thought he could feel, like an approaching cold wind, a sense of the mountain's immense solitude.

He walked on, listening eagerly to the crunching noise his shoes evoked from the rock; it was the only sound he could hear in the absolute stillness. Padre Paolo was too far ahead to be heard; and the faint breeze which had previously merged with the rushing of blood in his ears had expired some time ago. Instinctively, he opposed this glacial stillness with a stronger awareness of being alive than he had ever experienced. And yet, at the same time, he felt how the firm and stable reality in which he had believed for so long, was receding from him, dissolving on all sides, leaving him, not in a vacuum, but surrounded, accompanied, even spoken to in inaudible whispers, by something volatile, dynamic, darkly streaming and impossible to grasp.

If this indescribable sense of something vastly important hinted at the true world he lived in, if his real environment were something far different from the more convenient, easily identifiable appearances he had previously relied upon, it was urgently important that he should know more about it.

It had been unsettling enough to discover that gigantic and seemingly stable civilizations were whipped in their depths by demonic forces; it was intolerable to suspect that his own, seemingly so reasonable approach to practical living might have concealed the true aims of fundamentally unexplained—and, perhaps, inexplicable—strivings.

Though he still shied away from believing that his common sense had actually rested on an irrational foundation, he came to see, for the first time, that his hard-headed practicality had not been solidly anchored in logic, but balanced precariously on uncertain axioms; that his most reliable convictions were islands floating on dark streams of energy flowing toward unknown absolutes; that his most proudly rational intentions appeared so sensible only because they were fragments which, in their extension, would reveal their transcendental—perhaps mystic and perhaps fantastic—orientation.

He shrank from the sight of himself as a demonic being; perhaps, because he could not endure in it the blinding flash of the divine. His quick anguish, the vehemence of his reaction, his haste in scurrying back to shelter, disclosed to him how badly he needed the cocoon he had spun over the years. Almost astonished, he watched his mind working feverishly to repair the damage done to its pathetically transparent and yet vitally necessary blindfolds. For a while, he was still able to observe the self-deceptive devices used to block any view of eternity, to subdivide infinity, to put safe labels on the intangible, or to achieve a sense of security by trapping the unruly and sublime in meaningless, though well-sounding words; then the darkness became complete, giving him once again the illusion of living in a superbly reasonable, reliable, trustworthy and agreeably protective environment.

The sting in his foot, which had previously reached for his

attention, crawled up again; and he stood still to give his leg a moment's rest. What an ordeal every step might become if the raw area above his heel were enlarged, he did not dare to imagine. Nor what might happen if his fluttering eyelids should further impair and blur his vision.

When he walked on, he no longer asked wherein he differed from Crispian, nor what had given him the impression that in their depths they were truly related. With his mind under control once again, he recognized that men like Crispian were forever breaking through the steadily hardening crusts of a utilitarian realism. They would disprove the sterile conclusions at the end of every rational trend, they would deny that the human destiny had as its concrete aim a fatuous and perhaps repetitive self-perpetuation. And so they would frighten and disturb their fellow men while pushing them along toward the distant, obscure intent of mankind's wild and magnificent adventure.

But the Webbs in each epoch had to perform just as essential a task. They had to deny that any human goal was impractical, or it would never be reached. Men like himself had to solidify, foreshorten, make palatable all transcendental trends, even if it meant distorting the truth, even if they had to build false fronts to hide people's perplexingly unselfish strivings. For, strange and unreasonable as it seemed, rational men had to be persuaded that they were serving their own, egotistical ends, though in truth they were not; they could not live in full sight of their transcendental objectives.

And so, Webb thought, anxiously listening to his heart's strained efforts to send the blood racing through his veins, Crispian and he were indeed brothers. Irreconcilable extremes, incompatible, even opposing each other, they were nevertheless linked; they had to advance hand in hand. More than that, each had something of the other; in varying degrees the conflicting elements could be found in every person, as they were combined, to some extent, in Webb.

CHAPTER IX

THE PADRE, on reaching the oblique stone pyramid atop the promontory, awaited Webb's approach. Advancing toward the outer edge that hung in thin sheets over the vertical drop, he stepped on the largest rock which jutted out into the sky like a springboard to distant horizons. As he stood there, briefly scanning the widely scattered clouds, his attention focused on a fresh troupe, newly steamed up in the background. He studied the direction of the wind, evaluated the time of day from the height of the sun, and it seemed to Webb that his expression reflected concern. But before Webb had reached the slanted, craggy platform, the Padre had stepped off the rock and started to walk ahead, perhaps purposely avoiding to discuss his apprehensions.

There was something about the Padre's protective attitude which suddenly irritated Webb. A tired, sinewless rancor crept through him as he saw the strong figure advancing again; and before he could deflect its aim, it had flared into the unmanageable impulse to stop his guide, who appeared as rested and vigorous as at the beginning of the ascent.

Webb hailed him, and Padre Paolo looked back.

"I'm parched," Webb called, in as loud a voice as his panting lungs permitted. "I must have some water."

He was not sure whether he had made himself understood, for the mountain priest did not reply until Webb was nearly at his side.

"You will have to hold out," the Padre said. "We must save what little we have."

"I can't wait!" Webb countered, himself surprised to hear the harsh, rasping rage in his voice.

The Padre, half-incredulous, half-alerted, held his glance. "There is no chance to refill the bottle," he said quietly, "until we reach the brook below the glacier. It is still far. You will get thirstier yet."

"I don't care!" Webb blurted out. "I must have something to drink now."

Padre Paolo frowned and gazed reflectively at the small water bottle which protruded from the bundle of provisions he carried. He shifted the bundle from one hand to the other, away from Webb, as if he had decided that this ration had to be preserved. But before the motion had quite spent itself, he slowed down, ending up by holding the bottle in both hands; and it became painfully evident how difficult, perhaps impossible, it was for him to refuse help to anyone, no matter what the circumstances, even when he knew, as he did in this case, that charity might eventually prove harmful to them both.

Webb had observed the glowing up of that inner goodness which occasionally shone through the Padre's cracked, bronze skin, and he suddenly found himself loathing and despising it. An irrational, quite intractable desire to smash at that undeserved, unjustified, and somehow reproaching kindness incited him; he felt compelled to beat it down, to abuse it, or better yet—to prove it wrong.

"If I don't get some water, I can't go on," he lied, knowing full well that his thirst was by no means critical. The despicable lie, unpardonable under the circumstances, served his purpose so well that he felt no shame, rather some sort of perverse pleasure. The less he deserved to be helped, the clearer would be the proof that the Padre's charity was a folly, stupidly inviting its own deception and abuse. "I'm sick with thirst," he cried. "You have no right to withhold my ration."

For a moment, they faced each other in brittle silence. Then the Padre nodded, lowered the bundle to the ground and bent down, while Webb, with wild irony, watched him untie the string.

The mountain priest's hunched shoulders gave the impression that he was humbled, defeated, and Webb felt as exultant as if he had achieved some vast vindication of which he did not quite know the meaning. But this unwarranted sense of victory did not last very long. No sooner had he taken the bottle from the Padre, when a bitter taste seeped into his triumph; and after two or three gulps his throat contracted. He faltered, feeling suddenly weak, hollow, ashamed.

The Padre straightened up. When he saw how little of the bottle's content was missing, he looked up to scrutinize Webb briefly. "You can drink more, senor," he said gently. "There is no need to make yourself suffer."

The sudden pressure in Webb's throat threatened to prevent him from speaking. "We need every drop," he muttered.

"We shall manage, senor."

"We won't!" Webb erupted. "It was shortsighted of you to take pity on me. What are you going to do, later on, when I'll beg you for more, and you'll have nothing to give?"

The Priest looked at him, surprised. "I thought of that. I shall give you my ration." He noticed the suspicious quivering of Webb's lips, and hastened to add: "It will not be hard on me, senor. I am used to going long hours without water."

Webb closed his eyes to counteract the fluttering of his eyelids. He remembered that he had meant to ask the Padre for some ointment, but he could not bring himself to make any new demands so soon after his inexcusable treachery. "You can keep your share," he blurted out, pushing the bottle away. His voice was uncertain and hoarse, racked by the remote tremors of stifled sobs which tried to surge up as painfully and ineffectually as dry retching. "I only pretended to be so thirsty," he said, turning away. "It should have been obvious to you that I lied!" He broke off, realizing that his confession, far from being an admission of guilt, was actually a last, vicious blow at the Padre's unrestrained, overflowing generosity.

Padre Paolo pushed the bottle back into the bundle and tied the knot. More astonished than hurt by Webb's attempted abuse, which had neither impaired nor diminished his charity, he saw only the need to comfort Webb again. "Your nerves feel the strain," he said, without a trace of reproach. "It is my fault. We should have taken another rest much sooner."

Webb looked around the small platform. There was enough room for both to sit down, or for one to stretch out, to lie at the edge of the perpendicular drop, to rest, perhaps to sleep. The prospect appeared so alluring that Webb started to sway as if he were about to sink down on the spot. But a split-second later something inside of him pulled him up. An indefinable sound had alerted him; he believed to have heard the clattering of a small

stone, and he listened; but there was only the silence of the mountain. And the more keenly he listened to it, the more richly the
mountain's silence resounded with a variety of noises. There was
not only the rapid murmuring of the wind and the dry crackling
of the dust; there were the thousand whispering voices of the
pursuers coming nearer, the voices of all the dangers bypassed
and escaped below, the pointed rocks and the hidden cracks and
the splintered gullies, all thwarted, avoided, and yet not permanently defeated; all harpooned by his remembering nerves and
pulled after him, all drawing closer in baying, raucous, tooth-
baring pursuit—

"Let's go on," Webb cried out. The silence was restored as
dramatically as after a thunder clap, and Webb, jarred and bewildered, was about to seek some excuse for his shouting, when he
noticed that the Padre, instead of showing astonishment, held his
head slightly tilted, as if he too were listening.

A soft, dancing breeze came streaming down, wreathing itself
around the two isolated, forgotten, dusty men on the promontory's needle, pulling playfully at their clothes, before gliding
away into the sky's endless expanse.

"I prefer to go on," Webb said, his crisp voice cutting the
silence like a screeching blade.

The Padre nodded, no longer attempting to urge Webb to
take a rest, as if he had understood why the Consul, in spite of
his fatigue, had to go on. "Perhaps, higher up, senor," he said,
pushing the bottle deeper into the bundle, "we shall find a better
place to sit down, a wider plateau with no view of the mountain's
steepness."

He swung the bundle over his shoulder, crossed the platform
and started to traverse the thin spine, which linked the promontory to the ponderously rising flank of El Soledad.

Webb waited until Padre Paolo had reached the other side
before following him. As he balanced himself along the slender
bridge, he caught glimpses of the fan-like ribs that swept down
on either side, and he asked himself whether the Padre had also
seen in them the fleshless hand of death, and whether he, too,
had been swamped by the doubt and fear which threatened to
engulf Webb.

The trail, abandoning its caution beyond the bridge, renewed its assault on the mountain by leading directly over an almost holdless parapet. When Webb slipped two or three times on the smooth surface, which the Padre had negotiated without difficulty, his barely repressed envy and rage again boiled over. He felt like screaming at the Padre that there was no God, that it was wrong to help others, that the sick should be left to die and the ruthless to win—anything that would crash into the Priest's sleepwalking assurance. And while he was still seeking the most effective means to wound Padre Paolo, he became aware that his impotent rage was not directed at the black-robed man before him, but at the mountain itself.

He looked up. The twisted cliff above the parapet blocked his view, but he could sense, across the stony blindfold, El Soledad's gigantic presence. In a swift, surprising move, the mountain had swept aside the Padre, revealing itself as the true object of Webb's wrath and antagonism. It almost seemed as if the distant peak had approached, leaning down from its aloof altitude. For the first time it was near, nearer than it had ever been. There was a sudden, flashing contact between them; Webb felt the mountain's muted and yet fiercely alive tension, felt it in every quivering nerve; felt it as acutely as if El Soledad were crouched directly behind the cliff. And then the whirling excitement ebbed away, the tension ceased, and a moment later there was only the blank front of the rock.

He moved back, clenched his fists, then ran the two or three steps toward the parapet. A fiery hurt flared up his legs, when he scraped his shins in another attempt to swing himself over the rim. Succeeding this time, he fell, rolled into a furrow, and lay flat, unable to raise himself at once. The impact had left him pale and trembling. But the physical fall was not as laming as the after effects of the hallucination, the shock of knowing that he could no longer trust his senses, that his mind was beginning to give way under the prolonged, corrosive strain of the ascent.

He started to get up, but remained on his knees, panting. His brain felt clouded, he shook his head several times, angrily, wildly, and he succeeded in clearing his thoughts. But he could not altogether shake off the remembrance of his momentary obsession. He still felt as if the mountain had descended from its great height, had taken on the living form of a conscious, palpably real opponent, and was now watching him from every rock and gully.

There was a breathless silence in the wilderness around him. He sensed how the deceptive stillness turned into a vibrating immobility which hinted, not at a permanent balance of forces, but at a winding of energies before a swift and ferocious uncoiling. And again he knew that the mountain was near; his skin shrivelled, as though it were singed by the hard stares of a thousand eyes observing him from all sides.

The Padre's voice, hailing him from the entrance to a ravine, reverberated ever more loudly within the corrugated walls. Webb scrambled to his feet, signaled that he was not hurt, and started to climb hurriedly over the debris that littered the steep slope.

The blood throbbed more violently along his bruised, burning shins, when he recalled the Padre's prediction that the mountain would engage his mind in a relentless, unsparing conflict. While he picked his way among the somber, darkly glittering, almost bluish granite plates, he was keenly aware that some fresh element had been added to his struggle with purely physical obstacles. Some unexpected, fearful influence had arisen in his fatigue. And when he looked up to the waiting mouth of the ravine, he froze at the thought that every step carried him deeper into El Soledad's strangling embrace.

He had to take precautions, while there was still time. But he did not know how to protect himself against the recurrence of further, perhaps, even more uncontrollable lapses and delusions. Only one thing appeared certain: rather than attribute his compulsive states to some mysterious influence of the mountain, he would have to relate his symptoms to the unaccustomed conditions presented by his environment. He had to explain them as reactions to such concrete factors as thirst, lack of oxygen, or a general depletion of his physical and nervous resources.

The mountain, he stubbornly and somewhat defiantly insisted, was an inanimate mass of stone which could not possibly have any effect on his mind. For a while, he found some comfort in repeating to himself that the lifeless colossus, no matter how immense and awe-inspiring it was, had no power over him. But despite this logical appraisal, a residue of anxiety remained. He had to admit that the simplification was too crass; it did not encompass the whole truth, and certainly failed to explain all his symptoms.

He rubbed his forehead, his temples, his cheeks. He knew, after all, that a large number of myths surrounded most of the impressive mountain peaks all over the world. These giants could not have become the central figures of so many superstitions, of fairy tales and adventure stories told around flickering fire places, if they did not have the power to stir the imagination; if each, in its own characteristic manner, could not renew, time and again, in individual men the experience of the stirring, evanescent and yet overpowering, attributes which folklore ascribed to them.

Almost at once, there seemed to be a heightening of tension in the air, as if El Soledad had waited for this breach in his rational rejection to reveal itself more clearly. A slight link had been established between him and the rigid, unbreathing rocks lying about in inert pallor. He still insisted that it was impossible for any communication to reach him from their lifeless substance. But, at the same time, he found himself trying to read the enigmatic symbols written on their battered, eroded surfaces, querying how the blank tablets could project the meanings locked up within them, could convey and impress upon him the slow-rolling cerebrations, the inaudible sonority of the mountain colossus.

Some sort of hopeless lassitude surged and flowed through his muscles, while he wondered whether he had reached that stage of exhaustion in which people, lost in a desert, or after a long trek through a jungle, were known to have succumbed to hallucinations, to have been misled by weird visions, ending up, at times, as raving lunatics.

He examined the possibility with a curiously detached impartiality, and decided that his symptoms appeared to be of a different sort. For he could not as yet detect any weakening or blurring of his logical faculties. On the contrary, his brain seemed to work with an unusual lucidity, with a searching, almost clairvoyant comprehension. What was alarming, indeed, was an excess rather than a failing of his reasoning powers.

A shadow passed over him, grotesquely curling and twisting as it clambered over the rugged incline to his left. Looking up, he saw that it was cast by one of the clouds which, not so long ago, had steamed up in the distance. Much nearer already, passing, in fact, almost directly overhead, it vanished as swiftly as if it had prematurely revealed the massing of scattered forces around him, and was now trying to escape before alerting him to the destructive preparations progressing just beyond his field of vision.

Another cloud, streaking by directly ahead of him, was pierced and held fast by a needle-pointed spire near the far end of the ravine. Unable to float further, it dissolved its substance and unveiled, behind it, a distant crest, reaching to a dizzying height, white, sparkling, almost aflame in its sun-showered ascent. The view, remote and unreal above the dark ravine, overwhelmed him. On that titanic rise, he could imagine Prometheus, chained to the rock, undaunted, staring remorselessly and accusingly at the inexorable heavens. And had the myth not yet existed, he would have felt the need, in the face of this dazzling sight, to invent something similar, something that would express his impulsive response to the truculence, to the exalted and cloud-touching immensity, to that sprawling and heaving and rising greatness under the sky.

A few moments later, the gleaming titan disappeared behind the ravine's see-sawing sky line. And only then did it strike him that he might have to surmount that forbidding wall. With his emotions swinging rapidly from admiration to anguish, he understood how dynamically the mountain could affect his mind. Even excluding any more elusive and subtle influences, it was inevitable, in the most realistic sense, that the changing territory would force its variable content upon his attention. A murderous cliff could not fail to produce as its counterpart an emotion of fear, a prolonged incline would raise questions of endurance, an unsurmountable crest had the power to evoke the spectre of defeat and surrender.

And in this manner El Soledad could provoke any number of reactions, could play on the full register of his sensibilities, using his soul as an instrument which would reverberate to the chords struck on lofty spires, plunging slopes, and soaring towers, in the progression and sweep of the mountain's gigantic fugue.

When Webb emerged on a plateau which hung limply over the mountain side, he scanned the panorama, hoping to catch a glimpse of the peak. But he was still not allowed to see El Soledad. And so he could still not anticipate what the mountain had in store for him, nor in what manner it would choose to attack him.

Squinting, his lids hurting badly, he followed the Padre over the tilted plane when, all of a sudden, the glare which shimmered in tremorous sheets of heat alongside the high bluffs, condensed and flared into an image. Upon a depthless screen spun by gossamer light, there appeared a semblance of Esther, her radiant face framed by the earrings he had bought her on their honeymoon, her slender figure rising on the undulating air, her eyes distant and averted, though it was evident, nevertheless, that she was not indifferent to his plight.

At that moment, the Padre marched across the glare, and the hallucination splintered like brittle glass. But Webb still felt the enduring, never dormant pain, the yearning for Esther; and he longed for her and wondered what a different person he might have become, if she had not died so soon after their marriage.

Just then, the path veered sharply to the right, as if it were entering straight into the mountain. For the first time, rather than crawling along El Soledad's surface, they seemed to be penetrating the inner fortifications. On both sides, splintered towers rose high, alternating with broken slabs which shielded blind passageways, or enclosed somber caves, dead end lanes, and niches too pinched and low to enter. Shattered rocks, which had tumbled from badly cracked and patched breastworks, impeded their progress; and the Padre frequently had to retrace his steps before seeking a new way along the angular battlements.

There lingered over the ruins a welter of unsorted memories. Incongruously, the stones seemed to have retained the acrid smells of many unknown battles, while the anonymous fighters and their defeats and their deaths had long been forgotten. As the buttresses grew higher, Webb's view was more and more shortened. Blindly forging ahead, without knowing where he was going, he was reminded of something the Padre had said in the jungle near Irozco: "Imagine a man running, and he knows not why, nor where to."

By now, Webb reflected sardonically, he might know more of the 'why,' though he was as much, or even more, in the dark as to where he was heading. But what a long way he had come, he did see a few moments later, when the trail reached a gallery which permitted, across arches half-tumbled upon broken pillars, a breathtaking view of the depths he had left at dawn.

The mist had dispersed. The pass was sparkling quietly in the sun, its wavy hair-line crossing an inch to the left of the trees which had gathered in a circle of tiny dots to mark the spot where Crispian's painting was located. Seen from this height, the hut seemed to be situated in the narrow waist of an hour-glass, at a midway point toward which all lines converged from above and below, contracting from the wide mountain ring and spreading again toward the plains beneath.

It struck Webb that the painting's location reflected, in a curious way, its two-fold nature: a sensitized center, irradiated from above and below, registering, combining, and, by some unfathomable process merging stimuli which emanated from opposite poles.

In one direction, it was like a lens turned on the land below, absorbing the sights of the human spectacle; an eye gazing down on the earthly arena and projecting on the retina of canvas that part of the world which Webb had traversed in the past.

And in the other, it was at the bottom of a gigantic funnel which captured the distant sounds, the dim light, the speedy energies of remote stars, the pulse and throb of an expanding universe. Whatever faint echoes of the thunderous waves rolling through curved space trickled into the funnel, would become louder as they rushed down the narrowing cone, until, at the bottom, the accelerated sounds reached so high a frequency that their otherwise deafening roar could barely be heard by human ears. Or else, Webb reflected, the intensification could be compared to the effect of a magnifying glass which gathered and collected the rays from the sun's large orbit, focusing them upon a tiny spot, thereby generating the heat and ultimately the flame which had scorched out the gaping hole in the canvas.

The scenery, Webb realized, as he walked past the last arch in the gallery, had offered to him some sort of symbolic interpretation, not only of Crispian's painting, but of every soul's crossroad position. The tempting allegory, continuing to unfold its implications, pushed him to see each human life as a focal point in the universe; to regard the undefinable aura of consciousness flaring around an unexplored core as an intersection where infinite forces met, crossed, and shot past, their directions changed in as complex a pattern as the deflecting facets of a character prescribed.

It was a mystic concept, and he rejected it with almost convulsive haste, as soon as he recognized that it implied an interacting relationship with powers outside of himself; that it threatened to link him to the far corners of unknown worlds. He had long ago decided that he preferred to think of himself as a separate entity bounded by his skin, as an independent being free of obligations or fears, paying tribute to no one, indebted neither to a creator demanding obedience, nor to dark powers which had to be pacified by incense and sacrifice.

Perversely and unexpectedly, however, the allegory would not be pushed aside; it had clawed into his imagination, resisting his efforts to pry it loose. Burrowing even deeper, it set out to break open the illusion of his body's finite shell and to extend his dimensions far beyond the hard core of which he alone was sure. It was struggling to demonstrate that he was integrated in a scheme far greater than any conscious design of his own. It seemed bent on disclosing that he was at the center of a web tying him to those vast spaces which had sometimes responded to his wondering glance when, on his way home from the consulate, he had gazed at the stars' glittering procession streaming up from behind the dark docks.

For a while, as he stumbled over the granite, he resisted the mountain's attempts to draw him toward the supernatural. He had always distrusted the vaporous symbolism of the visionary, the mystic. No matter how tempting it was to solve life's irreconcilable contradictions by escaping from the realm of concrete concepts, it was an unreliable, treacherous method, inviting self-deception. It offered too much opportunity for psychological fancies and aberrations to parade as objective outer truths. And since it was impossible to determine where to draw the line between true insight and sickly fantasy, it was best to forego any beliefs, no matter how useful or inspiring, which could not be expressed in logical terms.

He looked around, challenging the maimed, blackened bulwarks, and he felt as if he had achieved a minor triumph over the mountain. But as he stared at the battered pillars, his uncertainty grew. In spite of his resistance, he felt his thoughts shooting out like lines fingering the unknown for a hold, their tendrils sweeping the darkness to weave him into the wider frame, the existence of which he had either denied in the past, or had tried to ignore.

It was, of course, to be expected that the hazards of the terrain, the dangers surrounding and awaiting him, would encourage a trend toward the superstitious, the occult, the arcane. The proximity of death, the ever more concrete prospect of a fatal accident, could not help but intensify that yearning for an immortal soul, which he had first experienced in the hut below. He now grasped, far better than ever before, the nature of the need he had suppressed so long; the need of a feeble being all too conscious of a perilous dependence upon physical functions, suspended between deaths from one heartbeat to the next; the need of a perishable creature, soft-fleshed, thin-skinned and without protective shell, forever seeking some assurance of safety and finding none; until, at last, one had no choice but to discover or develop in himself a sense of the imperishable.

He had to circle a splintered plate, and then he marched on. The Padre, he noticed, was heading toward a cleft in the high cliff which blocked the ravine like a dam. Something in the mountain priest's posture seemed to reflect fear; or, perhaps, Webb was projecting his own fear, when he realized that the Padre was seeking a way to scale that cliff.

A sense of pitiful vulnerability forced itself upon him. His fervent response to the intimation, to the possibility, or perhaps to the truth of an indestructible core in his make-up, proved to him, if nothing else, to what extent he longed to endure; how much he had been suffering from the realization that a falling stone, a minute drop of poison, a slight cut in an artery or a break of the fragile spine could end his existence, could end for him the sky and the earth, could wipe out the small conscious entity that was Donald C. Webb, eliminating him from the billions who now existed and would continue to live after him.

That this restless fear had been with him all along, he had never before dared to acknowledge. Until now, he had always flattered himself that he for one did not permit death to cast a shadow over his life; he had always taken a sober pride in his calm acceptance of the inevitable; he could not be terrorized by the inescapable dissolution of his personality. And in this manner, he had somehow managed to ignore the fact that all his best energies had been directed, since earliest childhood, toward assiduously and incessantly building, defining, and asserting his personality.

But here, amid these granite sentinels which mutely watched, or perhaps contemptuously ignored him, he could not even attempt to strike a pose of hollow bravado. They were not concerned with the anguish of one who could not be sure that he would see the next day's sun; nor would they understand or pity him, as he stumbled past them, shivering, feeling naked, no longer able to escape the sight of all he had so long concealed.

But neither could he recognize, all at once, how many lies he had used to pacify the greedily feeding fear of death that had been clamped around his insides, coiling around every vital passage, steadily tightening its grip despite all his efforts to loosen it, driving him to fabricate ever greater distortions while it insatiably consumed the more and more unbelievable arguments with which he tried to prove that it did not exist.

As a boy, he recalled, he had once attempted to imagine what it would be like if he suddenly ceased to live. Like many children who unconsciously hope to derive from the contrast a stronger sense of being, he had made a game of the attempt, since in any event it would have been inconceivable to him that he would not remain himself forever. He had playfully closed his eyes, and suddenly, while he stood there in the school yard, he had felt as if a black wave were flooding over him, and he had shrieked in terror.

Something of the same terror seized him now, when a stone, loosened by the Padre, came clattering down. Again, he had a flashing impression of a dark, insubstantial, far greater extension just beyond the visible environment which covered the blackness like a flimsy, but rarely penetrable skin. And again, as in his youth, he was compelled to scream, though now he was old enough to stifle the outcry.

The Padre, standing at the foot of the cliff, studied the narrow chimney. "You will have to observe me carefully," he said, "and remember which holds I seize, both with my feet and hands."

Webb nodded, watching closely while the Padre started to lift his heavy body inside the cleft. But when he imagined himself wedged into that same dangerous opening, he quickly lowered his glance. He had noticed, directly above, that recurring vision of a grinning death head which had lately started to torment him in many a sleepless night. In the past, however, it had always seemed to wait in the distance, patiently eyeing his villa. And since it had still loomed so far away in those days, Webb had not attempted to look beyond the dark grin of the skull, convincing himself that what might happen after one passed away was of no immediate concern to him.

That this was not true, he now saw far too lucidly while he approached the cliff. Hearing, at last, the warnings screamed at him by every toiling cell of his body, he realized only too well that the vulnerability of his organism had made death his constant companion, his ever-present shadow; that the grinning skeleton, instead of awaiting him in the distance, had walked at his side all along.

"What is keeping you, senor?" the Padre called down. "You must follow me directly. A man should not stand facing danger too long."

Webb started to climb after his guide. While he raised himself inch by inch inside the chimney, he discovered the grinning death head hovering at his side, monotonously asking him if he would now like to know what to expect at the end of life; or how near mortal danger he had come before realizing that death had never been farther away than it was just now.

He reached higher, scratched the back of his hand on a rough stone surface, and succumbed to a passing weakness when he looked at the thin trickle of blood pearling over his scraped skin. His faintness made it seem impossible that he could climb the remaining fifteen feet to the rim. He saw the Padre's head above him, his eyes peering down, intent, watchful, not yet concerned, but just then beginning to turn anxious.

Another step—and a stone crumbled under his foot. His hands, hugging a smooth rock, caught the weight of his body. While he searched for a new foothold, he saw far below, in a haze of weaving light, the hut in which he had reached his decision to climb the mountain. And through his whirling brain, in that seemingly endless moment of free suspension, flashed a mocking voice saying that his motive in risking his life was a harrowing fear of death, far more intense than he had ever realized; a dread of dying—which should have driven him away from the mountain instead of pushing him toward its murderous slopes.

"In any event," the Padre said, after he had pulled Webb over the side of the cleft, "you could not have fallen too far."

Unobtrusively, and yet overly cautious, in the manner of the experienced mountaineer, he drew Webb a few more feet away from the edge. "So it did not much matter that you sought a hold where there was none. But later, when we traverse steeper walls, you will have to be more careful. For as we go higher, the mountain will allow you no more mistakes."

He looked at the row of almos. perpendicular cliffs to their right, which ran like a palisade alongside the narrow strip they had reached. Though one could only surmise El Soledad's gigantic stature behind the see-sawing rampart, Webb's wrought-up imagination produced the illusion that the bulging, aching granite shields before him were gradually, tremblingly giving way under the immense weight that pressed against them.

The Padre's glance held on the glistening shields, as if he were trying to read the giant's mind behind the impenetrable armor. When he turned, he noticed the blood on Webb's hand. "Did you not feel the pain?" he asked, half-astonished, examining the torn skin.

"It isn't bad," Webb said, withdrawing his arm.

Padre Paolo looked up, struck by the crisp, taut quality in Webb's voice. "Indeed, senor, the wound is not deep." He hesitated, searching Webb's expression for any sign of widening cracks and fissures. "It will not hold you back—if you are ready to go on."

Webb nodded, and quickly turned away, hoping to conceal from the mountain priest whatever emotion his eyes might betray. But after they resumed the ascent it occurred to him that it hardly mattered what secret shame he betrayed, since it was not at all certain that either he or his guide would ever get back to the living; since, indeed, it was quite possible that their knowledge of each other might perish together with them in this eternally mute wilderness.

The Padre, wrapped in his own solitude, strode up the mountain side, veering to the right when the trail left the gallery and turned into a steeper passage which looked like a dry river bed.

For a while, there was no sound other than the brittle rasping and shuffling of their feet; the mountain was still. It remained lurkingly absent, as quiet and removed as if it had never exerted any pressure.

But the deceptive, and surely watchful, stillness did not mislead Webb. He expected another attack, and when it did not come, he felt disappointed. And then he became over-confident, and challenged the mountain, accusing it of using his fear of death to stimulate spiritual beliefs which could not be substantiated, no more by personal experience than by scientific fact.

He hesitated, growing uncertain. In his attempt to defy the mountain, he might have gone too far. There was, after all, the recent sharp turn taken by science, which had breathlessly announced, an instant before disappearing into an incomprehensible maze of mathematical equations that matter was not what one had believed it to be, but another form of energy; that both were different states of the same thing; that, in fact, energy was—

He pressed his hands over his eyelids to stop the frightful fluttering. His taut nerves warned him not to give in to the mountain, warned him that denial was of the utmost importance, perhaps a matter of life and death. And yet he did not know how to dispute that the spirit, a concept too close to energy to be separable, seemed to have displaced matter, had taken over the universe, had revealed itself, in a surprising reversal, as the sole content, the whole existence, the only truth and meaning.

A slanted, fiercely jagged, veined slab blocked his way. While he climbed over it, his body flat against the hard, rough surface, his feet pushing against cracks and fissures, his fingers clawing into hollows until they reached the frayed top, he thought, with savage self-mockery, what an opportune moment he had chosen to refute the existence of matter. He let himself down on the other side, dropped farther than he had anticipated; and the stiff, shocked, fall-absorbing cracking in his ankles reached his ears a split-second before the wave of pain hit and engulfed him.

Half-crouched, half-leaning against the rock, he touched the bones near his ankles and felt neither splinter nor break. He raised himself and cautiously shifted his weight first on the one and then on the other foot. He took a few experimental steps, and was not stopped; and so he moved on, though the pain persisted, rising and swelling and ebbing away, and in its pulse and throb holding his thoughts narrowly to its own concerns.

'A man in pain,' he deduced ironically, 'does not forget reality.' There was safety in irony, and he whispered inaudibly that even a trivial toothache was enough to stop the highest flight of fantasy; and he felt reassured by what he had said, and repeated it several times, with each hurting step.

El Soledad had not yet renewed its relentless pulling and driving and lashing. Grateful for the respite, Webb nursed his pain, hoping that the grinding ache below his thighs would continue to overshadow the greater torments that awaited him after his brief armistice with the mountain had ended.

And then he realized that there was no armistice at all. For the mountain, suddenly attacking from another side, started to ask him why he continued to exert himself, when he knew that, in any event, he would not reach Zapar, that he would soon be too bruised and battered and broken to go much higher. And to that unanswerable query, Webb could only oppose his pride. Taken unaware, he could only say that even to have failed was better than not to have tried; and knew, saying it, that he had neither blunted the mountain nor convinced himself. Flustered, relentlessly and mercilessly pressed for a better reason, he retorted angrily that he was not the only one who did not consider self-preservation the supreme aim in life; that all through history men had aspired, had dedicated themselves, had died for unselfish beliefs. And finally, driven into a corner, attacked, mocked, ridiculed by the mountain who was pointing at the pain he had nursed, pointing at it as he held it in his arms like a homeless kitten he had befriended, pointing at it as he tried to get rid of it and did not know how, pointing at it until he cried in wild defiance that he had indeed welcomed the physical pain, because it not only enabled him to assert his courage, but had brought him closer to the touch and the thrill and the whole inspiring experience of his spiritual strength—and cried aloud, and stopped in the midst of crying out, and swayed, and suddenly knew that the mountain, far from doubting his reasons, had tricked him into a confession he had never meant to make.

The canyon broke open, abruptly, bursting in wide splinters, as if it had suddenly lost the strength to contain the pressures that had built up within its walls.

Climbing past the breach, Webb noticed the crumbling, reddish flakes that enveloped the stones in the river bed, concluded that these boulders were softer, less resistant to erosion than the granite plates on which they rested, and looked up.

They had evidently tumbled from the gutted, rotting walls that enclosed the canyon. The overhanging bluffs, he discovered, were loosely holding bushels of ripe stones, which could crash down on him at any moment. A slight tremor might set them off; an echo of his footfalls might bring down some of those rust-flecked, top-heavy rocks. Instinctively, he tried to walk softly, even held his breath, and knew that it would avert nothing, but did not know what else he could do.

His mind, unable to find a way to protect him from the annihilation strung up above, started to curl away from the unmitigated terror to which it could not react. The meshes in the tissue of his awareness became loose; he noticed that he was losing touch with reality. And before long he knew that the mountain, though still silent, was not far away, and would soon reappear to press him deeper and deeper into himself.

It would push him, as it had for some time, farther into that inner world where facts, like quicksilver, escaped one's grasp, as they fled and danced away in search of more than one meaning; where truth became elusive, because it could not be tested or measured as unambiguously as on the outside.

There was some time yet to prepare for the next attack. It would undoubtedly come as another attempt to delude him with some sort of brain-clouding phantasms. It might tempt him with the assurance that injustice and crime would surely be judged and punished in some other world. It might lure him by promising that his own abstentions and his own modest merit had not gone unnoticed and would earn the small praise which the world had refused him. It might even flatter him by letting him see a divine purpose in his own unpardonable mistakes as well as in the sense-less, meaningless accidents and misfortunes that had marred his life.

And then, after he had been drugged by illusions, with his senses numbed, his alertness to ever-present danger and hostility lulled to sleep, the mountain would let him stumble on one of its mercilessly hard and excruciatingly real slopes, would brush him into the abyss, perhaps unintentionally, carelessly, at any rate un-reasoningly, with a cold equanimity in which there was neither design nor purpose, only accident and chance.

He lifted his eyes and stared at the rocks, forcing himself to calculate the approximate paths they might take if they fell. But none moved from its precarious hold. A small pebble slid to a lower edge, trailing a thin flag of dust. That was all, nothing else, no stir, no shift in the untenable balance, no crash.

There was not much more time, he sensed, before the next as-sault. The canyon's deep furrow rose in a straight line to a tri-angular opening at the end, to dark rocks gold-rimmed by an ab-sent sun, to a luminous patch of sky occasionally obscured by a cloud that rushed up to the passage and evaporated in long, wispy plumes of wind-blown mist. Reluctantly, and yet hastily, he turned from the iridescent patch of blue beyond the arroyo, distrusting the sky's profound radiance as intensely as any other promise of the mountain.

'The procession,' Webb thought incongruously, 'the faceless procession.' His nerves sprang alert; it was the second or third time that these unrelated words had echoed above his thoughts, reaching him as though from a great distance. He listened tensely; but though they seemed to have spiraled nearer, they still fell short of conveying their meaning if, indeed, they had any to con-vey.

Whatever the intrusion signified, he could not ignore it. In his present state, with his nerves supercharged in constant alert, a quarry waiting for an attack, a man beleaguered and invisibly circled by unknown assailants, he was not allowed to overlook the slightest irregularity; he could not afford to take any chances.

If he were accustomed to hearing inner voices, he told himself derisively, he would now be convinced that he had been con-tacted by some ghostly power. As it was, he only suspected some

subconscious association. He knew enough of the mind's complexities to realize that the most unintelligible vagaries could be
traced to perfectly natural causes. He had learned that modern
psychology could explain the most unusual reactions, the most
abnormal symptoms; that it had analyzed visions and voices as
a form of inner expression; that many of the phenomena which
had formerly suggested to the superstitious a mystic experience,
had since been exposed as deeply personal projections of a troubled
unconscious.

Quite possibly, his whole relationship to the mountain could
be explained in simple, psychological terms. He clenched and un-
clenched his hands, listening, waiting for El Soledad to counter
his defiant claim. The mountain had no answer, and Webb took
courage, convincing himself before long that in this new science
he had found a perfect defense, a matching shield against every
weapon in El Soledad's arsenal.

Indeed, by relying on this science, he could deny the mountain.
There was no need to invent transcendental schemes in order
to understand one's inner mysteries. For they could all be explained logically, the God-seeking and the spiritual experiences,
the longing for some absolute truth and the certainty of a greater
reality than that known by men.

He looked around, feeling absurdly strong and proud in his
newly won degradation from an inspired being to a partial mechanism propelled by compulsions and instincts. He did not mind
the loss, because anything was better than to follow El Soledad
into that holdless, uncharted, huge unknown in which the mountain wished him to lose his way.

The mountain remained silent; it was motionless and watchful, a spring coiled tight, with tremendous power in its unwinding.

A passing breeze brushed Webb's hair into his face. He ran
his fingers over his feverish forehead, brushing back the damp,
matted strands. He knew that he would have to be very cautious,
for he might be about to stumble into another trap set by El
Soledad. On one hand, it could be true that the mountain kept
quiet, because it wanted him to pass imperceptibly from the outermost conclusions of psychology into the very territory he feared.
On the other, the mountain's indifference might also be a cun-

ning device to make him distrust and discard his last, best hope
of protection.

The uncertainty became harrowing. 'The uncertainty of our
time,' Webb thought, 'the uncertainty of men in transit; of men
crossing borders, obliged to exchange their familiar currency for
new value, without knowing whether they were short-changed,
whether they were receiving counterfeit tender or true gold. In
a world gone mad with a progress that was either too rapid or too
slow, we are all men in transit,' he whispered, and wondered why
the psychology of men traveling had not been explored more ex-
tensively, and to what degree both present-day suspicion and
gullibility could be attributed to the insecurity of voyagers up-
rooted, moving, and homeless.

He wished he could defy El Soledad with something more firm,
more solid than the inevitably tenuous propositions of a science
which had been unable to penetrate the psyche to any depth,
until it discovered that it had to accept the irrational, the illogical,
the unrealistic as the main condition for further progress. He
wished its claims to be so strong that there would be no opportunity for the mountain to point to their all too obvious limitations; nor to ask if he really believed that these brilliant hypotheses
went as far as he would like them to go, went as far as to explain
the mystery of consciousness, the miracle of reason, and the twin
riddles of memory and imagination.

The canyon walls, he suddenly noticed, had moved closer.
Their upward slant was now more ferociously vertical, as if the
mountain had pushed them together in order to increase its pressure on him. Under that towering, judging, suspended blackness, he felt not only small and vulnerable, but strangely de-
nuded, bare of any argument.

The mountain was inexorable; it kept pressing him deeper into
himself. It had dissolved another line of defense, and was now
watching him err about disconsolately in a territory where psychological theories could no longer guide him, where nothing was
seen except the distant flare of life's innermost secret, the un-
reachable beacon, the undeniable and inexplicable fact of mind's
consciousness, man's ability to create images, to think, and therefore to be.

And still the mountain was not letting up. He was lost, without shelter, and still pushed ahead. But, at least, El Soledad could not drive him much further, he supposed, and clutched at that pathetically insufficient hope in the vast dread of his aloneness. The end was in sight, for now he was approaching that zone in himself which he had never been able to penetrate, where all his prior attempts to look deeper into himself had been stopped, where the most subtle and paradoxical inferences had always been deflected. He strained to veer away from the depthless, but by no means peaceful, quiet which in the past had reminded him of the clearings in the woods where the Druids venerated their gods. He suddenly remembered how the Roman soldiers sacking the temple in Jerusalem had expected to find the Holy of Holies a room filled with extraordinary and awe-inspiring symbols. And something of their nameless terror communicated itself to him when he visualized how they had rushed into a bare, unadorned emptiness where their swords had found nothing to slash.

Instinctively, he tried to withdraw, shrink back; but found that he could not escape. The mountain was blocking his way. This time, apparently, he would not be allowed to get away. El Soledad was closing the high, black canyon walls like a vise. Bearing down on him, at first softly, but imperceptibly adding weight, it moved closer to drive him over that inner line which he would not and must not transgress, which had to be hugged at all cost.

For across that line lurked the primordial experience known to men since primitive tribes first started to beat their drums against the silence in the forests and the quiet in their hearts. Behind that line lurked the experience which had caused the savage to distort the faces of his pagan idols, so that their ghastly grimaces should hide the vacant space behind them, of which the unshaped features were even more frightening in their unlimited potential.

Behind it, he suddenly knew, he would meet the certainty whether or not the shell of quiet were indeed as vacant as he had often assumed, as devoid of watchfulness and knowing, as bare of all potential harm as he had sometimes hoped a dark room would be before he switched on the light; or, more importantly, as he had hoped to find death.

He had craved that certainty, needing it as if all the peace of his days depended on it; and yet, when it seemed within his grasp, he could not reach for it. For he also dreaded that certainty,

dreaded the end of doubt and the knowing that the black realm
was truly the meaningless void he had wished it to be.

He remained at the threshold, paralyzed by indecision, listening to the silence which could signify either the quiet of emptiness or of ambush. He looked upon the apparent nothingness
within the dark frame, unable to discern whether or not it was
really no more than a blank screen upon which, in his youth, he
had projected his beliefs, his entreaties and unfounded hopes.

He stood immobile; because as much as he wished death to
be an end and a silence, he also wanted that silence to be alive.
It almost seemed that he confidently expected the dark room to
be empty, but would not enter it, because it might be. He was all
too aware of his maddening inconsistency, but could neither comprehend nor master it. And in his holdless confusion, he turned and
twisted to avoid the certainty toward which the mountain was
pushing him.

He knew that he had to resist; but it was not clear to him why.
He was not even sure whether El Soledad meant to overwhelm
him with the soul-consuming, blinding fire of a religious experience
which, in one flare-up, would render his entire past an inexpiable
sacrilege; or whether the mountain prepared to crush him with
the shattering disclosure that in an icy, mechanical universe all
striving, all rising, including his present life-risking ascent, were
vanities and a striving after wind. Near as he was to the disclosure,
he could still not foresee what it would reveal. And he turned
and sought to escape, but the mountain was blocking his way.

'The procession, the procession, the faceless procession,' Webb
thought, chilled, cringing, almost cowering as the words swirled
near and spiraled away. He tried to imagine a solemn cortege of
headless figures, but soon let the grotesque pageant drift from his
mind; and he forgot the bowing and scraping and mutely gesticulating parade, when he sensed that the mountain was renewing its
pressure, now bearing down on him in earnest, propelling him,
mashing him into the impenetrable globe of silence.

His breath dwindled; he felt suffocated, squeezed beyond endurance, unable to withdraw, to give way. He had backed up as
far as he could, and was about to be squashed. He saw no way to
pass inside that unyielding and yet non-resistant shell, no reasonable way at any rate, no calculable, logical way—until, all of a

sudden, in a flash of terror, he knew what was asked of him, what he had to sacrifice in order to enter.

He knew that to pass inside he would have to discard logic, his reliance on reason, his right as a rational being to judge and reject, even his hard-won ability to evaluate probabilities on the basis of past experience. He would have to believe, be guided by faith; he would have to trust. And still there would be no assurance that he would be able to understand that which could not be grasped.

At best, his restricted brain might not be able to conceive more than a semblance of those unimaginable truths. And at worst, he would become a helpless prey to the inconceivable, the never to be apprehended, a blind worshipper, a slave to that which, after having refused to reveal itself until it had obtained unconditional, uncritical faith, could inspire truth as well as delusion, and most probably both, in an entanglement which offered no longer any clues for discernment.

After driving him so far, El Soledad had not even kept its promise; there would still be no certainty. The possibility that one's trust might be exposed, at some point, to the most cruel awakening, to gales of cynical laughter, had not been averted. The mountain was asking him to surrender all safeguards, and offered no pledge in return. It wanted him to lay down his shield and his armor and to plunge into a darkness where anything from error to insanity could pervert his faith. And as reward El Soledad would not even offer a shred of evidence that the God he sought really existed. It made no promise as to the actual truth of those verities which religion, in its groping, symbolic, necessarily implausible and at best approximate manner, had so persistently sought to describe.

He would never accept such terms. He would not take that final, irrevocable step into the unknown, if it meant his end as a self-reliant, self-trusting man, if the password at the border were a whispered: 'I believe, because my reason has failed me. I believe, because I cannot know. I am ready to accept any revelation, because such is the coin of the realm I desire to enter.'

No threat of the mountain, no promise, no amount of pressure would induce him to bow to such a one-sided, tyrannical demand. If the mountain insisted on imposing such conditions, he would have no choice but to fight back with the blunt and absolute atheism toward which, in any event, he had always felt a stronger affinity.

The mountain did not stir; it was as quiescent, perhaps as stunned, as if it had not expected such ferocious resistance. But though it did not increase its pressure, neither did it budge. For a long while, it appeared to be undecided, perhaps deliberating, perhaps revising its impending attack. And as the quiet protracted, Webb came to see that there would be no compromise. While the seconds ticked away and his steps crashed over the eroded debris, he lost all hope that there was any chance of conciliation. He himself had to admit that there was no such thing as a partial belief in God; he could not offer in trade that genteel, civilized solution which had seemed so practical in the cities where religion and one's daily life could be housed in separate buildings. Here, in this death-strewn, echoing, ghost-ridden canyon, El Soledad would refuse to accept such a compromise. Rejecting all bargains, it would extract absolute negation—or total belief.

Webb felt an irremediable resignation descend on him, when he realized that he had reached the final impasse, the line where neither he nor El Soledad could budge, where the decisive battle would be fought. For he, too, could not compromise, nor give in. It was no use proposing concessions, for nothing he offered could remain confined to a limited area. The belief in an immortal soul would at once raise questions of punishment in the beyond. And the faith in an existence after death would soon cast its shadow over life, demanding a complete re-evaluation of all his views, his actions, of all he had done or had failed to do.

He understood, then, why he had both craved and refused the opportunity of knowing death's mystery. For as intolerable as he found the prospect of extinction, as much did he fear a re-appraisal of his entire life, in view of the vast guilt such a change in his outlook might uncover. He was trapped, a man caught somewhere between heaven and the gallows; a man no longer quite young, no longer quite of the earth; a man much concerned with his shortening future, desperately needing a hopeful faith, but debarred from any re-orientation by a past lived when the sequence of tomorrows had seemed to last forever, when the days had crowded up in endless succession.

His past, suddenly weighing on him, had turned enigmatic. The facts were all clear, incontestable; but their interpretation would depend on the perspective in which they were seen. Nothing was ever quite dead, he recognized; even the days gone by, long buried, long settled, were now ready to leap at him, revived, incited by the whiplash of the mountain. El Soledad wanted him to see them with the eyes of one who would live beyond his grave; and he refused to look at all the waste, the senseless failings, the unpardonable breach of faith with himself. But he knew that the mountain would not leave it at that; it would batter at his unbelief, hammer at it, attempt to break it down. And he would have to resist to the end, because his only alternative to denial was to convict and condemn himself.

He also knew that there would be no armistice in this war, no mercy and no escape; that the brief pause in the battle was soon to be ended by a more violent assault than any he had yet endured.

When he saw that the canyon was widening, he assumed that the attack would have to come before he reached that funnel-like opening which framed a sky throbbing with the pulse of racing clouds. He wondered what view awaited him at the canyon's rim, and why he did not hear the whistling of the wind which lashed the clouds past the blue oval, and how much of the turbulence was—

It was then that the mountain struck.

Not openly, not in a frontal attack, as he had hoped, not even from any side or from an ambush, but from inside him. Ignoring all his defenses, disdaining even to brush them aside with a stroke of its giant hand, not even battling to break down his refusal to believe, it suddenly asked why he had betrayed his God. It did not question his belief; it took his faith for granted; it asked why he had broken it, dealing with him, not as if he were a sceptic to be convinced, but a renegade, a traitor to his own self and to all he knew to be true.

The shock, the surprise, the sharp, unforgiving indictment were too much for Webb. There was no prepared defense, no sanctuary, no reprieve. There was only the deadly canyon, with its ripe stones, and its cold menace, and all the balanced forces it held in suspense and threatened to unleash. And there was his pent-up rage against that unyielding intimidation, against that long-awaited and never-fulfilled terror. He picked up a stone and threw it to force devastation from its perch, to oblige horror to make good on its promise, to detonate the fuses so that nature, after the explosions, could regain its equilibrium, and fear would find an end in its own undoing.

He saw the stone curving toward a shredded rock far back in the canyon. A moment later the front part of a cliff detached itself, toppling lazily before sliding down to a lower terrace in a cloud of dust. And without waiting to see where it would land, he turned and ran ahead. He heard one, then two, then several volleys, a reverberating and a crashing, explosions multiplying of their own momentum. He saw the Padre wheel around on top of the rim, and look down on him, and signal to him, with distorted features, that the canyon was falling.

He ran and felt his nostrils stung by the acrid smell of burning stone; and he caught a glimpse over his shoulder of dust rising in white, fluffy pillars. The pillars were narrow and moving and six feet high—like phantoms, like figures following him, like a ghostly procession. And with that he recognized them, and his thoughts screamed, 'the faceless procession.' At last, it had caught up with him, but not in the way he had expected. For it did not pass him, nor was he allowed to watch the marching parade as an uninvolved onlooker—for here he was, himself leading the faceless procession.

He ran, ran hard, ran faster, with lungs failing, his heart in uproar. He ran higher and higher, while the canyon's rolling thunder swept over him. He saw the sky's blue turbulence swaying nearer, with more and more clouds streaming across the widening oval. The clouds, white and smoky, raced along the sky, as if they reflected the phantoms below—two processions meeting in a mirror, so that he also ran toward that from which he was running away.

The Padre was to his right, not far any more. But he seemed small as the canyon's rim descended and the sky's intense radiance billowed over the breach, immense, shot through by flames. And suddenly it was no longer the Padre standing there, but his portrait, as Crispian had depicted him on the canvas. The radiant blue glowing over the gigantic panorama became the background painted by Crispian. And at that instant Webb also saw himself, his own portrait, the enormous figure of the thirteenth apostle, rising from below the horizon, with one foot on the distant crest that was shaped like the one on the canvas. Advancing across the glimmering firmament, marching higher, bestriding the sky, he was followed by the columns of other thirteenth apostles, by the featureless parade of clouds streaking beneath the burning blue.

He collapsed on the rim, his eyes fixed on the grime and the rotting stone. He panted, writhed, fighting off the hallucination, the hypnotic glare of the painting, fighting Crispian who had made common cause with El Soledad by portraying him as the thirteenth apostle. Both the mountain and Crispian had joined in a cruel accusation, the one by asking why he had denied his God, the other by painting him as a man of good will, pointing up his failure by showing him as something he was not, as a thirteenth apostle. And he raged against the indictment, refuting it, with his lungs beating against the ground, with the blood hammering at his skull, and his hands clawed into the flaky rubble.

The sweat dropped from his face, blackening the dust which registered in minute tremors the concussions roaring up from the collapsing canyon. His inflamed eyes, though averted from the sky, noticed how the shadows cast by the swift clouds were crawling over him. And when he looked up, he knew that his face was turning dark, while the clouds, the faceless batallion of thirteenth apostles, marched past the sun, stamping, treading, stepping over him in an inexorable procession.

CHAPTER X

It was not until shortly after three o'clock that Webb's battle with the mountain reached its decisive phase.

They had left the rim and the canyon and the pall rising over it. For a long time, they had seen the fine dust swirling up from sporadically renewed slides. Then the trail had led them up through a series of terraces, its back broken again and again as it lifted itself and fell over one platform after another; and the canyon, during the same period, had receded in stages, finally dropping from sight altogether.

It was around that time when Webb flung his first accusations at the mountain. He raised his angry thoughts beyond the view-blocking terraces; and he challenged El Soledad to come forth from behind all its screens, to drop at last its concealments. With his nerves strung taut over the thin edge between fear and fury, he mocked the mountain's refusal to reveal itself, and scornfully derided its unfair strategy of wearing him down by gradually stepped-up harassment.

His taunts fell off the stony walls, leaving no dent. There was no response, no shift in the interlocked defenses. Impassively ignoring all his provocations, the mountain continued in hiding, permitting him to see everything else—the shimmering horizons, the steaming, tumultuous ocean of clouds below him, at times even a glimpse of the foothills—all but the central fact of its own monstrous peak. And Webb had no choice but to climb on blindly—not knowing El Soledad, but feeling the imponderable shadow on him; not knowing God's inscrutable purpose, not even certain that there was such a purpose, but suspecting, nevertheless, that he was supposed to fulfill the undivulged duties derived from it. Again and again he rebelled against that cruel, senseless, unnecessary secrecy, but the screens shielding the invisible did not move aside, and his insurrection only served to make him feel his helplessness more keenly.

The trail swung to the left, and for a while ran alongside the high shelter of a crest. The wind ceased; at the same time, light and visibility were sharply reduced. They had passed into a large cloud which clung to the mountain side, an ivory hull as motionless as a ship behind a breakwater. While they moved cautiously across the cottony twilight, with the Padre's black robe looming up and vanishing in ghostly shreds before him, Webb wondered what steep plunges were hidden from their view. It occurred to him that they might be crawling along El Soledad's left arm, of which the long, hard, majestically outstretched, protective sweep had awed him when he had first seen it from the valley. And he drew closer to the dripping rocks on his left, remembering the perpendicular chutes that ran down from the ridge.

But he was not sure whether they had actually reached the crest; not even later when they rose, moth-like, from the cloud's steaming roof, and crossed to the other side of the ridge. Once again exposed to the wind, they trudged along a rectangular slope, their field of vision narrowly framed by tumbled rocks at the bottom, by the crest above, and by patches of sky on either side. Longing to look beyond his limitations, he suddenly realized that he, who was not allowed to see very far, could himself be seen very well, was entirely too visible on this slope, was exposed to view as clearly as bacteria on a microscopic slide. And at once, feeling himself watched, he looked up, quite involuntarily, as if to meet the glance of the eyes peering down on him from the incendiary blue above.

The sun's glare rushed at him, stabbing at his pupils, breaking through and igniting on his retina a shower of luminescent whites and yellows which then turned into black spots that remained with him long after he had been compelled to avert his glance. Looking down, he watched the dark circles glide over the stones; and soon he wondered whether his own thoughts could be seen as well from higher up; how much of his anger, and his weakness and, perhaps, of his guilt was exposed to that hidden eye staring down.

The notion disturbed and dismayed him; he tried to put a stop to his thoughts, imposing the hush which follows a confidential conversation after an eavesdropping stranger has been noticed. For a while, then, he solely concentrated on pulling his body up the slope, as unreasoningly and stolidly as he imagined a horse with blinders might drag a heavy sleigh up a snowless road.

But in the midst of not thinking, he came to ask whether, in the absence of present thought, his past might be read and judged. The question absorbed him. For even more disturbing than to feel oneself watched every minute, was the possibility that all the things one had forgotten and would never again be able to recapture were somewhere recorded; were, perhaps, considered and debated this very instant, while he, unsuspecting and utterly ignorant of what was going on, was not even admitted to the deliberations, was not allowed to defend or explain himself.

The mere assumption angered him; it seemed preposterous. How could a fair judgment be rendered, he ironically demanded, when the accused himself did not recall most of the good or the bad he had done. The whole notion of a Last Judgment, indeed of any condemnation, was absurd. For certainly the proof of guilt, if not guilt itself, would be obliterated by time's paling memory.

He taunted the mountain, ridiculing the old wives' tale that everything was written down in a book of life. The problems of keeping such voluminous records, he laughed, must have been so staggering that the whole system had undoubtedly broken down long ago. For a while, he amused himself by visualizing a myriad scribbling pens getting snarled up in a vast and hilarious confusion. And he defied El Soledad to convince him how any sort of order could be kept or restored.

The mountain, still impassive, withdrawn but tense, vibrating in its coiled immobility, did not react to his sally, leaving him to his amusement without interference. It was not long, however, before his laughter ran dry of itself. In an unintentional association, he had remembered a psychiatrist's report dealing with the case of an U.S. subject accused before an Italian court. In reply to a direct question the psychiatrist had claimed that, theoretically, nothing was ever totally forgotten; that it was all etched into one's mind and could conceivably be recalled.

The citizen, though receiving every assistance from the consulate, had been convicted in a fair trial. And the expert testimony now threatened to condemn Webb in the same way. For the old wives' tale seemed to have found the most unexpected, scientific corroboration. An accurate record was no longer so un-likely, if one considered that people were carrying their own judgment books around with them, making their own entries, at all times.

For the next half hour, he struggled against his own imagination which showed him how the tightly wound convolutions of his brain were to be unfolded after death, spread out like crumpled paper. And a superior gaze would thereupon read on the flattened surface the full story of his life, would know all his secrets, guarded or forgotten, by studying the implacably true record on which every lie, self-deception, each fleeting moment of his life was as minutely recorded as on a photographic plate.

It was then, a few feet below the ridge, with the sun coming out of the clouds in a white rage, that his smoldering conflict with the mountain broke into open combat. The Padre, after lifting himself into a gash within the escarpment, stood still, in frozen awe, a petrified silhouette against the glazed, blaring, wildly fluc-tuating sky. And Webb guessed instantaneously why the Padre did not advance. He knew that El Soledad had at last stepped out to meet them; and a few moments later, when he stood at the Padre's side, he caught a flash of an icy, gleaming, glistening splendor, of a glittering majesty so powerful, so dazzling that he was blinded and had to close his eyes.

The Padre did not move. Squinting, Webb discerned at first only the aura of El Soledad, a mirage of white, a spectral radiance embedded in the blue of the sky. The peak flared quietly in a steady, searing flame, while all around it the clouds raced, whirl-ing over the snowy fields, streaking their shadows over the long, bluish glacier. And then, as he opened his eyes wider, it suddenly seemed as if the clouds were arrested; and, instead, it was the sunlight that came swirling from the heights, pouring down from the summit. At the same time, he no longer heard the sound of the wind, but the torrential rush of the light cascading down from the jagged crown below the peak, thundering past the cliffs until the fiery flow fell and broke on the glacier.

Though his eyes were cut by the harsh reflections from a thou-sand sunlit spires, he could not avert his glance. Spellbound, he watched the brilliant flood being rocked back and forth in the glacier's basin, rising until it brimmed over, splashing like a surf

against the dark moraines. And then it poured down in a deluge
that burst into towers of spray, scintillating and flashing in rain-
bow colors as it touched black rocks with sparks of fire.

"Senor!"

Webb turned back. Without realizing it, he had been walking
toward the mountain, and the Padre, who had hailed him from
below was now coming up to him. "I notice you are limping."

Webb nodded. He had quite forgotten the sting in his heel, and
was about to go on, when the Padre turned him around. "Take
off your shoe," he said, in a voice so commanding that it allowed
no discussion.

Webb obeyed, and they saw the small oblong wound dug into
the flesh just above the ankle, purplish toward the outer rings,
and carmine red where the blood had coagulated.

The Padre was kneeling before him, examining the torn skin.
The wind draped his black robe in a half-circle over his legs. "You
must have felt the pain long ago," he said, his voice not as compassionate as Webb had expected, but sternly reproachful. "Why
did you not mention it?"

Webb shrugged. He knew there had been a reason, but he
did not remember it. All he could think of was how insignificant
the wound seemed when compared to the shining heights El
Soledad was here exhibiting in boastful and imperious splendor.
While the Padre pulled off the shredded skin and prepared to
bandage the wound, Webb had to lean against the large, flat rock.
He spread out his arms, in order to balance himself, digging his
fingers into whatever shallow dents they could find. And thus
facing the steady, white-blue flame of the mountain, he kept
thinking of past courage and future aspirations; and how his daring ascent had been imperilled by a wound so small that millions like it would not add up to a visible spot on one of the mountains snow-capped bastions.

His eyes hurt; but when he averted them from the searing
flare, he saw that the sapphire sky was tinted with more somber
colors at the far ends where the storm was gathering its tensions.
He sensed the tremendous power building up in that deepening
midnight blue, and he turned back to the greatness rearing up
ahead. With no hold other than the rock at his back, with his arms
open in defenseless spread, he stared at the colossus, overcome

by his insignificance in the face of the titan's sky-bursting height. And yet he did not submit; he asked accusingly whether such power could ever do more than smash opposition, whether it could also raise the weak from their sadness and hurts.

The sun grew dark; a cloud had fled beneath it, and while its shadow passed across the peak, Webb unaccountably sensed a wave of sadness welling up from the depths of the rocks, a deep sorrow crossing El Soledad's brow. For a while, the high towers gazed down at his feebleness, at his determination to go on, which was no longer the determination of conceit, but of one broken, aware of being powerless, of one going to his death in order to condemn the superior force which had engaged him in too unequal a contest. Then the cloud raced on, and the mountain's armor flared up, once again as glittering, as stern and merciless as before.

The Padre had bandaged the ankle. He picked up a stone and flattened the leather in the back of the shoe, hammering it into a smooth surface. "It will be much better," he said, returning the shoe to Webb.

The wind and the light raced across their silence. Webb had expected his guide to propose, as on previous occasions, that they should turn back. But, this time, the Padre did not even ask if Webb needed a rest.

Instead, he got up and brushed the dust from his robe. "We have no choice but to go on," he said, avoiding Webb's gaze. "We have climbed too high to return. From here, it is nearer to the glacier cave than to the valley and Santa Rosa."

Webb had some difficulty tying the knot on his shoe. "There may be no time to reach shelter below," Padre Paolo said, still not willing to face Webb directly. Apparently, he had been far more troubled by the clouds than he had shown until now.

"Can we make it to the glacier?"

"It is possible, senor. But I cannot say."

"How far is it to the cave?"

"It depends. Two hours. Perhaps more."

"And how soon do you expect the storm?"

The Padre's glance passed from the gray dance of the clouds to the deepening pockets in the bright, unnaturally brilliant glare where the midnight blue poured into the sky's greenish tints.

"There may be no storm at all," he said, picking up his bundle. "The clouds mean little enough. It is the heat of the sun that predicts worse. There is too much burning in the air." He looked at Webb, fully, without concealment, and there was the same fear in his eyes as in Webb's when he said: "But it may all pass without any harm to us. One cannot be sure with El Soledad. It may have passed within the next half hour."

'It won't pass,' Webb thought, hastening after the Padre, who now advanced along the top of the crest at a faster pace. 'It is gathering around us, it will burst right over our heads.'

He could not have said what made him so sure. Perhaps, it was the ancient, absurd superstition of the tempest and the sinking boat, and how the storm would not let up until the crew had discovered which one among them was guilty and had sacrificed the culprit to the sea in order to placate the angered elements.

'If it were discovered that I was the one to be cast out,' Webb whispered, noticing how the wind, in racing past, snatched the sounds from his lips as if to carry them to unknown destinations, 'I would be dropped a thousand feet from the crest.' He saw himself crashing down on a ledge, with his skull cracked open and all its most hidden convolutions exposed to view. And only then did he become aware that he could not possibly be the accused and had nothing to fear.

Below him patches of light raced toward the depths. He was now able to see that the trail was indeed crawling along the left arm of El Soledad. For a long while they would be exposed to an uninterrupted, full view of the ice-clad armor and the gleaming peak where powerful winds swept up snow which streamed up from the back in a sunlit, spectral corona. He was trying to guess at the decisions locked up behind the stony countenance of the giant, but could not foresee its plans, and only came to suspect the fury of which it was capable, the excesses to which it could rise.

A tremor, touched off by his fluttering heart, ran along the crevasses, the heaving crags, ran and warped the fields, ran and embraced everything in one mass of writhing anguish, even the towers and minor peaks which had already raised their spires like supplicants imploring mercy, seeking to placate the great wrath that was gathering around the summit, to pacify it before it was unleashed. And he, a dwarf among these strong satellites, he who needed protection more than any of them, sought words of prayer that would avert the worst, but found none, found his thoughts mute, found his heart dry and empty. He craved submission, and could not bend his knee. Everything in him shouted that he should beg to be spared, should pray that the tempest would not come to pass. But despite the panic of emotions responding to the immemorial dread of nature's cataclysms, he could no break the iron grip of his brain. He could not erase from his mind the modern knowledge that nothing he would do or say, no magic or incantation, could in any way influence the differential in barometric pressures, the variations of electric charges, which predestined the course of the storm in a blind and senseless unfolding.

And so, he alone, in a wind-swept territory where everything seemed to be scurrying for shelter, was passing helplessly under a black sun, parched, tearless, bare of any response to the gathering outburst, without prayer, without hope even of throwing himself at the mercy of an understanding judge. He alone, straddling a crest where gashes ripped out by previous storms hurried to dive into shadows, had no recourse, nothing to support him in that worst of all intervals between the approach of catastrophe and its inevitable fulfillment.

The sun came out. In a pent-up yearning for its former serenity, the landscape glowed up; then was extinguished; then lit up again. The sun stood high, as though raised up on shafts of light. Clouds approached, reached with flaring thunderheads for the sun, and failed and passed on. Never entirely submerged, the sun rolled alongside of Webb behind boiling, screening mist and smoke, again and again flung high on geysers of foaming luminosity which sent their jets soaring through the stained vapors, the smudged, rapacious clouds.

Then, for a while, the turbulence seemed to lessen. The wind was slowing down. There was an incipient calm in the air, an evenness in battle, a hope, as if peace might yet prevail and the storm be turned back.

He did not dare hope for a change. More likely, it was only a momentary lull, a period of grace granting him time to prepare himself. If so, it was no use, for he could no more prepare himself to die than he could placate the thunder and the lightning. He had lived on the assumption that nothing was demanded of him, that he had nothing to fulfill. After a lifetime so lived, he could not reverse his conviction without incriminating himself. He had to die as he had lived, prepared to plead total ignorance of the law rather than admit evasion or breach; it was better to hold down panic and uncertainty than to confess how often he had suspected that the gift of life had indeed not been entrusted to him without any obligation, without any expectancy.

He had no possibility of making his peace with God. But neither could he come to terms with himself. And that was more harrowing still. For the mountain might say to him, *Since thou hast driven out thy God and hast made thee master of thyself— why canst thou not account for thyself?*

He saw no way to reconcile himself to his end. He had known some rare and fortunate people who had met death, not meekly, not resignedly, not even in the assured faith of an awakening, but nevertheless as peacefully as if they had blossomed and ripened in an unresisted flow of seasons. But as for himself, he had not lived fully or happily enough to trust whatever might come after; nor could he look forward to a welcome rest like someone who, after a full day, looks forward to sleep at night.

He looked toward the descending sun, now passing as a bleeding red orb through a sheet of haze, now swirling up above brooding clouds. And he prayed, without knowing that he did; he asked for another few years of life; he begged to be spared this time. He implored the sun, the firmament, the clouds; he pleaded, and whispered, and cried his plea into the wind. And yet, in the midst of pleading, he had to let up, when he realized that he was begging for a respite—not because he had loved life so much— but because he had not loved it enough.

He was stopped, his yearning's impetus shattered by the contradiction; and for a while, before the blind need could surge back, he drifted, rudderless and spent, on the undertow of his confusion. The mountain had defeated him once again. It was forcing him to admit that those who had lived happily did not resist giving up all their good fortune; while those who had not loved life enough, and had not enough good reasons to cling to it, resisted

death, loathing it, as if their unspent portion of love and happiness had turned into hatred against that which was forever to
preclude its fulfillment.

To die well, it seemed, it was necessary to have lived well.
While he, who had quarrelled with life, also quarrelled with death.
He thought of Esther, of her small face pinched and pale on the
hospital pillow, of her hand's gentle touch, while she begged him
not to quarrel with fate over her dying. And then he recalled her
brown hair wrinkled softly among the flowers, her eyes all quiet
in her young face, in that twenty-four year old face where life had
not yet drawn one wrinkle, in that young, dead face—

He clenched his fists, not raising them, and yet holding them
tight in unforgiving anger against the mountain. Their battle was
not over, not by far, not just because El Soledad had shown him
that his plea for more time was irrelevant and could not be ac-
ceded to; that, no matter how old he would get, all he had left
undone, unlived, unfulfilled, would always rear up and make him
fight death, past senility, sickness, and agony.

A shadow passed over him. The sun had drowned. Black clouds
were steaming up like smoke blowing high, like gushers erupting
with pent-up pressure. Inexorably the mountain was gathering the
storm around itself, unmoved as it watched Webb scamper toward
his death. The wind was rising, and in its dark rush it seemed to be
repeating the mountain's words: *Since thou hast made thee master
of thy life, why canst thou not account for thyself?*

The Padre fell—and Webb cried out—and watched, paralyzed, as the black robe rushed down one of those long trenches
that curved out like chutes to nowhere. A moment later, the
Padre, with a twist of his body, had rolled away from the trough,
slowing his fall before slithering to a stop on the jagged rim.

He got to his feet, unhurt, and climbed up. The wind drove
hard at their backs, and the mountain priest, despairing of making himself heard, waved at him uncertainly, almost embarrassedly
as though to apologize for his failing, and went on.

Straddling the crest, Webb leaned into the wind, moving cautiously while he passed, in three short steps, the spot where Padre
Paolo had slipped. He envisioned himself in the Padre's place, but
grew dizzy, and had to stop. As he tried to steady himself, he was

caught off guard by the sudden realization that he would have been to blame if anything had happened to Padre Paolo; that he could be held responsible for another man's life.

He hurried ahead, refuting the charge, disclaiming any guilt. He had made no effort to persuade or induce the Padre to join him in the ascent. And if the Padre had felt that he should not let him go alone, it was his own decision; for no one had forced him to adhere to the belief that he was his brother's keeper.

The mountain was eyeing Webb across sudden rifts in the clouds; its gaze rested heavily on him. Perhaps, it wanted him to admit that the Padre, if not obliged to slow down for him, might be able to reach the shelter of the glacier cave before the storm unleashed its full power. Perhaps, it expected him to urge Padre Paolo to hurry ahead and be saved. But he could not face the prospect of being left behind in that enraged solitude; he would soon go insane if he no longer saw that strong figure ahead of him, indefatigably leading the way with trustworthy broad shoulders hunched steeply into the wind.

The sun's empty eye joined the mountain's scowl, pleading with him to admit his guilt, pleading with him like a mother, imploring him not to persist in his error, to accept his punishment without further arousing his father's wrath. He protested his innocence, but she would not believe him. And when he raised his face toward the light and the warmth, ready to admit anything for her sake, it was too late; the sun's glow and gentleness had fluttered away behind rapidly lowered vapors. Groping through the twilight, he would have been willing to confess any crime—rather than see her cry—if only someone would tell him why he was at fault, what wrong he had done. But no one came to clarify the reproach. Only a cloud dragged its shadow over him as if it were that of his father striding forth from his study, with the iron ruler in his hand catching a glint of the dim lamp in the hallway.

The wind rose to a higher pitch; and then he saw, in the volatile dusk, the drifting of fog and mist, the nebulous phantoms hastily passing, gesticulating, pointing him out with cottony arms, perhaps whispering among themselves that here he was—the guilty wretch responsible for the stormy clouds brooding around El Soledad's head. He asked for an opportunity to defend himself;

but the withdrawal around him turned into flight, as though in incredulous awe that he did not prostrate himself before the storm erupted in thunderous condemnation, in a paroxysm of elemental fury that would sweep him off the face of the earth and imperil them all.

His dread of standing alone under the searing gaze of the mountain was such that he begged those who fled to charge him with something he could repent. But in their haste of getting away from him, no one stopped to let him know why he had to be shunned. Like any mob, hasty and eager to condemn, they had pointed at him, without pointing out his guilt. And now they were gone, and he was alone, standing like a gladiator in a deserted arena, spotlighted by the mountain's stare. And he would have to fight his solitary battle, and find his own misdeeds in the silence of all those who knew and watched him from the circumference, well beyond the burning glare of the mountain's eye.

The wind was whispering something to him, but he did not understand it, and it scarcely mattered, because he was now baring something, of his own volition, which might be considered a guilt. It seemed like taking a perilous risk, a show of brazen courage that would have evoked a gasp from any crowd, even from the tough mob that had forsaken him. Yet in truth it was no more than a feint. For he knew that the mountain could not blame him for that accident, long ago, when the avalanche had crashed down on Cliff Williams, maiming his childhood friend, crippling and warping the future of the boy who, at college, had depended on him, trusting and admiring his judgment more devotedly than anyone ever since.

It was a feint only; and yet he felt relieved that he had unburdened himself. Again and again, over the years, Cliff's image had returned to him, always stirring up an indistinct self-reproach which, however, he had at no time been able to justify. For even on the night when he had had to inform Cliff that his bride had broken her engagement, when he had wrenched the bottle with the barbiturates from his friend's hand, wrestling with him, pushing the cripple to the floor—even then Cliff had not betrayed that he harbored any rancor against Webb. Though sobbing and raging, and in his frenzy even cursing the doctors who had saved his life by amputating his leg, he had, nevertheless, not blamed any of his friends for leaving him too long in the snow. And neither then nor later had he indicated that he had expected them to race down the path of the avalanche, instead of choosing the safer, but longer way around the ridge and up from the valley.

No one could have climbed down that icy, steep slope, as the Canadian guides had subsequently confirmed. It would have been suicidal. And so there was not the slightest possibility of reproach, even though by the time they had reached him, it had been too late; his leg, badly broken, was frozen and could not be saved. In the bitter cold, they had peeled off their jackets to keep him warm; and then, on a sled, they had drawn him over a field as white as that now swaying before his eyes, at the base below El Soledad's highest spire; a white field at dusk, with Webb and Esther out front, rushing ahead of the procession to meet the rescue team coming up from the village.

Another procession, reminiscent of the faceless cortege, of the dust pillars in the canyon, of the clouds marching overhead in his hallucination, of the thirteenth apostles in Crispian's painting. A cold blast from the whirling wind caught him full face, twisting him around. Instead of ignoring his feint, the mountain seemed to have brushed aside his defense. Webb waited; and when there was not the least contradiction of his claims, he knew that the charge against him was of a deeper and even more serious nature.

The air stream whirled away, leaving him to himself, leaving him like all the others; leaving him shunned and forgotten in that icy stillness beneath the immense, sentencing gaze of the summit. While he hurried along the crest, he had to take ever larger steps over mounds and gullies, as if his legs were growing shorter. With layer after layer of camouflage peeled away, he felt as though he were shrinking in size; he came to see himself as a dwarf. And it was this dwarf, if not he, who conceded in a high, whinnying voice that for many years Mr. Webb, nicknamed at college Donald C. Quixote, had nursed his pretended avalanche-guilt in order to cover up a more profound failing.

But no one, not even the dwarf, would tell him what that failing was. The silence in the dark arena was as electrifying as that of a large crowd holding its breath at a moment of supreme tension. They all knew his dereliction. Only he, who stood alone in the center, only he, under a flood of light, did not know what he was hiding from the blazing eye.

His college friends were still passing over that far-away whiteness below El Soledad's peak, as if the mountain would not permit them to drift from his sight. While he watched the hushed columns, he recalled their impassioned discussions on how to help their fellow men. In those days, they had been on the verge of taking their place in a world shaped by their fathers, and did not like the shape of that world, and deliberated in endless bull sessions how to set it right.

Noticing that his friends detached themselves from the distant snow, approaching on drifting clouds, he wondered how many of these young idealists had grown into men of goodwill without shedding their fine convictions; which ones among them had turned out to be thirteenth apostles, retaining their faith and fulfilling their enigmatic destiny, while he had lagged behind as a renegade openly rebellious and still not repentant.

Few in that tightly-knit circle of friends would have deserved Crispian's praise, if praise was indeed what Crispian had meant to express in the mysterious figure of the thirteenth apostle. Certainly not Eddie Fless, who had been convicted, years later, of fraud. They became anything but evangelists, followers of the great call. Unless, of course, Webb had misunderstood what the thirteenth disciple represented, who he was; unless there were more facets to Crispian's portrayal of this unknown apostle than he had so far perceived.

The figure, which until now had stood before his eyes in clear and well defined outline, was melting like a waxen image of a saint, giving his imagination a vaster range to the degree that the contour was losing its shape. He recalled that the thirteenth apostle had meant more to Crispian than a faithful, unswerving disciple; more than just a simple and dependable believer. In his notes, though sketchy on that point and perhaps intentionally enigmatic, Crispian had also characterized the apostle as one "who was called, but not chosen."

Why would anyone be called, Webb questioned, if the person so summoned was not to be chosen? The vapor streak ahead of the Padre was blown up into an indistinct silhouette which rose up to join the procession of other thirteenth apostles. Watching it, Webb tried in vain to read in its posture and gestures whether it was haunted, whipped, commanded; or seeking itself, seeking its own meaning, its mission, its duty, seeking and failing to find the truth of its undisclosed conflict with the power which had issued the call, seeking to understand the rejection while marching interminably in restless, brooding columns toward the cruelly withdrawing horizon.

Since the thirteenth apostle was one who had not been chosen, Webb thought angrily, it would indeed explain why only twelve disciples had become known to posterity. But it did not solve the mystery, he protested in sudden accusation, why this additional, superfluous, unwanted supernumerary had been called, if he was not to be accepted.

It did not explain, he charged, why some man, content to ply his trade in Galilee, a shoemaker, a rich merchant, perhaps a young fisherman—a man wanting no more than to eat and drink and enjoy the fruit of his labors, and to live in peace the days of his life—would be called from his hut, from his fenced-in villa, from his garrison. It gave no reason why someone would be drawn from his home, drawn to suffering, loneliness, and sacrifice—if in the end, in spite of his obedience, he would be refused, was not chosen, not admitted to whatever place or thing he had been called.

The wind was low; the wind was still; it rarely became violent now, except in those sudden updrafts which shot in hard gusts from the steaming, boiling, clouded depths. He watched the tongues of mist that followed in their wake, the frayed flags, the vapors licking up the crest like pallid, cold flames torn from smoldering fires at the bottom. He would see them approach, and would go blind when they passed over his shoulders, separating him, at times, from the Padre, or else enveloping both in one solitude of darkness—before uncovering again the thin crest and the dizzy plunge on each side.

There was, Webb cried to the mountain, no more incomprehensible cruelty in all creation, no more tragic fate than befell those who were called, but not chosen. A deep-seated bitterness, a never-before-admitted wretchedness lashed at him, when he visualized the rejected apostle erring about the holy land in Bibli-

cal times; when he thought of the many like him who had roamed
the earth since their obscure ancestor had commenced the faceless,
anonymous drift.

He imagined a young man in Galilee who had left his parents'
home in obedience to a call he had heard, his soul having been
picked, sensitized, marked in childhood perhaps, or even at birth.
Searching his duty, as yet undivulged, he wandered about, helping
the poor along the way, giving of his substance to all who crossed
his path, generously, not avoiding anyone, not disdaining or condemning, still without guile or experience, taking both the leper
and the thief to his heart, because he considered everyone, if not
equally good, at any rate equally deserving.

Wherever he heard of a cause, or of a leader, there he went. He
was ready to offer himself, to give aid, to support. But time and
again he found that the causes he was asked to join were false, and
their leaders corrupt. Until, in the course of his travels, a rumor
reached him which sounded unlike any other he had heard; a
rumor that a true prophet had at last arisen.

Webb's own heart reflected the joyous surge of the young man
who set out to join Him who had called. But he did not find the
prophet at once. He would hear of him passing through a city
with his twelve disciples. Yearning to become the thirteenth, he
would rush to that city. But by the time he arrived, the crowds
flanking the streets were so thickly clustered that he could not
break through to see him. Again and again he would be turned
back, here, there; he always missed. And each time he grew more
bewildered, and his heart became heavier, since he knew that he
had been called, and it seemed like his fault when he failed to
get through.

When he was told of the triumphal entry into Jerusalem, he
rode there as fast as he could. He hurried to the house where the
twelve apostles had gathered for the last supper. But once again,
he, the thirteenth, was not admitted. He stood in the dark courtyard and knocked at the closed door. He shouted that he, too, had
been called. But no one came to let him in; no one would even
tell him why he had not been elected, why the door was not
opened for him.

And so he stood outside the house, alone, at the fringe of the
beam of light falling from the window, in which he occasionally

saw the silhouette of one or the other of the twelve apostles, those fortunate ones who had been chosen. And then the lights went out. Still he remained, waiting until they would come out. But they had left by another way, as he learned when the crowds rushed by at dawn. Only then did he move on, knowing at last that now it was too late, that nobody would ever come to inform him why he had not been admitted, nor why he had been called.

He was on his way back to his village, when he heard of the arrest and the crucifixion. The news, sprawling across the road in monstrous, multi-tongued accusation, blocked his return home forever. And so he kept wandering, not knowing why or where to, seeking to understand the summons he had been unable to fulfill. Through the centuries, he was seen, here or there; sometimes alone, sometimes in a group with others like him. And sometimes in a large crowd of men of goodwill—for there are many who are called, but few who are chosen.

I have called thee, the mountain said. *Hast thou not heard my call?*

And Webb flinging back: "I heard and I obeyed." He paused, before bursting out: "And I curse the day I listened. I wish I had not obeyed!"

Distant peaks flared up everywhere in the dying sun's fire. In flaming rows, they rose from the pale horizon, drawing nearer, as though alerted that the thirteenth apostle's great dispute with Him who had called had begun; or rather that its ancient echoes, still haunting the dusk and the high altitudes, had returned, unanswered and as grave-less as in the past.

If thou hast heard my call, the mountain said, *why hast thou rebelled? Why hast thou broken away from me?*

And Webb, in angry defiance: "Why was I betrayed? Why was I called to help build a better world—when none can ever be? Why was I called to love all men, when they will never cease to hate and kill?"

Clouds, in turbulent drifts, kept gliding past each other, now hiding, now accentuating distance; always tantalizingly on the verge of disclosing the very end of space, yet never parting quite long enough to permit more than a glimpse of yellow sky nearby, a crimson crest below, a hint of agonizing mystery far, far away.

And from that great distance, from the bottomless pit of time, came the mountain's voice, saying: *Men are born good. There is truth, therein is hope.*

And Webb erupting: "Man is not good. Man lies, steals, destroys. Man is born with anger in his heart, learns to fear and is taught to hate. Man—"

He broke off, constrained by a surge of repugnance. He had never learned to voice his disillusionment with that eager self-justification he had so often noticed in others. To acknowledge man's incorrigible stupidity, selfishness, and corruption still hurt him as much as in his youth, when his untested, idealistic beliefs had first clashed with reality. But since then, as he occasionally suspected, he had adjusted so completely to his pessimism that he needed it—needed his misanthropic outlook like a drug addict who first used morphine to soothe his pain and then can no longer function without it.

If thou hast known that it was I who called thee, why hast thou lost faith? Why hast thou not followed to the end?

And Webb shouting back: "How could I keep faith in men, while bombs exploded? Who could have passed through industrial slums and retain hope in science and progress? How long could I trust the promise of the future?"

The wind, in dusky waves, drove its moisture into Webb's eyes. Through half-closed lids, he saw that the horizons swayed; at that moment, it seemed that the world was being rocked on its pivot, with ferocious forces on either side pulling at its innermost balance.

Men are born good, the mountain said. *And if thou hast despaired in thy brothers, thou hast turned from me and my whole realm and all I could have given thee. For thou canst not withdraw from others without withdrawing from thyself; and thou canst not lose faith in thy fellow men without losing faith in thine own worth.*

The mists, gleaming in refracted light, wrapped themselves around Webb. It was actually the other way around, he thought, —one usually lost faith in oneself before losing it in others. But whichever came first, it hardly mattered, since an inseparable link remained. And he raised his hand, brushing the tangled hair from his eyes, brushing aside the web that was weaving around him.

Thou wast born with a love in thy heart, which cannot be divided, the mountain said. *And if thou hast tried to withhold it from thy fellow men, thou hast withheld it from thyself. For if it be not allowed to encompass all, it will embrace nothing—thyself no more than thy brothers.*

And Webb, momentarily sheltered from the mountain's gaze as he passed into a cloud, felt cold and shivered in that most barren loneliness, known only to one who is separated even from himself. He wondered whether the mountain could understand how one's too ardent love for the human race might be turned into anger and contempt. And just then he stepped from the cloud, and the blare of light and multitudinous sounds was again upon him.

Men are born good, the rocks far and near sang out, echoing in an indefatigable chorus the mountain's words. *Therein is truth. Therein is hope. And so thou hast had no excuse for turning from thy earlier faiths. Thou hast no right to blame the evil of others for leaving undone the good that was thine to accomplish.*

And Webb quickened his pace, hurrying after the Padre, while the gale whined and moaned in clefts, or suddenly roared at him from hidden gaps. Voices such as these, he thought, might have hounded the thirteenth apostle, pursuing him from one desert to another. They were the implacable furies set upon the heels of one who had first been rejected and was then accused of disobedience; of one who had rebelled against his utopian strivings and had cast off his white-robed beliefs like stained clothes soiled by the world; of one who was to be punished because he had dared to accuse the accusers.

If thy excuse was that thou hast seen too much evil in the ways of the world, thou hast not looked deep enough, the stones sang out, their soaring, exuberant tones followed at once by the ringing chorus: *For men were created good.*

And Webb, clambering along the crest, denied it, emphatically, vehemently—disturbed only when he realized that his rejection was no longer a matter of free choice; that he had no alternative to his acrimonious denial. For even if he were less assured in his convictions, he could not budge from his position. He was too deeply committed to his bitterness. As long as he adhered to it, he could continue to regard himself as a disappointed idealist. But if he should waver or even reverse himself, a whole system of self-justification might be endangered or collapse. Because then, indeed, he would have no excuse for having left the battlefield; he would truly have to consider himself a renegade, a traitor to the cause of Man which, at one time, had appeared as the greatest cause of all.

Man is good, the rocks sang out, exultantly shifting their shadows and dancing in ecstatic, intricate ceremonial patterns. *Join us*, they called to Webb, *for thou, too, hast been created good.*

A fear which, a moment ago, had still seemed remote was beginning to settle in his heart. It was indeed fortunate, he thought, that he was so justified in his repudiation of the jubilant claim; that his pessimistic view of the human animal was derived not only from personal experience, but from the sum and substance of modern thought, from the sober appraisal of the individual as an organic machine, soul-less, will-less, product of environment and circumstances, expendable and cheap, his total worth in chemical ingredients being no more than a few cents.

Men are born good, the rocks sang out. He tried to ignore the child-like, trustful chorus, but the sounds struck at him from all sides. These voices did not understand, he thought with mounting bitterness. Their ancient faith had been conceived in a time too far removed from the present. And so it bore no relation to modern man's discovery that he was not only far lower than angels, but hardly above the beast and the savage; that beneath his thin, civilized veneer raged a vast hell of murderous, irrational drives—

Men are created good. Again and again, the rocks repeated the refrain, half-singing and half-speaking it with the granite voices of Biblical prophets, passing the words from one to the other, and closing the circle, and sending them around once more, so that not a syllable could drop into the steaming, clouded depths.

And Webb, listening to the Biblical words, wondered what the prophets of old might have said, had they lived in this day and age—through depressions, mass destruction, genocide; through all of man's mechanized inhumanity to man. In Babylon, those great seers had sung: 'Thou shalt love God with all thy heart and all thy might.' But had they been present while their people were fed into the ovens at Dachau on a smoothly organized assembly line, the voices of these giants would surely have burst with the expiring disbelief of musical instruments flung away or smashed.

If I have not lost faith in men, the mountain roared in reply, *why shouldst thou want to despair?* There had been anger in the mountain's words, but also pain and a sadness so great as to dwarf compassion. *Why dost thou see only the murderers, and not those who opposed them?*

And Webb fled along the crest, embattled, torn, longing to be one with the mountain, but held at a distance by his past; by the guilt of betrayal he would have to take upon himself should he confess to a renewed faith in men. As previously with his fear of death, he was trapped; for he could not now believe in the grandeur and the high destiny of the human race without asking himself what he had done to further it—no more than he had been able to believe in an immortal soul without submitting to divine judgment the use to which he had put his days on earth.

Hopelessly implicated in the clinging, shaping tissue of his time, he could not extricate himself from the web into which he had grown. He could only see the truth as it had been given him within it; and that truth was that more people had been slaughtered in this century than ever before; that more children were starving, more crimes committed, more injustices perpetrated; so that, if the mountain were to hold out hope in man's future, too much evidence would rise in opposition.

The mountain remained hushed in vibrant anger, its immense gaze perhaps circling the earth where it saw the ruined cities, the bombed bridges, the tank-threaded forests, and the long, silent rows of white crosses amidst rich fields, fertile enough to bear a plentiful harvest for all. The mountain, perhaps, did not know that men would fight wars, not for gain, but for destruction's sake; that borders were crossed, not to acquire new territory, but to live hate rather than swallow it. Perhaps, even the mountain had failed to grasp that human beings, alone of all creatures, had learned to transform unfulfilled love into hatred, to pervert it into sadism and masochism; that more often than not suppression, deceit, and abuse were practiced to inflict pain, pain for pain's sake, without any thought of gain or benefit, and sometimes even to personal disadvantage.

The mountain, perhaps, was too set in its archaic ways to have perceived that the whole recent surge of civilization had increased the pools of latent hatred as swiftly as its power resources and energy production; that it had multiplied the stimuli inciting individual hostility, while, at the same time, reinforcing the technological means of public suppression, so that the constantly building up pressures had to be diverted to the outside in frequent eruptions.

Or, quite possibly, the mountain had not yet recognized the paradox that in a period most preoccupied with economic theories, food had actually become abundant, while psychological problems had moved up to a place of paramount importance. To such an extent, indeed, that future historians might be impressed less by the scientific advances than by the upsurge of torment and suffering as the modern mode of life, as the chief pattern in which thwarted love and strangled joy had come to express themselves, in what might some day be called the century of the sadistic-masochistic rise.

I have heard thee, the mountain broke into his thoughts. *I have listened, and have considered everything thou hast found.* There was a pause, and Webb held his breath, chilled and anguished, as if not only his beliefs, but he himself, were to be judged, this very moment.

And with all thou hast said, the mountain continued, *thou canst not change the truth—thou canst not change that man is good!*

The voice had withered the shadows in a wide radius. And in its soaring radiance, Webb's rancors and despairs felt small and worthless; so that, although his stricken heart continued to send up more accusations, the words turned to dust on his tongue and could not be spoken.

And so he fled along the trail, a somber figure straddling the crest, product of his day and age: unhappy if he despaired in Man, guilty if he did not; and thus sentenced to inner dispute, either way.

CHAPTER XI

JUST BEYOND, beating an indistinct pulse as he approached, stroking past him in imponderable waves, was the unknown.

Always just ahead—intensifying, more alluring, inciting the wildest passion known to man—all that was undivulged had started to glimmer before Webb's eyes as though it were about to be shot through by the first glow of clarity.

Yet the darkness, though increasingly palpable, remained. While he climbed over the ridges and crests, which Crispian had scaled before him, Webb's soul reached out, reached beyond itself, reached toward knowing, ever more impatient, more tormented—beating at the bars of its prison—

The darkness remained.

There was a stir in the waving folds of the opaque, everywhere a thinning and dissolving of impenetrable substance. But no revelation loomed up, no secret wisdom projected itself upon him, no knowledge came from the outside.

The more he strained to look beyond, the more his gaze was turned inside. He would feel on the verge of penetrating to the core of some all-important mystery—and, instead, he would see himself as a child, standing by the window of his little room, a forlorn, barefoot figure in a nightshirt. He would seek to brush the pale image aside, but instead it seized on his mind, clung, spread, stubbornly, hypnotically. Distant at first, lifeless, immobile, the small boy seemed to be moving across the tunnel of years, more and more rapidly, until he broke from the past, almost tangibly real, recaptured not only with the heat of searing tears in his eyes, but with the spatial feel of the room, the nearness of the little bed, the cold touch of the linoleum on the floor.

Since Webb's struggle was not with his past, but with the mountain, he saw no apparent reason why this remembrance should have burst forth from a welter of forgotten and buried days; unless the mountain had some undisclosed purpose in wanting him to experience once again, as vividly as in those remote, juvenile fantasies, all the dangers lurking in the little room. A thin slit of light from the hallway had pushed a promise of warmth and security beneath the door; but the boy was not allowed to reach the nearby asylum, for he had been sent to bed. And inside his room, trapped in darkness, were all the nameless, shapeless anxieties, the remembered hurts and failed tests of the day, transformed now, glowing with fiery eyes in every obscure corner. There were, waiting for him everywhere, the dismembered fragments of witches and dragons, gliding across one another, or weirdly riding on each other's back—and he, unable to sleep, was at the mercy of all these indescribable, changeable threats, for he had been sent to bed, by parents insensitive to the menace of the dark.

He was beginning to suspect now why the mountain had drawn forth this memory among all others. That night, for the first time, a new ghost had come into being; a limp, dreadful ghost, at whose appearance and passing everything—trees and houses and fences—fell down and wilted. Screaming, he had rushed from his room. His mother, meeting him on the stairway, had embraced and soothed him. But then his father had come from the study and had refused to let him stay up. Deaf to the pleading of the boy, insisting on principle, granting no exception and allowing no reprieve, he had forced the child back into the loveless prison of night and obscurity.

A rootless panic, remote and unreal, was wafted toward Webb, like musty air in a cellar. And, all at once, did it become clear to him why El Soledad, in their uncanny tug-of-war, had pushed him back upon that incident. For on that evening, the seed had been planted from which sprang his present conflict with the mountain. On that night, the little boy at the window had pressed his hands together, praying, wishing with all his heart, wishing fervently that no other child should ever be left alone in the dark. Blocked by his father, the boy had made up his mind to obtain for others what he could not obtain for himself; he had resolved that, when he grew up, he would devote himself to the task of protecting all children from tyranny and injustice, from fear and lack of affection.

The clouded, sinking valley far below, Webb noticed, was dimly illuminated by spasms of flickering light. In a lull of the wind, he grew uncertain whether El Soledad would really fulfill the threat of the gathering storm, or would destroy them by some other means, as yet undivulged.

The clouds closed in again, forcing him back into himself. He knew now where the powerful surge of idealism, which had stirred in his youth, had its point of origin. It had not been too difficult to trace back to its source the swift, seemingly invincible, almost jubilant impetus of dedication and self-sacrifice which had swept him along at college.

But he could not see clearly where, in the dark churning waters of time, of daily drifts and imperceptible currents, he had been driven from his course; at what point he had first lost his innocent beliefs, then his zest and fervor; or how it had come about that his fervent altruism could have congealed into so embittered a pessimism that now, as he climbed over hazardous cliffs, he found himself locked in irreconcilable conflict with the mountain.

I have asked thee to do thy duty, the mountain said. *Why hast thou turned from me?*

The mountain gazed down on him from its stupendous height; the mountain did not know what it was like to fight windmills. The mountain, most likely, did not count progress in terms of life-times, or even centuries. Perhaps, it did not think that the sort of progress Webb had believed in was important at all.

Neither did Webb any more. But at high school he had believed in it with all his heart. At college. After the rise of the new inventions, as Professor Velliczek used to express it, when electricity, radio, all the means of communications, had broken up every static form of life, every petrified social stratification. "We are living in a period," Professor Velliczek had told the class in one of his succinct, sarcastic, and always fascinating lectures, "when science has achieved one of the great breakthroughs in history. Our advance is so hasty that the pioneer and the home-steaders are practically proceeding hand in hand. Indeed, you might say, we are all living at the spearhead of progress."

At that point, he looked up from his notes, causing Webb to shift uncomfortably, since it always seemed that the nearly blind professor was seeking out his face. "But unfortunately," Professor Velliczek continued with that faint, melodious accent of his, "a spearhead is not always a wise head. And possibly for that reason we have not yet learned to distrust the Victorian axiom that all progress is good; we still believe that it is bound to be not only technological, but ethical, social, functional as well—perhaps even sensible—and all that without any willfully directed contribution from us. By some inherent magic, if taken in ever greater doses like medicine, it would induce politicians to devote themselves to the good of the people, diplomats to peace. And before long, war and poverty and senseless strife would have become memories of the past. Why, then," he inquired, his gentle, thoughtful, warm eyes peering at Webb from behind glittering glasses, "has nothing of the sort happened? What the devil became of our panacea? Why doesn't the damned thing work as well as our latest carburetor?"

The bell, at that moment, rang out; and the white-haired professor, leaving his question unanswered, stalked from the room, trailed by aroused students who went on to argue the problem outside, in the courtyard, on the street. These youths of goodwill, eager, intelligent, and inexperienced, these vigorous, unresigned, unwarped, unmellowed, and far too logical reformers coagulated in little groups, discussing, quarrelling. And inside one such cluster was Donald C. Webb, the son of a Philadelphia high school teacher, surrounded by other young men who had been called from their homes to help mankind progress toward a better future.

Their language was different from that of the young fishermen on their way to Jerusalem; but the tasks confronting them might not have changed too much; and surely the enthusiasm and fervor of these young Americans was as great as any in past centuries. And among these fledgling apostles none was more ardent than Donald Webb, whom some of his friends considered a little naive, a little too impatient, perhaps too intensely dedicated, though no one questioned his good faith; Don, who stood there, inquiring why there should be so much conflict in the world when the solutions appeared so simple; why there must be a gap between recognizing an error and its correction, between the discovery and application of remedies to defects so obviously harmful to nations and individuals alike.

If there were men who could have answered their questions, they did not step forth. The guiding spirits of the epoch were too busy hacking at what they proclaimed to be false, hypocritical, and unnecessary beliefs. They had found it easier to tear down than to rebuild; and, besides, more acclaim was to be had by negating and ridiculing. In order to amuse the crowd, they continued to chip away at the rubble—long after the statues had been smashed. And while the need for vigorous reaffirmations increased by leaps and bounds, the wreckers could offer no other counsel than to endure the desolation with aplomb. As their ideal hero they could only project a man strong enough to sit bravely on the ruins.

Young apostles on their way to Jerusalem, dazzled by the claims of charlatans, sidetracked by clowns, tricked by medicine men, taken in time and again by that motley and gifted crew which gathers to amuse and sell wherever a crowd streams to the market place.

Young men of goodwill gradually losing their way. But in spite of disappointments, the cynical view, which could have solved so many of their perplexities with a shrug and a wink of the eye, remained unacceptable to them. It held out no hope, suggested no remedy; it was designed only to make the status quo tolerable. But they refused to take the easy way out, as so many others did. They were a minority swimming bravely 'against the stream'—swimming against that disillusioned, hard-voiced, emasculated crowd which receded like a weary surf from World War I in the form of the 'lost generation.'

Pebbles awash in the wild currents of the times. Their goodwill adrift like flotsam—to be gathered by those who would use it for their own selfish, evil, ambitious ends. Goodwill deceived or thwarted—"but goodwill, nevertheless," Webb cried to the mountain, "no matter how or by whom it was abused."

Instead of going out for amusement, they gave of their time to help others. Like Esther who, in addition to her studies, held down a part-time job as a social worker in one of the worst slums, impairing her health by overwork, risking insult and attack when she returned home late at night.

"I still have to go back to old Mrs. Lejeune," Esther had told him that evening after he had taken her to meet his parents for the first time. The introduction had been disastrous, with his father in a particularly bad mood, and behaving abominably.

And Don had said nervously: "You have an exam in the morning. What time do you have to get up?" And she, smiling: "Don't even remind me. I bet I'll be so sleepy, I'll get everything all muddled up." And he: "Then go home and get some rest." And she: "I have to bring Mrs. Lejeune her pills. If I don't, she's liable to get drunk again. The old smartie claims she needs something to kill her pain."

They were walking alongside the fish markets, treading across a welter of dripping boxes that overflowed with the pink gills, the glittering scales, the torn dead mouths of bass and tuna and sliced-open salmon. Neither of them had as yet referred to his father's insulting condescension—though Webb's rage boiled up every time he gazed at her delicate, calm, almost saintly face, at the faded, outmoded chiffon dress—her best—at her finely shaped forehead on which danced the highlights reflected from the wet asphalt. "I'm sorry, Esther," he finally blurted out, "I didn't expect him to treat you like that."

"It wasn't bad, darling," she smiled, anxious to conceal from him how disappointed and hurt she was. "Can't really blame him. If you were my son, I also wouldn't consider any female good enough."

"That wasn't it, and you know it," he grumbled. He wondered whether he should tell her that the vindictive old high school teacher had slighted her because she was neither sufficiently affluent nor socially prominent enough to provide a means of revenge on his more successful colleagues who had advanced to university positions. But he hesitated to mention anything that might cast a shadow over future years of marriage; and when his anger welled up again, he muttered: "He's no good, Esther. Don't be taken in by all his sanctimonious drivel. He's nothing but an old hypocrite!"

"Don't say that," she broke in quickly, "he's your father." And he, in his rage and shame: "I'd rather you didn't stress it. You don't know how hard I've tried to see only the good in him. But I can't make myself blind. Like tonight—the way he set out to impress you. Holding forth on the nobility of humble spirits. And me knowing all the time that if one squeezed dry a thousand like him, there'd be less goodness coming out than you have in your little finger."

And Esther, alarmed: "Don, I won't let you talk that way! It isn't true!" And he: "Isn't it? I wish I didn't know him so well. Ever since I can remember, it has troubled me. Like the time he fired the gardener who used to take care of our front lawn once a week. I was a kid then, and I saw the old guy cry and beg my dad to keep him on, because he needed the job. He even promised to work twice as hard as any younger man we could get; but my dad turned him down, and then all the neighbors fired him too, and that's the last anybody ever heard of that old man. But my dad kept right on reading Emerson's essays to us—every night after dinner—and I used to stare at him, wondering why he never did any of the fine things he always talked about."

And she, near tears: "Stop it, Don! I don't care how bad he is, or what he's done to me. He's still your father, and you ought to respect him."

"Don't, Esther," he begged her, "don't ever say that to me! Because I want to respect him. I want it more than anything in the world. More even than keeping my own self-respect. You don't know, Esther—you just don't know how awful it is when you can't look up to your own father."

At that moment, a policeman came between them, and when they got together again, they walked on in silence, stepping over puddles, passing hallways that reeked with the sour smells of poverty and stagnation. And then, after they arrived at the tenement where old Mrs. Lejeune plotted to outwit her arthritis by drinking herself into a stupor, Webb looked up, scanning the crumbling fire escapes. "What keeps you going, Esther?" he asked. "Sometimes I wonder—how you can go on without ever getting discouraged?"

And Esther, searching her handbag for the pills: "Discouraged? Why should I be?" And he, kicking a can along the gutter: "Always doing things for others. Are people worth it? Is anyone worth the trouble?" And she, turning to him, astonished: "What's come over you, Don? Just because your father—" And he, cutting her short: "It's not only my father. The drunk we passed at the corner—calling you a dirty Jew." And she, smiling patiently: "Why should that upset you? He was drunk."

He gazed at her, thinking that if he could paint he would portray her like this—with the street lamp in back of her soft, luminescent hair—and would call the picture 'The Madonna of the Midnight Lantern,' or 'The Saint of the Festering Gutters,' or some such crazy thing. But he did not mention anything of that to her, and only asked: "Doesn't anything ever get you down?" And then he had to wait until a man and woman in the adjoining house ceased screaming at each other, before he could add: "Aren't there days when you get tired and want to give up? Don't you ever lose faith in people?"

And she, quite perplexed: "If I did, what else is there?" And he: "Nothing. That's the worst part of it. There's nothing else— nothing at all." And she, drawing him close, searching his expression: "Don, you haven't lost faith in people? You like them, don't you?" And he, nodding: "Sure. Maybe too much." And she, saying quickly as the quarrel in the adjoining tenement turned into a brawl: "Don, too much can be as bad as too little. Either way— it can ruin a person."

With his eyes fixed on the shoddy, yellowish windows behind which the woman was being beaten, he said inattentively: "I know. But where do you draw the line? What's too much and what's too little?" And Esther, holding him tight, protecting him against the animal shrieks of the woman whose wailing rose above the dull thuds of blows and the cracking of furniture falling or thrown: "Don, you can't help everybody. There's only so much you can do, and that's all. You can't remake the whole world overnight."

Not overnight, and not in a month, and perhaps not in scores of years. In the meanwhile, however, it was small comfort to hear that progress needed time—as that young professor had told them, when their political science class toured the soup kitchens outside the city. Because time seemed more like an enemy than an ally, while they crossed one of those cardboard-and-spit jungles where life was a battle from day to day. It was hard to wait until the future would make good the world's promissory notes, while they gazed at the wide desolation of tin cans and refuse and slimy trenches; while Webb listened to the rain drumming on the corrugated, leaky huts, and watched, together with Esther, the undernourished, rickety kids crawling and playing in the mud.

"How can one learn to be patient?" he countered Esther's plea that night, after they had finished the Friday evening meal at her parents' small, musty apartment, which had become a second home to him. "The more you need, the less you can wait. The trouble with time is that it does not move at the same speed on all levels—and for all people."

Her parents had gone to the synagogue, and Joshua, her younger brother, was out playing baseball. While Esther cleared away the dishes, he was thinking how slowly time crept over the graphs and charts which the dispassionate professor had shown them that afternoon; with what majestic dignity it paraded for the statesmen and economists who congratulated themselves if they had arranged a conference for the coming year—and how urgently it raced for the hungry and sick, for the baby with the bloated belly that might not live to see the next day if it were not properly fed before evening.

"Don't let it get you down," Esther said when she returned from the kitchen. "The first time I saw that awful place, I also was sick for days." And he, nervous and distraught: "Are you telling me—one gets used to everything?" She set down the tray, almost dropping it, causing a silvery ringing of glasses. He saw that he had hurt her, but did not know how to apologize. "No, Don," she said quietly, "one might get numb to pain—but one never gets used to it."

She gathered the cups from beneath the candles which her mother had left on the table. They had melted away an inch or two since her father, the hunched Jewish tailor with the wrinkled, serene, mild face, had lighted them before dinner, chanting those thousand-year-old blessings over the slender, perishable objects that would not last the night. They were still burning; and their flames were still as bright as they had been when they shone on her mother's joyous, blissful smile—which always seemed so peculiarly extended by the slight scar she had received during a pogrom in Czarist Russia.

Time was a myriad things, he thought, while Esther went back into the kitchen. He could not even make out whether he should regard these tiny fires as short-lived, because they were so perishable that they could be put out by a passing draft; or whether they ought to be considered the Olympic bearers of a spark already aglow in ancient temples, proclaiming the existence of an eternal God.

Hypnotized by the small, orange-blue, solemn flames, he questioned whether that eternal God would be able to judge from these undistinguished white shapes, so similar to all other candles ever made, that a millennium or two had passed. And perhaps for the same reason, a passing God might also have failed to observe the twelve year old girl they had seen that afternoon, crouched in front of the corrugated hut, with the rain dripping into her tin-plate of watery soup; perhaps she had escaped notice, because there had been so many other little girls exactly like her in past generations, with similar budding breasts on the verge of blossoming up to nourish more children who would grow up to bear others .....

Esther had returned; looking up, he saw her breasts across the candle flames, and he longed, yearned, strained to take her into his arms, to embrace that lithe, soft figure, to forget, to push the whole world outside a flaming orbit of love, of a tenderness without measure or end. His hands started to tremble, and he turned away, quickly, guiltily; but he was pursued by the rain-soaked, ripening bosom of the little girl; she met him just below the shelf where the hunched tailor kept his Torahs and Talmuds, sitting there with her waiting breasts—waiting until she was old enough to be embraced and give the fruit of her womb to a callous, indifferent world that forced youngsters like herself to cook their food in rusty cans over an open fire—

"What's wrong, darling?" Esther asked, coming quickly around the table. "You suddenly turned pale. What's troubling you?"

"Nothing." He looked away. He did not know how to explain to her all that had flitted through his mind. Abstractions meant little to her; theoretical discussions still less. She was the only one in their group who never participated in their frequent, almost incessant debates on how to achieve utopia. And yet, she did more to help people than any of the others—almost light-heartedly, without questioning her motives, as if it were self-understood that she had to give of her time to those who needed her, as if it were the most natural and unproblematic thing in the world.

She took his hands, alarmed. "Don't torment yourself, darling," she said softly. "You're doing all you can. That's enough. That's as much as anybody can ask of you."

"Is it?" he asked bitterly. "Has it ever occurred to you how little we accomplish—when you consider how much ought to be done?"

"It's no use, Don," she said, imploringly. "You'll only make yourself sick. You've got to stop thinking that way."

"I can't!"

"Try, darling. You've got to give yourself a chance. Just because you couldn't change your father doesn't mean you can't rest until you've straightened out the whole world."

He wheeled around, stung by the truth of what she had said. "It's not only my father," he stammered, knowing that, as right as she was, there was more to his hunger. "Did you notice," he asked, "the kid with the scratched knees we passed this afternoon?"

A dark, quick moisture flowed into her eyes: "The little girl.....?" And he, nodding aimlessly: "The way she looked after us—with the wet thin dress clinging to her—showing her—showing her skin...." He swallowed. "Suppose she'd been our child?"

And Esther, imploringly: "Let's not suppose. Please, Don! I don't want to think of it." And he, insisting, though the soft warmth of her body streamed through his sinews to inundate his brain: "Why not? She could have been ours!....And we passed her!" His arms grew rigid. "Everyone of us—we just passed her. Suppose, some day, it happened to our child—if we wanted to bring one into this world!"

And Esther, crying out: "If? If we wanted to?" And he: "Yes. I mean—if. I'm not sure whether I want a child. Not if it might grow up to stand in breadlines, or be killed in a war."

"Since you're not sure, Don," she said, her eyes unnaturally bright in the light of the candles, "since you don't have enough faith to want children—then I'm not sure I want to marry you."

The din of streetcars and angry motors, the busy shuffling of feet and the blaring of a victrola pressed into the apartment. For a moment, they stood listening, both very pale, very quiet. He sensed that he had gone too far, and desperately tried to think of a way to retract, which would be both honest and not hurt his pride. He found none. He stared, helpless and flustered, at the red wine on the table, remembering how her father, the hunched, overworked, witty, and unendingly grateful refugee from the pogroms in Russia, had raised the goblet to praise God who had both flayed and preserved his people throughout their long history.

"You'd better go," Esther was saying. He looked up. He had not expected her to be so brusque. In their other disagreements, it had always been she who offered to compromise. But then he understood that this was no mere rift or quarrel. To her, marriage was more than a union between two people—it was an act of faith. She would not give herself to a man who did not trust the future sufficiently to want a child. She had once told him that a child was the greatest affirmation of which two people were capable; it was to proclaim that mankind would endure and rise, it was to believe in the sense and meaning of all creation, in the ultimate protection of a wise and almighty spirit.

On his way home, he was nearly run over by a motorcycle. Once, when a drunk pushed him from the sidewalk, he almost gave vent to his pent-up misery by driving his fist into the sallow, pimply face. Containing himself only with difficulty, he rushed on.

Back in his room, he threw himself on the bed. The warped, low ceiling had never seemed so deserted, the cramped walls never so confining; he could hardly breathe. Lying in the dark, he imagined her parents returning from the synagogue. They had looked forward to a celebration—because that night, after weeks of secrecy, he and Esther had told them that they were engaged. And now that great joy was spoiled for them, that happiest of all the days they had spent in the adopted country they loved and admired so much.

'But not through my fault alone,' he thought, digging his nails into the blanket. For if he had been lacking in faith, Esther's love was also wanting. She had shown him that she did not love him as much as he had expected, not enough to forgive everything, not enough to sacrifice all—as he might have done.

And suddenly, about an hour later, there was the soft knock at the door. Without awaiting his answer, she rushed in. She turned the key in the lock. It was the first time she had visited him after dark; and while she took off her coat, she looked around the room as if she had never seen it before. She would not let him switch on the light, and she would not let him talk. There was to be no concession on his part, and no condition on hers.

But at the last moment, a rush of shyness came between them and kept them apart. He drew her close—and suddenly all hesitation fell from them. Suddenly there was only the great want of two beings, surrendering at last, embracing each other, finding one another outside of time and place, far from the brooding stare of fate and its mysteries and all its unresolved intents.

Her indistinct face, turned to him afterwards on the pillow, reflected neither confusion nor regret, only an unbounded trust and love. And while he stroked her damp forehead, he asked himself, with naive and awed wonder, whether the great miracle of life was now starting to unfold in her, whether they had both joined before the altar of indestructible hope to proclaim their faith in the future.

But it was not until several months later, two months after they had eloped to New York to get married, that the physician's tests revealed her to be pregnant. And another month passed before she contracted the fatal pneumonia in the unheated apartment of an invalid aunt, whom she had nursed through an attack of rheumatic fever.

After that, there was no warmth in her hands, and no stirring in her dead breasts, and no life unfolding in her womb. There was only a black cortege traversing a void and murderous world that crushed those who loved it. There was only, many years later, an immense, stern mountain in a remote part of the world, saying to him: *Why didst thou turn from me, when thou hast heard my call? Why didst thou not follow to the end?*

CHAPTER XII

THE WET rocks gleamed and glittered beneath the overhanging bluff, where the Padre had stopped. A sudden fork in the trail had made him uncertain. He alternately scanned the right prong which rose swiftly to a jagged ridge and there disappeared beneath the sky, then the left, which wound and curved aimlessly in the general direction of a tremendous, forbidding, sheer wall that plunged down thousands of feet into a mist-strewn abyss.

Webb saw the indecision on the Padre's haggard, exhausted features; the chafed lips trembled, the burnished, scraped skin was strung taut over the cheekbones. While the wind sang and roared around their niche, Webb's glance wavered to that frightful wall, where all color dissolved in one blinding, metallic glare. Soon everything began to swim in front of his eyes. He leaned against the smooth rock behind him; his arms and shoulders grew limp; he felt himself sliding down. He still realized hazily that he had come to a rest on a broken stone, half-seated, half-crouched; then fatigue, long repressed and accumulated, streamed from his muscles and engulfed his mind.

The Padre was shaking him, pulling him up.

"Senor! Senor!"

"Leave me alone," he stammered, struggling against the hard grip.

"We have to move on."

"I need some rest."

"Not now, senor," the Priest was saying. "We are fighting time. The wind has let up, but the storm is still approaching."

"You go ahead. I'll follow you. In a few minutes...."

"If you close your eyes once," the Padre warned, "you will not get up."

"I don't care," Webb sobbed, while the mountain priest pulled him from their momentary shelter and out onto the swaying

239

path. "I don't care if I never get up....I've got to have some sleep!"

He managed to wrest his arm free. For a moment, the Priest reeled quietly in front of him, still watchful but apparently resigned. What was ominous, however, was that the black shape kept floating nearer, reaching out to support him with one hand beneath his left shoulder. And then, all of a sudden, the Padre's other hand flicked up; without forewarning, he slapped Webb's face, hitting him hard, two or three times. And when Webb, after a moment's stunned surprise, cried out, Padre Paolo struck two more blows, hitting him so brutally that Webb, in a surge of black rage, leaped at the Priest, seized his throat and wrestled him to the ground.

It all happened in a few seconds—the insane strength unleashed by his fury, his strangling grip, the choking, gasping, the rolling toward the edge of the slope. And there, the sudden clearing of vision, the pulling back—a moment's stillness while his reason, focusing once again, made him understand what had happened and why the Padre had assaulted him; why it had been necessary to provoke his anger in order to break the spell of his fatal lethargy.

Breathing spasmodically, Webb stepped aside and watched the Padre get up.

"Forgive me, senor," the Padre said softly, his hulking chest rhythmically widening and narrowing a gash ripped into the black robe by the stones from which he had risen. "But I had no choice."

Webb nodded. He meant to thank Padre Paolo, but his throat was dry and choked; he was too tired to speak. The careening landscape rolled and pitched across his vision like a stormy sea. When they started to move ahead, he vaguely wondered which of the two trails the Padre would select. He hoped that they would steer clear of that atrocious wall on the left; and when he saw the mountain priest turn to the right, he was relieved, and followed him numbly toward the cloud-swept sky.

The path, almost directly behind the fork, swung sharply upward. High stones, piled one upon the other like a stairway for giant steps, opposed their advance. Climbing had become difficult once again; whatever truce might have been in force was shattered in a new rage of battle.

There was no more reprieve in sight. Attack followed attack, in murderous, slow-rolling waves of fatigue, of fear and despair. The mountain did not let up; it entered into him from all sides; it poured itself into his muscles; it was the dust on his tongue and the weight on his heart. It coiled around his skull, and it kept asking why he had turned from his duty, why he had not followed to the end?

He defended himself. He offered answer after answer; they were neither argued nor rejected, but simply gobbled up. And then he was asked for more, for more, more—until he grasped that the mountain, like a clever prosecutor, already knew the truth and merely permitted him to stammer his way toward a full confession.

He fell silent. Caution clamped itself around his breath. There was, perhaps, not a single lie left in him. But broken, splintered truths were secreted away everywhere, strewn over all parts of his being, like a malignant disease. At any moment, he might accidentally fit another fragment into that composite picture of himself which the mountain wanted to see.

To prevent any clear view, he had to keep the pieces of the jigsaw puzzle well mixed. He could truthfully say that he had never distorted or ignored anything; his integrity would not have allowed it. But his piecemeal honesty, by stowing away facts in separate compartments, had always precluded that flashing fusion, which the mountain was now straining to bring about.

The mountain tore at him; the mountain clawed at him; it burrowed through his insides.

From here and there, it brought forth images, sentences, faces, harried remembrances. Against his frantic resistance, it fitted them into a flow of continuous developments; it wove and spun them into one simultaneous texture on which his life appeared, like a ghost never before materialized.

He shrank from what he saw; he ripped and slashed at the tissue. He could not bear to behold that shape of a soul striving and erring amidst the cross-currents of a world in torment, battered and hammered beyond recognition while it tried to stay afloat on the torrential rapids of large events and crowds too numerous to be under anyone's control.

He wiped the sweat from his forehead, from his cheeks, his neck. The skin and bone, he suddenly felt, were in the way; they kept him from seeing the inner face which had been molded— and probably disfigured—by the complex interplay of outer pressures acting on his native potentialities. He had never been able to delineate what might have been his own true self. To know himself, it seemed, he first had to subtract the influences of his time. But here, on these slopes, still more was demanded of him; here he was also asked to see himself against the further extension of the mountain's realm, not frequently noticed in daily life—yet always present, like the fog-bound shores along a river.

His eyes remained fastened to the iron sheen of the granite running down the trail in a thin stream. He did not dare look up; he sensed that the fog and the mist were lifting—the mountain was peeling itself free. He was not prepared to see himself against that uncanny background; he felt as panicky as a strutting actor who notices that the scenery behind him is slowly withdrawn, but who must continue to read his artificial lines, in front of the high, black, unadorned wall—because there are no others he has memorized.

Lifting himself over an embankment, he ripped the skin between his thumb and second finger. The sight of the blood sickened him. He tumbled ahead into the shelterless wind, casting about in vain for some protection against the voices howling around him.

He swayed. The inhaling abyss, drawing off all the air around him, leaped nearer, ready to receive him. Trembling, he pulled himself higher, clinging to one precarious hold after another. He wanted to explain to the interrogating rocks why and when his present conflict with the mountain had begun. But no motivation would remain with him—except one expressed long ago by Arthur Warren, who had been the most unlikely of the young apostles in their group: 'How can one go inside a church, when there are beggars on the steps?'

They had been crossing the campus, when that ancient accusation had found its modern expression in Arthur. The handsome son of a wealthy exporter, normally self-controlled, even suave, had voiced his indictment in such contemporary lingo as—"rotten," and "the whole foul mess," and "when you see some of those guys get away with it, it sure makes you sick." But what he had meant to say, with lips twisted by some deep and unexpressed hurt, was as old as: 'Why does not the race go to the swift, nor favor to men of skill? Why is evil permitted to flaunt itself, unpunished? Why is there no justice—no rhyme or reason in the blows of blind fate?' And again: 'Why are there so many ragged, ill, flayed, beaten, hungry beggars on the steps leading to the house of God?'

The wind howled fiercely around Webb, ripping, tearing at him. But it could not snatch from him the memory of Arthur striding across the sunlit campus.

For a long time after that day, Arthur had joined every picket line he could find, holding up placards to a newly vacated sky, as if he were demonstrating against God and all the lies and consolations of organized religion. It was his way of expressing his sudden conviction that man was betrayed, left to his own devices, and had to shoulder responsibility for himself, if he hoped to improve his lot. And not until much later, when Webb saw him again at a reception in Washington, had Arthur succeeded in returning to the fold. By then a father of three beautiful children, respected trustee of his church, he had managed to creep past the unanswered questions—which still barred Webb from any truce with the mountain, as unsurmountably as that ridge in front, with its vitreous crown of steel-gray, inflexible granite bluffs.

He blinked the moisture from his inflamed eyes. Through a tear-streaked haze, he saw that the Padre, suddenly staggered by a cross-blast, lurched to the side, stumbled, and held himself up on a rock that was shaped like a tombstone. For a moment, the black figure hung limply on the arch, held up only by the force of the wind, pressed hard against the surface, almost squashed. Then the limbs moved again; the body pried itself loose, and resumed its tortuous advance, gradually regaining its equilibrium.

The sweat ran down Webb's shoulders in thin, hot rivulets. There was no let-up, no respite from the stinging voices. They kept repeating the great questions that ran through his mind; they aped them in shrill mockery, swirling around him, racing away and quickly returning—but always without answer. He watched the Padre's robe clatter in the wind, and he wondered what the mountain priest's reply might be, if one or the other of his Indian parishioners would suddenly ask, in the dusk of a little clay chapel, why God had forsaken them?

The Padre, no doubt, would attempt to illuminate by some fairy tale what he himself could not understand. Committed to his faith, he would have no choice but to explain Barrie's unpunished viciousness to the Indian miners wounded in the shaft explosions. Or if, during a drought, he happened to be praying in vain for a cloudburst on a sun-scorched plaza, his arms spread wide over the mute, querying, bronze faces, he might notice some rebellious youth break ranks and walk away, turning his back on the cross held high by the mountain priest. And again Padre Paolo would have no choice but to rush after him and try to bring him back.

But what would he say, standing there among those emaciated Indians, in the glare of an arid sky? What doubts would pass through his mind, while the shadow of the cross crept slowly over the sun-baked plaza, nearer and over him, offering him the choice of crucifixion on its three black stumps—as it had always offered it to any man of goodwill dedicated to help his fellow men?

And what would that young, self-reliant Indian reply, if the mountain priest tried to defend God by explaining that a constant amount of evil, an irremediable mass of misery, might be preserved on purpose—as a test, perhaps—as a touchstone upon which generation after generation of individuals had to prove their worth, their good or bad intentions, their moral strength?

The truculent boy was not likely to believe that no better answer had ever been found to explain men's incomprehensible failure to achieve peace, to help themselves, to enter paradise though they kept inventing the means with which to build it. He would turn from the Padre, as Webb and his friends had turned from any defense of the status quo. With the young, hard energy rippling in his muscles, with all the exuberant vigor in his sinews and tendons, he would not wait for the Padre's prayer to take effect, but would labor to irrigate his barren acres and make them more fertile for himself and others.

The wind drove a squall of rain and sleet into Webb's face.

While the drops slithered down his burning skin, his glance passed along the saw-toothed horizon that was eerily lit from below by long-forgotten suns. Beyond those dark rims were cold fires of fervor and enthusiasm thwarted, of hopes squashed and left bleeding. "All religions are at their hearts outcries of pessimism," Professor Velliczek had once told the class. "As they must be, of necessity, for their sole preoccupation is to answer the insoluble questions raised by the human tragedy."

And the class had listened to him in hostile silence. They did not want to believe in tragedy, they refused to hear anything that might dampen their enthusiasm—those dedicated fighters for a better world, the young lions striding down Hudson Street, striding into battle every minute of the day. They would rather have no explanations than the apologies of any theology that might also serve as an excuse to leave misery tolerated and injustices unresisted.

"It's crazy," Bill Barton had sputtered after a lecture dealing with mass starvation in India. "Half a million gods nodding approval while watching those hungry skeletons crawl through the dust. You'd figure the untouchables would be smart enough to get up and do something for themselves."

"They won't," Tom Sears mused. "They believe in that superstitious bunk. Everybody gets taken in by propaganda." He always suspected propaganda, though he was not always sure who disseminated it, or to what purpose.

And Clem, who continually argued with Tom, contradicted at once: "Goes a lot deeper than that. When you're miserable, you need something to hold on to. Can't blame people for grabbing any kind of consolation to tide them over."

And Webb, his steps at that time still buoyant, his face not yet lined and furrowed: "Naturally. That's why it's so popular. It's the kind of comfort that makes everybody happy—not only those without any hope this side of paradise, but the ones who've got everything they want. Sure makes it a lot easier to watch others suffer, when you believe there's a divine purpose to it."

For a while, then, as they strode down Hudson Street, there was silence. Until Eric, the quiet, moon-faced boy said: "Maybe God wants us to be unhappy. It'd certainly explain a couple of things my Sunday school teacher never could clear up for me.

Things like—if God is all-powerful, why doesn't he take a hand in straightening out this botched-up job down here? Doesn't he care? Or does he refuse? If so—why? Why doesn't he help us wipe out evil?"

And with that, Eric lapsed again into his customary silence; and they drew away from him, slightly uncomfortable, because they could never make out how he felt about religion. Nor did it ever become clear to them, not even much later, when they heard that Eric had gone as a missionary to the South African diamond fields, but had resigned from his church after a year. He had, however, declined to be shipped home—as he wrote them, in a high fever, the day before he died. He had stayed on to continue his work at the mission's hospital, until he met—on a sultry evening blood-soaked by a huge, moist sun—the single tiny mosquito he had been awaiting. And after he was infected by it, the mosquito had whirred back into the sky, leaving him below in the dust of the red, heat-blistered veld....

At that point, his strange, incoherent farewell letter had come to an end, fading in a soft spiral. And the minister who mailed it to them had added that Eric, after making his peace with God, had asked that the enclosed leaflet be sent to Clem Hopkins or Arthur Warren.

It was a stained, discolored petition, of the kind they had circulated by the dozens in their Sturm-und-Drang period. And when Clem Hopkins and Webb walked home that night, after leaving Arthur Warren, they had stopped at a quiet hamburger stand, where Clem opened the leaflet, smoothing it down in order to read it. In the dim, uncertain light, the fat print had seemed both rebellious and remote; it called upon the voters to support the construction of a new school—a proposition which, Webb remembered, had been defeated. As they sat there, they avoided speaking of their dead friend, who had asked such intransigeant questions of his Sunday school teacher; and they recalled their own shock upon discovering that there was no one to protect them in the big hole their elders had ripped into the sky, no one to lead, guide, and look out for them; no one to help them unless they helped themselves.

The sleepy short-order cook had brought them their coffee, and Clem had crumpled up the leaflet which Eric had kept so long.

Dropping it, he had watched it roll away; and before it had dis-appeared beyond the murky sidewalk the last words they could see on it were:—BUILD THE SCHOO—, of a school that had never been built.

"A herd of Parsifals," Professor Velliczek had once called them, as usual concealing his admiration so well in a sharp-tongued barb that it escaped their notice. Perhaps, if they had been less burdened by their noble, urgent tasks, not quite as tense in their hurried quest for the Holy Grail, they might have understood that his irony actually covered both affection and the highest esteem. But the brilliant old man, abhorring sentimentality, gave no hint of his true feelings. Only on one occasion did he refer to them as —"young, brazen giants, sprouting in the land of unlimited op-portunities, with no patience for learning because they are so fidgety to give their last full measure of devotion." And then, lowering his voice to a gruff mutter, he had added something about their naive and awesome unselfishness, perhaps without parallel in history.

Better than anyone else, Professor Velliczek had understood what powerful compulsions drove them to accept responsibility for the state of national and world affairs. God having died at the hands of their elders, they had grown up in the twilight of the morning after the orgy of debunking. The young generation had arrived too late to join in the clamor and tumult—the revel-lers had passed away, leaving only the debris of spent passions, leaving the world as empty and silent as a mansion wherein the master had been slain.

They had hoped to inherit freedom—and, instead, they in-herited despair. In the first flush of revolt, they had considered themselves liberated; but soon it became apparent that people felt more oppressed, once the divine could no longer be used to oppress them. Contrary to all expectations, in the dawn of murder, the rebellious sons found themselves more inescapably in bondage, although the severe, demanding lord and father, at last overcome, lay murdered above and would not dominate them anymore.

Suddenly on their own, they saw that there was no one left in charge, nobody they could rely upon to keep the world running—for better or worse, fairly or unjustly, but at least under some sort of plan. The spectre of chaos arose. As day drew upon them and life clanked onward with its relentless demands for a million decisions, they huddled in fear, increasingly aware that they had swept away more than a mummified despot, more than ancient superstitions—they had also killed the belief that they were protected—they had murdered trust itself.

For a while still, slogans such as survival of the fittest, natural selection, evolution, cast a child's spell over the fearful sight of mankind's beheaded body, of which muscles, nerves, limbs continued to twitch and jerk, no longer restrained by a supreme and benevolent mind, individual nerve centers running amuck.

"But the spell," as Professor Velliczek had pointed out in his last book which had provoked so much controversy, "could not be kept up indefinitely. In an epoch already made insecure by the thrusts and jolts of burgeoning progress, by the sweep of ever more unpredictable innovations, the lack of foresight could not long be denied nor ignored. Too much, we realized, was happening in disconnected laboratories, board rooms, council chambers —without liaison, coordination or master plan; no one knew what it was all leading to."

The next paragraph in the book had caused so many heated discussions on the campus that it was reprinted in the college newspaper: "By the time the spell had faded, we felt like passengers in a bus racing down a mountain road. Suddenly awakened, we saw that the driver's seat was empty. Panic broke out. Somebody had to take the wheel and pull the brakes. And the young generation, rushing to discharge its duty, abruptly found itself saddled with a responsibility far beyond its age and strength."

The old teacher's head, like an indestructible ghost, flickered across the sleet and mist. Wherever Webb turned, those thick bi-focals, behind which one could only suspect the penetrating glance, peered at him, looming up in a passing cloud or in the mountain's steaming rocks. The wrinkled, translucent, finely veined face had lost none of its serenity over the years; a wise and devoted mentor, he still seemed to be contemplating Webb's progress into storm and chaos with an untroubled compassion —with concern, but also with the diffidence toward the present of one who has looked far into the future and knows that the sun, though often obscured, cannot be abolished, and will again rise in days to come.

"The sacrifice of these courageous youths will surely leave its mark—but sacrifice it will turn out to have been, inevitably," Professor Velliczek had subsequently written, in an intrepid attack upon his critics, which had fanned the glowing embers of controversy to a raging fire. "For in the endeavor to drive out, once and for all, not only Cain and the Golden Calf, but injustice, poverty, oppression and any other atavistic, perennial wrong, this generation of young American liberals has tackled a task more gigantic than any undertaken by their boisterous ancestors, the pioneers, the scouts, the trappers; a task more forbidding than the early settlers' trek to the West, more dangerous than the conquest of nature or the construction of machines to achieve mastery over land, sea, and air. For here they have engaged in conflict with obscure elements deeply embedded in human nature itself; here they are coming to grips with the age-old problem of leading Adam and Eve back into Paradise, against the opposition of every conceivable type of fire-breathing monster, against stupidity, selfishness, intolerance, ancient prejudice; and, worst of all, against Adam and Eve's obstinate, flailing refusal to be dragged back to the place for which they pretend they eternally yearn."

The fledging apostles striding down Hudson Street. Eager. Impatient. Extreme. Supremely confident in their assurance that they had been called. Strong and proud; and as yet not even suspecting that they might not be chosen.

Webb felt the cold seep through the hollow of his bones, like water dripping in dank caves, when he remembered how little they had understood Professor Velliczek at the time. It had seemed strange to them that he should be so impressed by their courage and self-reliance, which they had taken for granted. It had seemed stranger still, when he had warned them of the heartbreak in store for them.

"I know, it is a bad thing to be a prophet of gloom in a dancing, sunlit city," he had once chuckled to Webb, as they crossed the park on their way to a symposium on future designs in architecture. "But if I could only get you young dreamers to listen, I would not hesitate to warn you, day after day—even at the risk of being stoned to death on the campus."

And Webb, as yet not even suspecting any cracks in his confidence, had smiled indulgently, while Professor Velliczek, warming up to his Cassandra role, chortled: "Beware, I would cry! Beware! The claws and scales of those old dragons are sharper and deadlier than you can see from afar!" Stopping near a marble fountain, he had stabbed his pipe in the general direction of Webb. "Go out to fight them, by all means! Fight them with all your strength, since you must. But don't expect them to sprawl dead at your feet—immediately after your first attack!"

Chuckling, the slight old man with the fearless, untiring mind, with the dazzling personality and the disarming, wrinkled, at times almost puckish, smile had walked on, ambling alongside a flower bed that was flaming with the rich colors of fall.

All around them, the wide green lawns glittered under the fine drizzle of the sprinklers. Though evening was upon them, there were still many children in the park, playing, shrieking and laughing. The future seemed too well secured in growth and health to inspire or even tolerate fear; and Webb had listened, as often before, to Professor Velliczek's forewarnings of the pitfalls and perils ahead, without any real apprehension.

For the past two or three months—ever since Professor Velliczek had first advised him to consider a diplomatic career—they had frequently talked and walked together, sometimes outside the library, sometimes on their way home, or around the campus. For some reason, perhaps because he foresaw that Webb would need more guidance than others, or, possibly, because he had come to recognize in him a rare and as yet unformed intensity of striving, Professor Velliczek had recently taken a special and most flattering interest in the ardent, impulsive, strong-headed young man.

Together they would search out Webb's true aims in life; they would probe his ambitions and examine his qualifications. Though Professor Velliczek's time was at a premium—he was not only the most renowned and venerated member of the faculty, but a world-famous authority on international law—he was never too busy to see any one of his students who needed guidance, advice, or assistance of any kind.

"Don't think of me as a teacher," he would tell them. "I dislike the word. I detest it almost as much as the term 'indoctrination course,' which has lately become so popular in hurried mass education. It makes me feel like a tree surgeon who grafts extraneous seedlings upon servile and inferior trunks which—," and here he had turned to Webb with a humorous twinkle in his eyes, "—do not thereby become improved." Again he had chuckled. "Call me anything you like—a midwife, perhaps—since all I want is to bring out what is already in you. Or, at moments when you feel less kindly disposed toward me, when I have irritated and exasperated you, you may call me a gadfly—a scourge—anything but a teacher."

In spite of his facetious protestations, however, he was a true teacher, a magnificent teacher, a teacher in the classic tradition —to whom education was more than a profession, more even than a vocation; who was not content to instruct his students inside the classroom, but considered it also his duty to counsel them outside, to help them find themselves, to inspire and prod them, to discover their latent talents and direct them toward the hazy goals of their faintly stirring aspirations.

He even extended practical assistance to them, often introducing a deserving student to influential alumni who, having been previously helped by him, rarely refused his requests. He had offered, for instance, to give Webb letters of recommendation to some State Department officials he knew. And when Webb enthusiastically accepted, Professor Velliczek had written forthwith to Washington, announcing Webb's arrival—two years ahead of graduation.

And still, no matter how liberally he gave of his time and energy, he always seemed to feel that he had not done enough. He was consumed by the desire to bring out the best in them; he unrelentingly strove to awaken in them a sense of purpose, an awareness of a nobler mission in their lives, which would be enduring enough to withstand attack or diversion long after he would have ceased to watch over them, long after he could not protect them anymore, long after his impending retirement and death.

To what extent he had succeeded, Webb sensed at that moment when he realized that even now, after so many years, the dead teacher's influence could still make itself felt in him. In the sleet and mist ahead, he again saw the white-haired mentor's dim silhouette, half-turned away, half-watching him, awaiting his approach as if their ghostly appointment had been arranged a long time ago; as if Professor Velliczek had foreseen that, in spite of all warnings, Webb would some day rebel and swerve off; would deny that he had ever been called; and so would be forced, in the end, to ascend the deadly slopes of El Soledad.

"What a pity it is," Professor Velliczek told Webb that day in the park, "that we must make the most important decisions in our youth, when we're least qualified to make them. At no time do we need stronger convictions to guide us—at no time are we less competent to judge their merits."

Momentarily withdrawing into himself, the old teacher listened to the shuffling sound of their steps on the gravel, before shaking his head. "It is, of course, just as well," he chuckled, "that every new batch of young fighters refuses to believe the tales of the returning warriors. If you were to pay any attention to the warnings of those who've already suffered defeat, no battle would ever be fought, no progress even attempted." His wrinkled, mellow smile faded. "And yet—how much heartache would be avoided if we could only eliminate that damnable static of the inner ear, which prevents understanding between different stages of maturity, between old and young, parent and child, tutor and student—a static which scrambles the meaning of perfectly intelligible words until such time as we are ripe to comprehend what is said to us. Too bad, too, too damnably bad, that there should be so little communication between us; that we pass each other on different planes as it were, in full sight of one another, and yet unable to grasp what the other shouts."

He glanced at Webb; and when he saw no response in the young man's expression, he turned away, raising his hands in vague wonder and then dropping them helplessly. "Sometimes I ask myself," he mused, almost inaudibly, and yet with some sort of stirring emphasis, "what use is experience, if it can only teach us the error after the deed; if—in its deepest personal sense—

its lessons cannot be conveyed? What good, indeed, is wisdom, if it comes only to those too old to act?"

And Webb, walking with his head high, was obliged to slow down in order to remain in step with the much shorter, frail, angular man, who seemed so curiously bent forward at the waist —not like a reed broken, but rather like a bird perched and about to take to the air.

"Why do you consider it so necessary to impress upon us the possibility of defeat?" Webb inquired, puzzled rather than alarmed, unable to understand why Professor Velliczek—himself the most fearless and positive of men—should be so troubled by what he called their "brittle, brash, and unjustified confidence."

"Perhaps, you'd better ask," Professor Velliczek smiled, "what use can my warning be to you, when at your age you need reassurance more than discouragement?" He waved his pipe in that incomplete and indeterminate arabesque which always struck Webb as a symbolic shrug of the shoulders. "What use, indeed, when your youth and immaturity demand hopes more than common sense, promises of victory more than truth, more even than caution—since you must counteract, above all, the many uncertainties produced by your lack of experience?"

Whenever Professor Velliczek fell silent, Webb felt even more keenly the spellbinding powers of this extraordinary man. More often than not his students disagreed with his uncomprising and unorthodox reasoning, and yet, though he might sting, annoy or upset them, he never failed to interest, to stimulate, and even to captivate them; whether or not they liked to hear what he had to say, they could not help hanging on his words.

"You young Americans," Professor Velliczek continued in his lilting, melodious accent, "are an astonishing new breed. So sure of success in anything you tackle. Wonderful. I can't cease admiring you, while at the same time feeling concerned for you." He waved his pipe again, this time in a more definite motion, which reflected his increasing preoccupation. "Progeny of a giant land, you've been raised in the belief that all things are possible. Magnificent obsession on the part of an otherwise eminently realistic people—but since your ancestors have made the wildest dreams come true, they've earned the right to proclaim and uphold that splendid myth. And yet, though it has proved itself to be the most useful of all errors, it is also the one which contains, beside the basis for your greatness, the seed of your tragedy."

And Webb, untouched by doubt, aware of no error, tragic or useful, noticed that the old man's slumped shoulders had straightened up. Whenever a new thought surged through him, Professor Velliczek would become alerted in every nerve and sinew; his thin cheeks would then seem more translucent, his wrinkled, fallow face suddenly aflame.

"Remarkable new breed," the old man exclaimed after a while, "different and wonderful. You're such an extraordinary mixture of the practical and the visionary—half-idealists and half-realists. You're composed—one is almost tempted to say: glued together —of so fundamental an antithesis that the question arises how well you'll succeed in managing these irreconcilable and unmingling opposites. One may even ask whether you're viable at all. And one can't help but await the answer to this question with breathless suspense, since on the outcome of your inner conflicts depend not only your own fates, but, considering the growing power of this nation, the fortunes of most other peoples in the world."

He tapped out his pipe and stamped the ashes into the gravel, nodding to himself, as if to confirm his thought. "When you go abroad, my boy," he resumed, as they strolled past a star-shaped lawn, at the center of which a clumsy statue squatted stolidly, "you'll encounter a great many misconceptions about Americans. Which is, of course, hardly surprising," he snickered, "since you're often as baffling to yourselves as to others; since, in view of your innate contradictions, you frequently find it difficult—and sometimes impossible—to understand yourselves."

He hesitated, then added in a more serious vein: "The fact is that, contrary to your own opinion, you're actually a very complex people. Your open, frank manners, though absolutely sincere and heart-felt, are in effect misleading; in spite of your demonstrative simplicity and unaffected forthrightness you're not easily fathomed."

They were stopped at the bridle path when an amazon, riding past them, raised a cloud of dust which swiftly separated into sunblown pillars and then swirled quietly toward the gothic arches underneath the high-crowned trees. Professor Velliczek, blinking near-sightedly as they crossed the nave formed by the bridle path, had apparently seen neither the rider nor the dust and pursued his thought without interruption: "Half-dreamers and half-doers, you appear to some as unabashed materialists, and to others as naive charity-dispensers. But the fact is that you're neither—because you're both—you're both unmitigated utilitarians and uncorroded idealists. And what's more, you can't be one or the other, since you are, in truth, like the centaurs of old, a composite breed. Indeed, your contradictions are so irresolubly entwined in you that the resulting tensions either tear you apart, or drive you to erect the tremendous structures of your achievements—to raise and build the high, airy vaults of faith and concrete fulfillment."

As usual, Webb tried to resist the thrill which Professor Velliczek's enthusiasm always evoked in him. A sense of modesty, even shame, prevented him from being as whole-hearted and un-restrained in admiring his fellow citizens, as was Professor Velliczek. He would find fault and shortcomings where the foreign-born teacher saw none. He would feel the need to criticize his country, not from any sort of alienation or bitterness, but, on the contrary, to hold down pride, to preclude any unwarranted self-glorification in the community's achievements, past and present, in which—he was honest enough to admit—he had but an un-earned and indirect share.

And yet, as he listened to Professor Velliczek, he could not help seeing himself as an heir to noble traditions which had proved their worth on the hard anvils of history. He felt himself touched, clasped, embraced by whatever it was that tied and joined him to the millions of unknown and never-to-be-encountered people between the shores of the Atlantic and the Pacific. He tried to visualize all those unidentified men and women, but could not; and yet there stirred in him a sense of kinship with all those dreamers and seekers who had this in common with him that they shared the same borders and were alone under God; who moved about, settled, built homes; who worked, plowed, planted, loved, married, raised children; whose daily efforts pushed the life-blood through the veins of the land, whose unrecorded words and un-noticed deeds kept that good earth alive and the country's vast, rich, generous heart beating; and who, believing that they were pursuing their happiness, were actually pursuing the great unrealized and uncomprehended dream—their own, as well as that of their ancestors and children's children.

Fleetingly, then, he recalled how, as a little boy, he had vowed to protect all other children from darkness and fear, from injustice and lack of affection. He wondered whether this initial dedication, having grown and matured in him, had culminated in his present wish to join the civil service, to devote himself to the people for whom he felt responsible, to serve them in some capacity, to represent them abroad.

Professor Velliczek, he noticed, was watching him. The old scholar, apparently, had not just been discussing an abstract subject close to his heart. More likely, he was once again nurturing, purposefully furthering and nursing that sense of mission in Webb which, after first discovering it, he had since sought to strengthen and render invulnerable to future doubt and disillusionment.

"We were speaking of extremes," Professor Velliczek mused, as they approached the pond in the center of the park. "How will you handle them? The gift of compromise is really quite alien to your nature. As immoderate as the very size of your country, as uncontrollable as your intemperate climate, you would no more be capable of self-limitation than the dust storms sweeping across your western plains, the blizzards roaring down from the North, or the scorching heat in the South. You'd be as indifferent to any petty achievement as one of your great rivers to a drop of water. You think in large terms: and, once you have conceived an objective, no matter how Gargantuan, you'll drive toward it—until you're stopped."

He stood still, pointing his pipe at Webb. "Visionaries as well as realists—and extreme in either direction. The dreamer in you conceives great visions. And I would say to you—dream on. Dream your gigantic fancies until they've become reality. But don't let the realist in you demand that they come true overnight. Don't wake up, one dismal morning, and expect them to have materialized; and when you observe that they have not, don't rage against your splendid visions, for it is not they which have betrayed you—but your own impatience."

For a while, they walked on in silence, beneath trees laden with the golden browns and yellows of decaying leaves. Amidst the autumn's ripening dusk, they found a bench, which alone was still enshrined in a simmering patch of evening sun. And after they had sat down, Webb said: "I doubt that I'd ever let go of my dreams, much less rage against them."

"You might," Professor Velliczek said, groping distractedly for his tobacco pouch. "If you were only dreamers of great dreams, there'd be less danger. But you're also a pragmatic nation. You believe in results. You feel that any ideal which is worth believing in is also worth setting into practice. And if you can't bring to a successful conclusion whatever you've set out to do, you're apt to decide that the whole attempt was wrong, if not in basic intent, at least in planning or execution."

He broke off; he pondered; the intensity of thought pounded the blood through the veins in his temples; waves of energy, gathered up from nowhere, beat and lashed the sunken chest, the brittle frame, the hunched shoulders.

"Extreme also in that direction," he cried. "Absolutely admirable, the way you want accomplishment. You're impatient with delay; you want no excuses or explanations, you're not interested in philosophical theories why something can't be achieved. You are, in short, as vigorous in your will to accomplish—as you are in conceiving the grandeur of your blueprints!"

A falling, circling leaf touched his shoulder, before plummeting to his feet. For a moment, while it had rocked, floated, hung in the air, the present had seemed suspended, as if the future, for once straining to reverse its course, was about to escape from the past and take the dying leaf once again to its blue heights. But then, in a swift and mellifluous surrender, time proceeded to follow its ordained course.

"What would be the use of drawing blueprints," Webb asked, "if one didn't try to realize them?"

"What use indeed?" Professor Velliczek assented. "But in the gap between concept and fulfillment, there's the time of tension, the time of battle, of hope and despair; the times of the small victory and the large defeat. There's the brittle point in you, the juncture where extremes are joined, where you are apt to break."

In the distance, Webb saw a nurse arrogantly pushing a baby

carriage across the lawn; and whenever, in later years, he thought back of that golden autumn afternoon, he would always remember her starched whiteness, as she stiffly traversed the wondrous shafts of light pouring down the dark tree canyons.

He would also recall how close he had felt to Professor Velliczek at that moment, closer than ever before, pitying the small, wiry, fiercely independent old man, pitying his wisdom and his doubts and his relentless questioning of everything that others might take for granted. For to Webb, at that moment, there had been no need for either wisdom or inquiry, since truth had stood before his young soul, had bared itself in a way that Professor Velliczek could no longer comprehend, had shown him the body of victory in the distance, the firm promise of fulfillment above the smoke of battle, above the time of conflict, of hope and despair.

Never again could Webb have been so impervious to Professor Velliczek's premonitions as at that instant when he stood at the outer edge of the springboard to the future and saw an elusive vision of something enduring and fine and inevitably triumphant, a composite view which could not conglomerate in Professor Velliczek's heart—no matter how ardently he loved and praised that brave new world he had discovered only in his adult years. For the gigantic fresco projecting itself before Webb was actually a mosaic composed of countless minute impressions: of a camp fire in Montana, of a train thundering over the great divide, a little boy wading in the Gulf of Mexico; of stories told on the steps to the village store, of the shouts in the bleachers and the bridge game in the country club, of the voices and sounds and murmurs on all the main streets, the pungent smells in the stock yards, the flashing lights on Times Square, the splintered and fused and indestructible strength of what Professor Velliczek described at that moment as—"the will to realize the oldest dreams of mankind, on the part of a nation of pragmatic idealists."

Webb sat up; there was something incongruous in the juxtaposition of the words: pragmatic and idealist, which had struck his sensibilities like a slight electric shock. "Are you aware," he asked, "that a pragmatic idealist might be considered a contradiction in terms?"

"Indeed, I am," Professor Velliczek exclaimed. "That is why I have chosen it. How else could I circumscribe a contradiction in life? And between these two words, can you hear the flash and cry of conflict? The crashing cymbals? The crackling of tension? Just listen, and you will hear the secret turmoil and travail of men predestined, forced by inheritance and tradition to make their dreams come true. Listen carefully, and you'll know that you've reached the battlefield, the great arena where the extraordinary drama of this country unfolds."

He paused, but only briefly, and then continued, more rapidly now, sweepingly, almost elatedly: "If one had to sum up your special mission, your characteristic role in history, one could not avoid seeing you as pragmatic idealists. For in this respect you are different—different from other idealists in the past who conceived utopia but could not work toward it—different from other pragmatists who merely sought to solidify their own position under existing conditions. To most other people, the ideal has always been a direction rather than a goal that can actually be reached. But to you, whether you consider felling a tree, plowing a straight furrow, moving a mountain, or abolishing strife among men—it is invariably a concrete and immediate objective."

The billowing dusk rustled its satin shadow beneath the trees. Leaning back, Professor Velliczek scanned the blurred distance. "You must succeed in anything you undertake, or feel defeated," he pondered, speaking quietly, as though to himself. "But who is to say that you cannot succeed? That utopia is forever out of reach? Who is to predict how long and impassable is the road to an ideal, to a dream come true?"

They kept battling windmills—and they felt increasingly bewildered by their defeats. They did not understand their setbacks, at home or abroad—in the voting booths on main street, or in the council chambers of the League of Nations.

Rebuff after rebuff kept them permanently off balance. They began living in a constant state of disappointment, in a creeping sort of consternation. Success in making the world a better place was so slow in coming, if at all, that it appeared non-existent. They had been prepared to battle corruption and injustice, but they did not know how to deal with the sluggish inertia which blocked, even more effectively than any active antagonism, their drive for reform and innovation.

Theory, so invincible in the abstract, broke down in the realm of personal experience. It broke down at the end of Hudson Street, in front of the shoeshine stand, where for months they had tried to educate the pock-marked Czech—who polished their shoes most expertly, but refused to become enlightened in local politics. He called them "a bunch of smart-alecks too young to know anything about life." And he continued to vote regularly for the candidate who had the gangster support, and then, a week later, resumed paying off the racketeers without ever connecting the two phenomena in his obstinate mind.

"Beats me, how a guy can be so stupid," Harry McKenzie snorted when, on a drizzly morning, they had left the shoeshine stand.

"It's guys like him who make you want to give up," Clem had said, with a half-hearted chuckle that withered quickly in the silence of the others.

And Buster Griswold, who later became a phenomenally successful salesman, had tried to disperse their discomfort with a joke. "If you ask me, the old nut is right. Fact is," he had grinned, waving at a pretty girl in a dress store, "we don't know enough about life." He was fat and clownish-looking and convinced that no woman would ever love him. That afternoon he had been particularly moody, because he had lost out on a business commission. But since he always promoted something, spending much of his time between classes on the telephone, they had not taken his loss too seriously—except Eddie Fless, who related everyone's setback to himself, as if to confirm his constant apprehension that he would never amount to anything.

"Sure is a tough world," Eddie had said. "You sit in your room and try to make sense out of things, and it all seems so easy. But then you go outside—and you just can't figure out people."

And Webb flaring up: "What's the matter with you guys? You run into a single old fool, and you're ready to throw in the towel. As if the whole world stopped at Hudson Street!"

The world did not end at Hudson Street. It was enormous, as vast as the unexplored promise of all young beliefs; and in its remote spaces the hopes that had been shipwrecked nearby could still set sail. In indistinct terms such as mankind, the people, the human spirit, one could still forget the imperfections of one's friends, one's own shortcomings, all the frustrations daily encountered.

Escape, evasion, at first a constant necessity, soon turned into a mode of thought. Trapped in one impasse after another, they withdrew from reality, imperceptibly, wherever its immalleable evidence clashed with their preconceived notions. And by degrees, what had once been spontaneous dedication became a flight into idealism.

By removing one's convictions from the battle zone of practical experience, they found, one did not yet have to surrender them. And thus it was possible to postpone the confession of one's disillusionment—if only at the price of an ultimately more destructive collapse.

More and more frequently, they would avoid passing the shoeshine stand, sometimes stopping at the drugstore for coffee, and sometimes crossing to the other side of the street. They did not know why the pugnacious Czech made them uncomfortable; they still waved to him, they still mocked him, but now only from a distance.

Withdrawal from reality, however, though gaining them time, provided no solution to their fundamental dilemma. On the contrary, their tensions increased. For the rift between actuality and the abstract, once it had been initiated, kept spreading inexorably.

The higher their aims, the more sordid, even loathsome reality appeared by comparison; it soon fell so far below Webb's wishful thinking that life, in its undisguised wretchedness, looked ugly, dismal—repugnant to the point where he felt he either had to adjust his thinking to mud and filth, as most of his more sensitive contemporaries seemed to be striving to do; or else to escape still further into an isolation from which he could look back, with embittered contempt, upon the wastelands that fell so far short of all potential and imagined beauty.

That summer—the last before his graduation—Webb worked on a farm in Vermont, helping out a distant cousin of his mother. For three glorious months, there was a moratorium on his inner conflicts. All the quandaries of the city were forgotten in the labors of his sunburnt body, in the care devoted to tenacious, hard, but ultimately responsive fields; in the chopping of firewood at sunrise when the dawn painted the hills in somnolescent pastels and the dew glittered on evanescent trees embedded in meadows still gray and faintly steaming.

Twice, during that untroubled, robust, splendid vacation, Esther came up for weekend visits. They walked through the woods and bathed their feet in cold brooks and tried to fish and caught nothing. They made friends among the staid farmers, in spite of raised eyebrows at their uncontrollable exuberance; they were invited to hot cakes and maple syrup, and, late on both Sundays, Webb would drive Esther to White River Junction where she took the midnight train back to Philadelphia.

Then the summer had burned itself out. And Webb, back in the city, walked the same dusty pavements, among people who still scurried about with the same preoccupied, crafty, or care-worn frowns; who had never left their daily chores and worries, and thus could not even fall back on remembering the cool whispers of a silvery Vermont birch spreading its arms on a hill top.

Nothing had changed in Webb's environment; within a week, he was again enmeshed in the unsolved problems from which he had temporarily escaped. And yet, in the months that followed, he noticed a subtle transformation, a shy embarrassment, even some sort of estrangement, not only in himself but also among his friends.

It was their last semester. They had to prepare themselves for the practical exigencies of life. Reading the unemployment statistics no longer evoked compassion as much as the apprehension that their fine sentiments would be in the way, would obstruct or impede their advancement.

Experimenting with various attitudes and poses, they sought some sort of inner transition which would not leave them open to a charge of either betrayal or surrender. Without quite admitting to each other what they were about, they tried to adapt their convictions to the altered circumstances rather than relegating them precipitously to that attic in their minds where much useless learning and many outgrown ambitions were soon to be stored.

One or two of Webb's friends—who had been, in fact, the most outspoken—were also the first to glide away on felt slippers. But for most of the others, he noticed, the breaking-away process proved to be more difficult than might have been anticipated. They rubbed and scratched on their high principles like on old sores, but could not tear them off without ripping their skin. They hacked at their inhibiting compunctions, but could not scuttle decency; their exertions, in fact, only served to drain energy and to twist and warp their attitudes to a point where it became difficult to preserve or regain some sort of equilibrium.

With the struggle for survival looming ever larger outside the university portals, adjustment became urgent. They would break unless they learned to bend, to side-step, evade or resist. Anguished, Webb started to observe older men of goodwill, hoping to learn how they had met the same challenge. And thus he became alerted to those who stressed their bitterness in order to demonstrate that they were victims and not traitors to their beliefs; to those who had become more concerned with angry denunciations than with solutions to the ills they had once sought to cure; to those who derived a morbid satisfaction in citing instances of injustice, maltreatment, oppression—without any true sympathy, however, registering less compassion in describing sufferance than Webb felt in hearing about it; and finally to those who affected the superior sneer, originally worn like an easily identifiable mask over a supposedly bleeding heart—but imperceptibly hardening until the mask had become the actual face.

Even Professor Velliczek, Webb came to suspect, had once been a follower of the same blue banners in his youth, and was now a dreamer broken over the wheel of many disappointments. During the summer which Webb had spent in Vermont, Professor Velliczek had passed through a tragic period; his wife's youngest brother had been murdered in a concentration camp. He never spoke of it; he did not permit his personal loss to influence his views. And yet, one day when he lectured to the class on the progressive collapse of international law, there were, in his very animation, hints of an aching need to defend, against a cruel inner questioning, his beliefs in man's high destiny.

And among his students, more urgently than in himself, he battled with redoubled efforts the inroads of despair. He was well aware of their intellectual and emotional predicament; he strove to encourage them at every opportunity. "The breakdown of American idealism, if it should come to pass," he told the class that winter, "may well reveal itself, at some future date, to have been the crucial fact of our century. In the tremendous moral crises which have begun to endanger the very existence of the civilized world, this idealism will be as desperately needed in guiding the nation as was the overriding faith of the Founding Fathers in framing the Constitution, not only for this country's lasting benefit, but for the good of all mankind."

By emphasizing their role in contemporary history, he had hoped to inspire and strengthen them. But the cracks and fissures were already running so deep in most of them that his words struck them as reproach rather than encouragement. And, in any event, his gentle voice was beginning to sound curiously insignificant in the martial blare, the insane barking of dictators, the chaotic and delirious shouting in most parts of the tormented globe.

Even Webb, during that winter, sporadically withdrew from Professor Velliczek. He would start out, some evenings, in the direction of Professor Velliczek's home, but, somewhere along the way, he would veer off.

Or he would watch the impressive sage traverse the campus with quick, short, well-measured steps, the white hair bristling in all directions, the myopic glance fixed to the pavement or passing directly over him, without recognition, though sometimes at a distance of only a few feet.

But even then Webb would make no move to step forward; he would merely stand there, watching the old man pad away, wondering why the sunken, withered frame seemed so curiously unbroken though it was bent forward, at an odd angle, from the waist up.

And when, by chance, they finally met again, in the nearly deserted library, Professor Velliczek gave no indication that he felt hurt or even puzzled by Webb's protracted avoidance; he asked no questions—as if, indeed, he had understood and there were no need to explain.

Flustered, Webb sat down at the table where the tireless old scholar had been researching some obscure aspects of medieval philosophy. He was about to stammer some excuse, when Professor Velliczek interrupted, raising his hand. "In a time of defeat," he smiled, quoting from one of the Latin texts before him, "the beaten avoid their own shadows."

It was a sweltering evening. By the time Harry McKenzie and Tom Sears had joined them, the air in the library was so stifling that breathing became a chore. But once Professor Velliczek had started to tell them about some of the fascinating passages he had discovered in the medieval tomes on the table, they could not think of leaving. Involving them at once in the search of his ever inquisitive mind, he discussed with them such difficult theological concepts as original sin, the fall from grace, the whole question of man's inability to redeem himself without God's consent. And to their surprise it became apparent that their sharply rational teacher was willing to concede to these ancient doctrines as great a truth as to any modern interpretation of world conflict and economic struggle.

"But I don't see the logic," Tom Sears sputtered, for once too perplexed even to suspect propaganda. "How could these medieval preachers demand that people should redeem themselves by their own efforts, when they taught simultaneously that men could only be helped by God?"

And Professor Velliczek, evidently prepared for a question he had raised himself many times, reviewed for them some of the answers given by the various Church fathers.

Now and then his eyes would rest on Webb, whose mind had started to wander, drifting back to that day when Professor Velliczek had first spoken of the godless generation which had slain the lord of the mansion. Somewhere, he felt, a circle had been closed—a circle running from the proclamation of the great void in the sky, to the young generation rushing to assume responsibility for a fatherless world, fighting valiantly, but finding itself inexplicably thwarted. And now, as the circle had curved back to its starting point, there emerged with all the terror and judging stare of a bleeding head, the question whether men could indeed be saved, except by the consent of the God each man had helped to slay in his life-time.

"Assuming those theologians were perfectly logical," Harry McKenzie exploded, "you still couldn't transfer their philosophical systems to our time. Their premises just wouldn't make sense to us."

And Professor Velliczek, amused by their sense of superiority, proceeded to draw for them a whole set of parallels from the medieval dilemma to their own impasse. In the course of a dazzling display of wit, insight, and keen observation, he made them see that their need to motivate a continuation of their ethical endeavors in the face of mundane failure was as great as that which had plagued medieval man.

"Even greater," he concluded, "even more do you need the spiritual answer."

And Harry McKenzie, frowning suspiciously: "Why more?"

"Because, from the outset, you've been more certain of success. You're so convinced that all things can be 'fixed up'—if I may use your expression—you seem unable even to conceive that anything you tackle might not be accomplished." His glance wandered along the high shelves in the library, pausing at a hollow-eyed bust of Aristotle. "Historically, since this nation has never been vanquished, you know only one outcome—success. You've been bred and raised, one might say, in unquestioned expectation of victory. And, accordingly, you're well prepared to win; in victory, you're both magnanimous and modest." He waited, until a truck had thundered past the open window. "But how will you be able to take defeat? That is what I often ask myself. How will you stand up under prolonged failure?" He listened to the fading rumble of the truck, almost studiously avoiding a glance at Webb: "It troubles me more than I can say."

And Tom Sears, grinning confidently: "I suppose, if we'd ever have to, we'd learn as fast as anybody else."

And Professor Velliczek, shaking his head: "Not necessarily. You're inexperienced in failure—you might break. You've no background in retreat, no prepared positions to withdraw to, no technique for a wise and mellow acquiescence. You can't be skeptics—only believers or cynics; you're either outgoing and trusting; or embittered and angry. In one way, of course, this is understandable; it is the price you pay for that admirable vitality and energy of yours which never permits the majority to sit still on a fence; but such decisiveness must also be wearing and hard on you. Very hard."

Passing not far from their window, a newsboy yelled his grim headlines so gleefully that only part of what he screamed could be understood. His raucous shouts revealed something about a jealousy slaying, a bus crash with a score of critically wounded, and then the usual headline about a stern note sent by one remote, militaristic government to another, giving notice to the world that another diplomatic crisis was in the making. The folly of the blustering threat irritated Webb; he wondered whether he should seize this opportunity to tell Professor Velliczek that he was no longer sure he really wanted a diplomatic career.

"Love nest discovered! Read all about it!" the newsboy yelled; and then, without transition, he screamed something more or less incomprehensible about atrocities in a concentration camp. Webb noticed that Professor Velliczek's skin was drained of color, looked less translucent, more wrinkled, older; his personal loss, apparently, was still too recent to allow him the detachment he strove so hard to attain. And rather than adding to his burden, Webb postponed telling him that he might not apply for the civil service position already promised to him in Washington on the basis of Professor Velliczek's recommendation.

Professor Velliczek, closing the thick volume that had been lying on the world atlas, absently traced the outline of the western hemisphere engraved on the cover. "How fortunate you are," he whispered, "living in this blessed rectangle. How very fortunate that you've never had to acquire any philosophy of defeat—even if it does leave you less well prepared in any serious crisis."

And Webb, almost defiantly: "Can anyone be prepared for defeat? Were you ever, Professor?"

"Perhaps." The old teacher's thick bi-focals sparkled in Webb's direction. "You see, it was quite different for us in Europe. From earliest childhood, we absorbed through every pore a kind of long-range resignation, which hindered us in many respects, and in others came us in good stead. Quite, quite different. When one is born in the shadows of old fortresses, as I was, and grows up in the sight of cannons aimed down from their dark towers; when one's earliest memories are of underground jails and torture chambers and all the other implements of tyranny and suppression, one is not apt to forget that both persecution and man's aspirations outlive the day's evil. One is, in short, far better conditioned for a melancholy stalemate with evil."

And Harry McKenzie, lowering his bulky forehead like a bull

charging to attack: "Are you suggesting that we resign ourselves?"

"On the contrary. I wish I could teach you to hold out beyond defeat—beyond even the burial of hope. I wish I could impress on you that the national pragmatism, which has been so wonderfully useful in building up a continent, can—under certain conditions—turn against you. Instead of supporting you in adversity, the deep-seated optimism of the fixer and pioneer may actually render you more vulnerable to despair. And unless you can learn, in time, to unclutch, to let go of the fallacy that not only work but all beliefs must be submitted to the test of success or failure, there's no telling how far you'll recoil, nor to what extent you'll reverse yourselves."

His eyes, almost blank behind his scintillating glasses, were so myopic as to be nearly useless; but they also had a visionary quality, an inner sight which inspired awe and frequently the disturbing impression of standing before a blind prophet who saw not only one's present contours, but all one's future shapes standing behind one in a long row, awaiting their turn to emerge into the present.

"I wish I could teach you to forget about results," he continued, "and to learn, instead, that there's a moral opposite to the pragmatic absolute—the good deed sufficient unto itself."

The peculiar silence of a large library sang around them, while each of the four, preoccupied with the same insoluble problem presented by the moral imperative, sought his solution in a different direction. And before them, piled high on the table, the worn books contained the innumerable, tortuous constructions of the medieval thinkers seeking to justify their powerful faith in spite of pestilence, pilfering, drought; in spite of political disaster and perpetual wars.

"Perhaps, we are wrong to expect either victory or an end in the battle against windmills," Professor Velliczek said. "Perhaps, we must recognize that there's a link between the windmill and the cross, a deeper connection than our enlightened grandparents could have foreseen. For, in retrospect, it would appear that the windmill became to the free-thinking idealist what the cross is to the faithful believer. Both are symbols—interchangeable—for the identical thing." He paused, before adding almost hesitantly:

"In either case, the sacrifice demanded of us has remained the same."

A sudden chill made Webb look up. There had been a considerable drop in temperature; cold air came flowing from the glacier in a strong down-draught. When the wind briefly parted the mist, the gleaming ice flashed up in the distance, suspended for an instant like congealed lightning in the clouds. Then the feathery humidity closed around him, pressing him back into that harrowing solitude where he found himself locked in with his memories, a shadowy prisoner of regret, stumbling along labyrinths of missed opportunities, of errors and insights gained too late.

The higher he climbed, the deeper he seemed to sink into himself. Drawn unpredictably along tortuous channels, his memories followed no orderly sequence in time. 'Before' and 'after' would appear reversed—inexplicably so—until he discovered that he was not moving levelly across the past, but vertically from the surface to the depth of his being. Round and round as in a vortex, always lower, always faster, whirled helplessly along an unerring course, he tumbled toward that area of the vital break in him—

Again, the mist had lifted, this time almost straight ahead, only slightly to the left. And there, unexpectedly, the frightful wall which they had avoided when they chose the right fork of the trail, swam out of the clouds—gray and nebulous, trailing little flags of smoke like a burning ship on some monstrous ocean, afloat on steaming space without rudder or hope; and then faded again, gliding majestically into onrushing veils of the overcast, to vanish there in all its awe-inspiring grandeur.

Webb's breath broke from his lungs in short gasps. The path, contrary to all expectations, had led them back, in a wide circle, toward that atrocious chasm. It was, of course, inconceivable that their trail would come to a dead end at the edge of that impassable wall. At some point, it would have to swing away again; and, indeed, when he looked up, he saw that the Padre, struggling upward through the swirling clouds, had already started to swerve off, moving again toward the right.

Still, the threat had remained, somewhere behind the screening vapors. Webb scanned the clouds, but soon lost all sense of direction in their unceasing, turbulent shifts. He imagined himself suddenly stepping out on that sheer wall, thousands of feet over the abyss—and then, abruptly, he would hear the scream which always haunted his recurring nightmare—Cliff Williams' scream as he was swept down from the ledge, the scream piercing the avalanche's black thunder while they stood on the rim in a paralyzed semi-circle—

Sweat, in thin hot rivulets, scorched Webb's skin, as it always did when he awoke from the nightmare. They had not budged, while the tremendous sheet of snow cracked slowly, dipping Cliff Williams downward in a sluggish and almost astonished motion. They had not rushed to his aid, not one of the young apostles—not even Webb, who had been Cliff Williams' closest friend. They had watched him fall, roll, tumble downward, his body reduced to a limp ball of clothes, at times emerging from the infuriated mass of snow, bobbing up and down with flailing arms and legs, but soon buried again. They had listened to his scream and had not followed him, not even after his cries became muffled while he slithered to a halt at the bottom, and the snow filled up the dale around him, covering his wrenched body until only a brown sleeve and a gloved hand were to be seen. They had not followed him—not even after his last piercing outcry had been entombed in the white, powdery stillness of the quiet valley, and the perturbed mountains gradually sank back to a mute and icy rest....

During the long train ride back to Philadelphia, Esther had done her best to console Webb. Twice, from different stations, they had phoned to the Canadian hospital to which Cliff Williams had been taken. And when they learned that his leg would have to be amputated, something froze inside of Webb. Back in the train's cold, drafty compartment, he talked incessantly, like one who would not give silence a chance to make itself heard. Again and again he would speak of the accident; and yet, he could not clearly express to Esther the hectic, dim, shapeless sensations that had flashed through his mind during that fatal moment of indecision on top of the rim; he could not even admit them to himself. His entire outlook, before and after, had demanded the heroic sacrifice, the fearless extreme of unselfish conduct. But when put to the test at a critical juncture, neither he nor any of his friends had been able to live up to the ideal conduct they demanded of others, nor to the noble spirit they had taken for granted in themselves.

The hidden knowledge of a personal inadequacy was too intolerable to be confessed; it had to be anesthetized in some form. Unobtrusively, in the weeks that followed, the whole context of his views began arranging itself along changed patterns. To stand alone while admitting one's shortcomings, to bare one's secret deficiencies before others believed to be more perfect, would have been tantamount to condemning oneself as an individual in the presence of a superior group. It was far less painful to condemn all mankind instead—to take a dim view of the whole human race. And so it was hardly surprising that he instinctively chose to embrace a misanthropic pessimism—the only alternative offered to those who would otherwise have to despair in themselves, because their expectations had been unnaturally high in the first place.

Paradoxically, by a mere reversal of axioms, he could right his disrupted equilibrium. By turning his idealistic view of humanity upside down, he was able to raise his depressed self-evaluation. For if people were not as good as he had assumed, but basically rotten, driven by ruthless and predatory instincts, he could regain for himself some measure of self-respect.

In the course of time, this inner need to see the worst in others, to tear down, to uncover the despicable motive and to reduce the noble gesture to a show of hypocrisy, invaded all his beliefs. However, since it was neither an easy nor a swiftly accomplished task to revamp so many firmly held convictions, the transformation progressed only by imperceptible degrees, and was, in fact, not completed until many years had passed.

About two months after the accident, Cliff Williams returned to Philadelphia. But Webb could not bring himself to look him up at once. For a whole week he worked hard ringing doorbells to campaign for the new school proposed by the parent-teachers association in a crowded neighborhood. And when Eddie Fless dropped by his room one evening, ostensibly to return a fishing rod, but actually to talk about Joan, his girl, Webb handed him the petition at once. "I wish you'd sign, Eddie," he urged. "It's important."

And Eddie, signing without even glancing at the petition:

"Sure, Don." He signed anything, embraced every cause they suggested, donated and volunteered, always in the hope that by making the world a better place to live in, he himself would have it easier later on, would perhaps even manage to survive. His parents had once been prosperous, but had lost everything; and not only had they failed to get over it, but they had perpetuated the shock in their son. Needing help, he was offering help. He was as dedicated as any of the others in the group. But no cause he supported appeared to be strengthened by him; for he always seemed to make the others aware that it was he who needed support.

"Bad breaks sure always come in pairs," Eddie said, while Webb blotted the signature. And Webb: "What's the trouble?" And Eddie, looking quite pallid in front of the window, fingered the drapes nervously: "Sure couldn't have picked a worse time to lose my job at the gas station." And Webb, knowing what a hard time Eddie had working his way through college: "How much do you need to tide you over?" And Eddie, his small, sloping shoulders silhouetted by the garish neon sign over Clark's Tavern: "Don't need anything for myself. I'll get along. For a while, at least. What really hurts—is about Joan."

And Webb, looking up, startled: "What happened?" He had always liked Joan; she was not pretty, but sweet-tempered, light-hearted and generous. And Eddie, turning his thin, undernourished, agile little face, looking at him with that swift, shrewd, pathetic glint in the sad eyes: "That uncle who's been helping her out, passed away. Now she's got nobody. She'll have to quit college— unless—unless we find some way to pull her through."

And Webb, folding the petition, his hands trembling a little: "How, Eddie? How can we pull her through?" And avoiding Eddie's glance, he tried hard not to think of Joan, but of millions like her in the same predicament. He attempted to tell himself that with petitions such as the one he had just folded they would some day obtain laws providing aid for all hardship cases like Joan's, preventing the heartaches and hurts that were about to hit Eddie and his girl without any fault of their own. And then he turned away, swamped by the futility of all they were doing; but Eddie's haunted eyes sought him out, and all Webb could say was: "How can we help her, Eddie? How?"

And Eddie, picking up the fishing rod, spinning and twisting it between his thin fingers: "I don't know, Don. Honestly, I don't. I thought, maybe, since we always get up some collection or another, maybe the fellows could—"

The mountain gleamed up as the clouds split open, briefly unveiling the jagged peak behind the gaping, merciless abyss. There was a soft, dusky light on that vast snow field beneath El Soledad's crown, which the procession of thirteenth apostles had previously traversed, pulling the sled on which rested Cliff Williams' broken body. And though the silent phantoms had since vanished, there still seemed to linger, among the spires toward which they had moved, a waiting—not only Cliff Williams' and Eddie's waiting, but the waiting of everything that had ever waited for help which failed.

Quickly looking down on the trail, Webb remembered how Eddie had awaited his answer in his room, the pinched face a pasty gray against the neon light behind the window. "I wish I could hold out some hope, Eddie," Webb had said. "Of course, I'll take it up with the fellows, but I'm afraid there's not much chance." And when those swift, shifty, sad eyes had kept staring at him with that inarticulate confidence which has tried and cannot conceive disaster, he had added: "You know yourself how much more it takes to put a person through college—than to contribute a few dimes to one cause or another."

As he had expected, they had found no way to help her. A month later, Joan had left college. And some fifteen years thereafter, when Webb accidentally met Eddie at the Chicago airport, he first learned about Joan marrying a man much older—

"She didn't wait long," Eddie told him between flights, straining his voice to compete with the roar of a four-motored plane. "She couldn't afford to."

And all Webb could think of saying while they passed the ticket counter was a polite expression of sympathy: "I'm sorry, Eddie."

And Eddie, the swift, shrewd glint in his eyes now a hard glitter, smoothed the handkerchief in his stiffly padded jacket which concealed so well his sloping, defenseless shoulders. "Not your fault, Don. I guess you guys meant well. Even if you did have a lot of cockeyed ideas about people and things."

The impersonal, metallic voice of the public address system interrupted him with a departure announcement.

"Gotta catch the plane to Kansas," Eddie grinned, shifting his thick, expensively embossed briefcase. "So long, Don. And don't get me wrong. Best thing ever happened to me was listening to you guys bellyaching about all the things that are wrong in this world. Sure was the most useful education I ever got. That is, once I had sense enough to switch from trying to correct those injustices—to taking advantage of them."

He winked his eyes, waved, and was gone. Another two years, and someone sent Webb the small item in the newspaper about Eddie Fless having been convicted of fraud, and sent to jail.

The wind, in merciless frontal attacks, flung its compacted iciness at Webb, scouring his skin to a bleeding rawness. Whenever he tried to shield his face with frozen hands, he would recall Eddie's sad, haunted eyes; and their accusing glint was as hard to endure as the stinging gale.

Fighting his way upward, he thought of the day when he had received the clipping with the news of Eddie's imprisonment, some seventeen years after graduation; and he could not help comparing Eddie's debacle to his own successful career which, by then, had led him to a high point in his rise from the genteel poverty and anonymity of his family background.

Reading the newspaper item over and over, first in his office at the Barcelona consulate, later in a swank restaurant, and then at home, Webb had felt both upset and peculiarly irritated by Eddie's misfortune. The disclosure of his schoolmate's embezzlement had spoiled what had otherwise promised to be a most enjoyable evening, with dinner at the club and then a musical soiree at the house of the Countess de Neira. Phoning her, he excused himself, pretending fatigue. And he actually intended to retire early, but found that he could not dismiss Eddie from his mind.

Pacing in his luxuriously appointed study, as his former friend might have been pacing behind bars, Webb first tried to regard Eddie's crime with the proper indignation, and then with some sort of perfunctory compassion. But as time went by, and he could not dispose of Eddie's reproachful stare, he came to feel as if he were being led from the judge's bench to the witness stand and thence to the chair of the accused—where he was unaccountably convicted together with Eddie, and sentenced to an even longer term.

He could not fathom the cause of this morbid sensation. Looking back from a secure and high position upon his troubled youth, he felt more than justified in having freed himself of their college aspirations, their bankrupt illusions and romantic altruism.

Indeed, he had every reason to be satisfied with his subsequent course. Well-liked by his superiors in the State Department, careful not to step on anyone's toes, financially secure in consequence of savings judiciously invested for him by Tom Sears—now a top investment counselor in New York—Webb was convinced that he had reached a most enviable place in life. And in spite of Eddie's sarcastic stare, he could not see where he had failed his friend, nor anyone else—and, most certainly, not himself.

Mixing himself a drink, he acknowledged—with that pitying condescension he had lately assumed toward his fervent years—how much more life had to offer than he had realized in the tormented enthusiasm of his youth. And he refused to defend himself against Eddie Fless, a fraud, a petty thief, who had broken into his home like an uninvited beggar forcing entry to a feast, and now stood on the polished marble floor, reminding him that they had once been partners in that vast and reputable enterprise known as the brotherhood of men.

The bells rang on the belfry of a distant cathedral. Their sonorous tolling reminded Webb of his unpleasant afternoon at the consulate, when the refugee woman, whose visa he had been obliged to deny, had burst into hysterical tears. Such painful, distastefully emotional scenes had become more and more frequent, while an unrooted humanity, swelling from a trickle to a flood, stormed the consulates, seeking shelter from persecution. He would have liked to help that unfortunate woman, the widow of a physician who had fought in the Belgian underground; but he could not; and she had refused to understand why he was unable to circumvent regulations. Nothing, apparently, was more difficult for despair than to be reasonable.

If his career had led him to the ambassadorial level, or to any high diplomatic post, perhaps he could have done more for these innocent victims of tyranny. As it was, however, he had remained far too unimportant a cog in the big machinery to fulfill any of the high expectations Professor Velliczek had once harbored for him. And so it hardly mattered that he had turned his back on their utopian dreams.

The drink cooled his hand, as he sat in his comfortable arm chair, reviewing the spiritual legacy which Professor Velliczek had bequeathed to the young apostles from Hudson Street—on that unforgettable afternoon at his home, when he had unexpectedly announced his retirement. At the end of an impromptu and moving farewell, their ailing teacher had told them that the future would surpass even their highest hopes. "For the fact is that we can no longer prevent utopia," he had predicted. "It is coming upon us—not only with absolute certainty—but more rapidly than we dare to expect."

The young disciples had drawn closer, surprised by so unequivocal a prophecy. Sensing that Professor Velliczek had overcome the last of the many doubts with which he had struggled so long and so arduously, Webb had turned to Esther. But she had failed to notice his startled glance, her eyes being fixed, with rapt attention, on the old man's almost luminous face.

"To predict utopia while the world is at the brink of war and total chaos," Professor Velliczek had continued, brushing the embers from his pipe into an ash tray, "must sound to you like folly. Nowadays, indeed, no one in his right mind seems to take the notion seriously; it has become the fashion to refer to utopia only in jest, if one refers to it at all. And yet, my young friends," he had exclaimed, stabbing his pipe in a staccato rhythm along their circle, "the joke is on us—on all of us who have resigned ourselves to consider it a hope too absurd to be pursued, a visionary's hobby, a toy for idle minds. For it is precisely our realistic era, so preoccupied with exploring personal and international immorality to its absolute limits, which demands utopia as its most urgent and immediate objective."

His impish smile had flashed briefly across his withered features. Tim Hansen, whose phlegmatic bearing did not as yet indicate that he would some day be honored, posthumously, for extraordinary bravery in the battle of Guadalcanal, had wrinkled his freckled nose irreverently. And while they suppressed the laughter that rippled along their attentive faces, Professor Velliczek had continued: "Just as war and everything else is becoming more total, so also develops the need for utopia in a more absolute form. We're heading toward a future which will enforce idealism without compromise. And, paradoxically, the most hard-headed realists may well be the first ones to recognize that nothing much short of utopia will be adequate to meet the requirements of our altered circumstances."

His head slightly tilted, as if he were listening to an inner voice, he had added: "Something new has arisen under the sun—something the great preacher in Ecclesiastes could not have anticipated. Born in a static epoch, in which change was almost non-existent, he could only foresee an endless continuation of man's evil. But we, my young friends, are living in a dynamic period, in which direction becomes ever more decisive, as in all motion. And since our speed continues to accelerate, the ethical polarity, the opposite directions of good and evil, are bound to play an ever more important and concrete part in our lives, until, in the end, the utopian dream—"

The bells rang out. Webb came to with a start. For a few moments, the rememberance of that afternoon was still so vivid that a glow of youth and fervent dedication seemed to linger on in his somber study.

He buried his face in his hands, as though to blot out the vision of the young apostles' rapt faces, etched sharply and lastingly into the sleepless night, their eyes as clear, affirmative, and vital as they had appeared to him on that memorable afternoon. And though he still tried to regard his lost enthusiasm with that gentle irony he had so long affected, he suddenly found himself yearning for it.

He felt as if the merciful blanket of resignation with which, in the course of the intervening years, he had learned to cover his impoverished soul, had been lifted abruptly. In a chilling self-appraisal, he admitted to himself that his polished worldliness was a poor substitute for fervor and dedication in any worthy cause. And, for the first time, he questioned whether life had already passed him by—before he had even noticed that he was no longer part of that main energy stream with which the human experiment renewed itself from generation to generation; whether his attitudes, altruistic or skeptical, were no longer important to anyone except himself; whether he—as an individual—though by no means fully matured, was already the fruit dropped off, the branch wilting, the driftwood still swirling with the current, but without directed motion of its own, and gradually swept toward the stagnant pools at the side....

He got up, drawing the silk dressing gown closer to his chest. The task of building a better world was now in younger hands. He had done his share; he had battled; he had been forced down. Others would step into the breach; others would continue the good fight....

But what was to become of the wounded? No one seemed to have any answer for it, not even Professor Velliczek. How were they to live on? What solace was there for the broken idealist? What future was there for the disenchanted dreamer to whom even the refuge of cynicism was refused?

When he passed the open door to his bedroom, he thought of Esther, visualizing how she used to sleep, all curled up, with her cheek nestled in her elbow. The longing tore at his heart, and he quickly moved on to the dressing room. Taking off his tie, he remembered that he had promised to take the Countess de Neira to the bullfights tomorrow. She was an extraordinarily attractive woman, always beautifully dressed. Everyone would envy him. They would sit in a privileged section of the sunlit arena, gazing at the multi-colored, yelling crowd, while the shadows gradually pressed in from the East—shadows of death as black as the bull pawing the sand.....

CHAPTER XIII

If thou art called, the mountain suddenly spoke up, *thou canst not make the call undone. Thou wouldst either follow or rebel, but thou canst never live again as one who was not called.*

And with that the voice sank away, leaving no echo in the wind's chaotic turbulence. In an instant it had become remote, swept onward with all the other screaming, rushing, storm-whipped sounds. And yet Webb sensed that it had remained nearby; it was as imminent as the pallid, wreathed cliffs to his right, which now and then shimmered across the swirling mist like organ pipes in a ghostly cathedral.

A moment later El Soledad spoke again, this time over a burst of rain drops which splattered on the rocks, rapping the tense surface as abruptly as a hasty drummer sounding an alarm, and then ceasing as suddenly.

If thou hast tried to live as one who was not called, the mountain said, *it was because thou didst not want to have it true that thou wast summoned but not chosen.*

And again the voice fell away, and the wind, in haste and confusion, drove along its multitudinous sounds like a frightened herd. But again the pause was not protracted, and the words billowed up once more as swiftly as that cloud over the abyss had mushroomed from the brooding canyons.

But as thy friends have shown thee, each in his own manner, the thing one has loved cannot be destroyed, nor forgotten. For though men try, it will not die by murder. And though thou hast turned to fight it in many ways, it was not possible for thee to live again as one who has never been called.

As impalpably as it had emerged, the voice withdrew into the storm's savage and inarticulate sounds, abandoning Webb to a chaos of angry retorts and pent-up accusations, none of which he had been given a chance to express. Choked and shaken, he stumbled along the trail, sometimes holding on to rocks so that he would not be staggered by the short blasts which lunged at him from the air stream; and sometimes he was caught off guard, and then reeled dangerously close to the edge of the chasm.

Pulling back at the last moment, with his knees faltering, he would ask himself if it were not better to give in, to let himself slump and come to rest on a deserted patch of the trail; to lie there forever as one who had not reached the peak, nor safety, nor peace; to lie there with his paltry remains as unnoticeable from up high as the insubstantial ashes of a will-o'-the-wisp which had flickered along the monumental walls for a while, in the vain hope of finding a foothold, and was finally caught and extinguished so that it should no longer quiver across the giant rocks' preoccupation with infinite concerns.

With each grinding step, the yearning for an immediate surrender became more overpowering. At the brink of exhaustion, even death began losing its terror. An all too persuasive hopelessness painted ever softer shadows into the hollow-eyed skull which hovered once again in front of him, sometimes flitting over the ground or glaring at him from a grinning boulder.

He longed to sleep, and perhaps to dream—to dream that the monstrous convocation all around him was only a nightmare from which he would soon awake. For some time now, he had rarely envisioned reaching the shelter of the glacier cave. Instead, with the chances of survival steadily diminishing, a prospect of mute and inert repose offered itself as the sole remaining promise to one too tired to believe, too weary even to hope. And once, when the wind tumbled him against a boulder, he considered letting himself drop to the ground, and he actually sank to his knees.

What pulled him up was the sudden ghastly conviction that the mountain would not permit him to glide to a peaceful rest. The mountain, he sensed, had started to drive hard to the very core of his resistance, to the innermost pivotal area around which their whole conflict revolved. The moment he ceased running, El Soledad would bend over him and clutch at his head and look into his brain. And if then, in panic, he would attempt to escape, it would press him to the ground, while it burrowed deeper and deeper into his memory, breaking into obscure recesses to pluck from them the images, faces, scenes he had wished to forget.

A cold dampness of rain brushed over him. Convulsed, he started to leap up, but faltered and fell with his back against the boulder. A shadowy figure approached—and he gasped in voiceless terror—before the spectral appearance took on the Padre's features. He felt a strong arm pulling him up, and he saw the Priest's lips forming words, but could not understand what was said. And he did not care, because he could not permit himself to be distracted just then when his running battle with the mountain was raging to a time of decision. He needed all his attention to defend himself; and so he muttered something about having slipped and being all right again and perfectly able to go on.

He walked like a puppet, intent on concealing from the Padre how near he was to the breaking point. He had to be left alone while he beat back the mountain's heaving attempts to uproot all the most valid justifications of his entrenched pessimism, to fling him on his back as it were, in a complete and dramatic reversal of an outlook crystallized in the course of decades. He had to hold on, while the mountain pulled and tore at him and was about to wrench him loose, with leverage extending to cloud-swept heights, from all the anchors he had cast along the years in his inexorable drift toward shallow denials.

The mountain shook and jolted him, twisting and wrenching as violently as if it were still possible to spin back a middle-aged man to the crossroads in his youth, where he had turned from the outworn ideals perturbing his growth; as if the buried and forgotten avowals could again rise to struggle, in ghost-like and fantastic capers, with the acrid repudiations that had cleared the field; as if Webb, at this late stage, still had a chance to comply and change his direction once more to what it had been before an irreversible trend had led him from past days of disillusionment toward impending days of wrath.

Almost directly overhead, he saw the glacier's high blue gleam streaking past, like a comet's tail in a black sky, as blinding as the sun and yet without its warmth.

Then the sweat drenched his eyes; the glistening river of ice seemed to splinter into a thousand pearls of quicksilver, all dazzling, elusive, racing away to evade his glance, and, after a searing flash, leaving him sightless in the turbulent obscurity of a mist without spark, glow, or radiance.

For a while, as he staggered after the Padre, soft drizzles brushed past him in lulls of the wind. Again and again, he had to shake the moisture from his rain-soaked, gray hair; and when some drops rolled onto his lips, he recalled how the same thing had happened at a forlorn railroad station in Alabama where the rails had run in iron lines toward the horizon—unbending tracks laid down long ago, rails that could not be jumped—just as he and his college friends could not have escaped the grooves they had burrowed into the easily impressionable but iron-memoried matrix of time.

When he had last seen them at that class reunion in the plush Philadelphia hotel, every one of those aging alumni seemed to have undergone at least as great a transformation as he. And yet, while he watched them mill about in little groups, he felt sure that in each the apparent change was no longer an actual growth, but a mere continuation of patterns they had established long ago. Whether they knew it or not, they were prisoners of a million long-forgotten choices, arrived at in a past when they were too young and inexperienced to decide either wisely or well.

He, too, had been trapped in congealed habits, and was aware of it, though he had never recognized it as clearly as on that evening. Everywhere, in the glittering banquet hall, he saw facets of himself reflected—not in the mirrors that lined the walls, but in the obese, balding apostles gathered once again at a festive supper. Wearily he listened to the buoyant speeches and toasts; and after they rose from the long table, coagulating in small groups while sipping their cordials, Webb moved erratically from one circle to another, and finally retreated to a far corner, from where he surveyed his friends. For a brief and frightening moment, he saw them as puppets, twitching and gesticulating in response to invisible mechanism, strangely ritualistic in their polite manners, in their jovial conversation and benign smiles; and regardless of whether they were still ascending, edging sideways, or declining, they all impressed him as being quite incapable of changing their directions.

As for himself, he felt as if he had reached that moment of absolute stillness when the momentum of free flight has spent itself and the direction is about to be reversed. His ambition drained of all hope, his soul already stripped of all messianic dreams, he had nothing further to look forward to but peace of mind—or, perhaps, only an enduring armistice. And while he observed the perambulating alumni, he wondered how many of those prosperous graduates from Hudson Street still pursued unfulfilled hopes or merely strove to perpetuate their affluence and themselves; how many might still be kept awake—on an occasional, troubled night—by the inaudible echoes of childhood fantasies in which they had slain dragons, rescued the poor, comforted the crying, and had generally solved all the problems of the world as victorious commanders or absolute kings.

The majority of these prosperous apostles, no doubt, were still good men, striving to reconcile themselves to the hurt of not having been chosen; half-awakened dreamers groping in a twilight, which they could not make out, whether it was of dawn or of dusk; warriors who had withdrawn from battle to find themselves at war with themselves. They were half-men, bewildered and not quite fulfilled, craving they knew not what. And, like Webb, they all wore polite, casual masks, concealing from themselves and others those features that mattered the most.

While he slowly drank his coffee, Tom Sears approached, exchanged a few pleasantries, and left. Then Bob Tomlinson passed by, told an anecdote, and went on. But he was replaced almost at once by Buster Griswold, the super-salesman, who proceeded to surround Webb with his enormous bulk while forcing on him a detailed account of his great financial successes.

Listening distractedly, Webb felt more and more grateful for the shelter offered to him by his resignation. With an irony tinged by bitterness, he reflected how little there was he could boast of at this point. His superiors in Washington, although he had done nothing to antagonize them, had gradually lost interest in him. In fact, as he had lately realized, it was precisely his caution and his eagerness to please which had ultimately achieved the opposite effect of dissipating his bright prospects. So that, when Buster, finally breathless, implied that it was now Webb's turn to report his good fortune, he had no choice but to admit that he was sailing the next day to assume his consular duties in a little known place called Puerto Carribas.

Rather than mentioning, however, that this unimportant post, after so many years of loyal service, amounted to a demotion, he described the town as a beautiful harbor city, picturesque, quiet, and peaceful. And while he thus made it appear that he was eager to go there, it briefly struck him that Buster might also have been guilty of dissembling; that his yearnings, quite possibly, were also bereft of all hope—by fulfillment, perhaps, as much as his own by defeat.

At that moment, Harry McKenzie strolled over to them; and Buster, changing the topic, pulled a cigar from his tuxedo pocket and offered it to Harry, inviting him to "live well for a change—though it might be against all your principles."

And Harry, wearing no tie, his shirt collar defiantly open, refused. Ignoring the jibe, he took out his battered pipe, stuffing it methodically, while studying Webb with that blunt frankness which had always annoyed everyone.

"Quite a gathering," Harry said, nodding in the general direction of the banquet table, upon which still sprawled the rich debris of supper.

And Buster, winking his eye at Webb: "What's wrong with it?"

And Harry, pointing his pipe stem at a distinguished group in front of a potted palm: "Who would have thought they'd turn out like that?"

And Buster: "We're all getting old, you know."

And Harry, his wiry hair still flaming in coppery hues though a few gray streaks had also dampened some of its fire: "I wasn't talking about age. Just take a look at those squat pillars of society. Do-gooders who've done well for themselves. Knight-errants too paunchy to break another lance. Troubadours who've hung up their lyre in some tavern where a middle-aged matron's cooking made them forget both the dragons and the sleeping princess. What a sight! They're sure something to behold—if not to look up to!"

And Buster, with a twinkle in his eyes: "Relax, Harry. Not everybody can be a failure."

And Webb, noticing that Harry's skin turned a shade darker,

just before Harry said evenly: "Depends what you consider success?"

And Buster, who had always been Harry's best friend, growing more serious: "Come off it, Harry. Don't you ever get tired bragging that you're the only one who hasn't made good?"

A pause; and then Harry coming closer, his bony, broad-jawed face as rugged, as truculent and stubborn as ever, his clear gray eyes boring into Buster: "Made good—like you, for instance? You really think you're a success?"

And Buster, guffawing, his clownish face puckered up in huge amusement, though his hand trembled a little when he struck a match: "Sure am, Harry. But don't hold it against me. Not my fault. Some people just can't help getting ahead."

And Harry, deaf to the tremor in Buster's voice, as insensitive as always, pursuing him relentlessly: "You mean to say you really got the things you wanted? I don't mean all of them—just those that count?"

From all parts of the brilliantly lit room, smoke drifted toward Webb, together with the subdued murmurs emanating from similar groups clustered everywhere. When a waiter passed, they each took a glass of brandy from his tray, with Buster saying: "Maybe I didn't, Harry. But I suppose you got yours. Since all you ever wanted to prove was that the world is going to the dogs. You sure made it easy for yourself."

And Webb, remembering the frozen despair in Harry's eyes during their last meeting in Baltimore, wanted to stop Buster; but knowing what close ties still bound these two graduates from Hudson Street, he hesitated to interfere. And so he merely started to edge away, while Harry was saying: "It hasn't been as easy as you think, Buster. But through it all I've kept my integrity. At least, I haven't sold out."

And Buster: "No, you haven't. But neither have you bought anything. Nothing new, at any rate. Not since you left college. Why don't you give yourself a chance, Harry?"

And Harry: "What do you expect me to do? Trade in old ideas like used cars? Every year a new model?"

And Buster: "Just don't hang on to all that's stale and worthless. As if you could prove yourself loyal with that. For God's sake, Harry, get wise to yourself! Start moving the merchandise.

You're not fooling anybody by exhibiting all that bitterness in the shop window—just to prevent anyone from coming in and catching that the goods on your dusty shelves are all mildewed and shot to hell."

And Webb, in the movement of setting down the glass, turned back, intending to tell Buster how Harry, some fifteen years before, on the stairway of the Baltimore hospital had broken down, his face as white as his knuckles that were clamped around the bannister, rattling the spokes, pulling them back and forth as though to tear out pain by its roots, saying—

—'I couldn't Don! Maybe I should have moved away from that part of town—but I would have felt like a traitor!'

And Webb, pulling Harry away from the bannister: 'Stop it, Harry! Stop blaming yourself!'

'I couldn't have run off to live in one of those fine districts. Not with all these people staying behind.'

'No sense thinking about it now. Won't change anything—'

'Won't do my kid any good. If that's what you mean. Not anymore!'

'He'll pull through all right.'

And Harry's eyes wandering to the clock which had moved ahead two hours since the start of their vigil: 'You keep saying he'll be all right....' Suddenly, in a voice hoarse with anguish: 'What's taking them so long? Why don't they bring him out?'

'Sometimes surgery takes longer than they expect—'

'If there are complications!'

'There won't be! They've stopped the bleeding in time! The surgeon was sure they could save him!'

'You didn't hear him say—how! He didn't want Alice to hear that the boy's left side—his hip will be low—one arm shorter than the other—!'

Three more steps up the stairs, and then another pause, as they saw, across the spokes of the bannister, the worn woman at the end of the hall, slumped on a bench near the entrance to surgery. Her eyes wide and tearless, her hands clasped, she had not stirred since they had rolled her boy past those swinging doors.

'Don't let her see you that way, Harry. Don't make it harder for Alice!'

And Harry, his bulky, powerful forehead beading with sweat: 'She hasn't said one word to me! Ever since it happened—not one word!' And then, hesitating at the top of the stairs. 'How can I face her, Don? How can I ever face her again?'

'She's not blaming you, Harry. Nobody can blame you for an accident. Even if you'd moved to some other district, it could have happened just the same.'

'But I tell you, it was no accident—they pushed him—those kids! You don't know what they're like in our part of town. Animals! Poor, unfortunate children—but animals! Killers! Frightened of everybody—mostly of themselves. Ganging up on anybody who's different. That's why they pushed Tommy under the truck—because he wouldn't join their gang!'

'You can't be sure—'

'Can't I? Ask the grocer at the corner—he saw it happen!'

They had been pacing the hall; and as they approached Alice, Harry had broken off, turning, standing still, swaying, then stammering while they paced away from her: 'She knew something like that was coming. She kept saying we ought to get out. Remember that time you came to see us? How she said we ought to move away? For the kid's sake, she said. Remember?'

And Webb, watching a nurse push a creaky bed from one room to another, had thought of that dismal apartment in which he had visited Harry, a month or two before sailing to Brazil where he was to start his first term as a full-fledged consul. Proud of his promotion, almost brazenly sure of himself after his first taste of success, he had felt all the more surprised and perturbed that Harry was still living in so run-down a neighborhood. A graduate chemist, Harry could have afforded to rent a better place, but had stayed on, because any increase in comfort might have been interpreted as an outward sign that he had betrayed his convictions.

'Was I wrong, Don?'

In the vacuous hospital hall, Harry's voice had sounded uncertain. Yet, his coarse features, beneath the greenish light of a NO EXIT sign, had still seemed as truculent as if they had been sculptured by a blunt instrument.

'Can you really say, Don, that I was wrong?'

And Webb, still smarting in remote corners of his being from the disdain shown to him by Harry on that day, had stared at the surgery door, tempted to tell Harry that he had thought him indeed very wrong—wrong in despising all those who struggled to get ahead as if they were renegades who had made a deal with the enemy; wrong in believing himself unchanged, when actually he had changed as much as any of the others, only in an opposite direction; wrong in considering Webb a turncoat just because he had not appeared sufficiently bitter.

But with Harry's child fighting for life two doors away, he had not been able to say any of it, and had merely muttered: 'I don't know, Harry. I just don't know.'

And Harry, his glance anxiously passing over the surgery entrance: 'It didn't seem wrong at the time. Maybe it wasn't. If I had to do it over, Don, I might still decide the same way.'

And Webb had drawn back imperceptibly, as if Harry at that moment had grown tall and sturdy, had grown out of his leather jacket to cast a heroic shadow all the length of the hospital hall, all the way to Alice, enfolding that sickly woman who had given birth to their strapping, strong, wonderful son, now on the operating table. And Harry, his shadow enveloping that care-worn girl, the oldest daughter of an irresponsible window-cleaner who had deserted his wife and eight children, had stammered: 'I wish I knew, Don. I wish I knew the right or the wrong of it. I wasn't so much of a stubborn fool as you might have assumed. I saw as well as any of you that we weren't doing any good for the people we'd wanted to help. But then, just sneaking away, wasn't the answer. Not for me. I wasn't cut out to be shallow like some of the others. With me, it took. If you can't help someone, at least you can stay with them.'

'What's the use, Harry? If you were drowning, would you feel better if the person who couldn't rescue you decided to drown himself at your side?'

An interne had rushed from the operating room, disappearing into the laboratory. White as a sheet, Harry had walked toward the swinging doors.

'Don't expect me to tell you what's right for you, Don. I only know that I'd cut my throat the day before I'd ever ask: What's the use? Because that's never a question—it's always the excuse of someone who's already made up his mind to quit.'

And Webb, stung as so often before by Harry's blunt honesty:

'Maybe I didn't quit. Maybe I'm just not the type who beats his head against the wall. Maybe I've decided that doing even a little bit of good is better than either ruining yourself or doing nothing at all.'

And Harry, no longer listening, blocked by the closed surgery doors: 'Why don't they send someone out—let us know how the kid's doing!'

'They will, Harry. Just as soon as they—'

'As soon as they know...?' He had looked down. And then, for the first time, the tears had brimmed over, streaking down the coarse skin on his hard face: 'Why did they do it to him? He wasn't doing anybody any harm. They didn't have to push him....'

'Don't, Harry....'

'The poor kid....What'll I tell him when he grows up? When he can't go out to play ball or dance? How can he help hating me?'

'He won't....'

And Harry, standing in front of the surgery doors like Abraham before the altar on which he had been commanded by God to sacrifice his son Isaac: 'What was I to do, Don? Should I have turned and run from all I believed in?'

—Soft murmurs reached Webb from all parts of the crowded banquet room. A waiter had stopped in front of him; and Webb, noticing that he was still holding the glass he had been about to set down, put it on the tray.

Only a short while could have passed since he had crossed to the table; Harry and Buster were still standing in the same spot, with Buster guffawing at that moment, blurting out between boisterous peals of laughter: "You're a card, Harry. You really are. Fact is—you're not looking to fix up things—you thrive on all that's wrong in the world. Why, if the boys in the various governments ever got together to patch up their differences, they'd put you clear out of business. Yessir, that's what they'd do. Clear out of business."

And Harry, standing tall and straight like a massive block of black basalt: "When that day comes, Buster, at least I'll be able to say to myself that I've waited for it."

And Buster, with his incipient baldness shimmering wanly beneath the smoky light of the candelabra overhead: "Fine, Harry. That's great. But in the meantime, you're allowed to shave off your beard and cut your hair, no matter what vows you've taken. Relax that granite face of yours and dance around the table—like that—a skip and a hop—" Hugely amused, Buster danced a few steps, with the bulk of his exuberant belly bouncing and flapping in reverse rhythm.

But Harry, unsmiling, refused to accept Buster's invitation to laugh at his expense. "No use trying those salesman's tricks on me, Buster," he said. "If it makes you happy playing the fool, go ahead. But don't expect me to place a large order for that kind of amusement."

And Webb, impulsively moving forward, wanted to put an end to their argument, telling each of the two friends how little they actually knew of each other—telling Buster how Harry had stood in front of the surgery door like Abraham in front of the altar, while an invisible surgeon performed the sacrifice which had been extracted from his loyalty. And then, turning to Harry, he could tell him, with equal justification, how Buster had run into him in Rome, shouting—

—'For cripes sake, if it isn't good old Don!'
Yelling Webb's name at the top of his voice, Buster had bounded across the Via Veneto, brushing aside people like a mighty walrus parting small waves. And once he had reached Webb, he had started to pump his hand, slapping him on the back; and finally, over his protests, dragging him to a bar, where his booming voice, issuing from ruddy cheeks and a fat neck, had soon attracted general attention and universal dismay.

It had been a distressing meeting, for it had seemed that their diverging careers had left them nothing in common. Buster had been a picture of prosperity, satiated, almost bovine in his contentment. But, perhaps by force of habit, his manners were still aggressive; he had behaved, in every respect, as the successful, high-pressure super-salesman. In the course of overly jovial conversation, he had not neglected to inquire discreetly how much Webb was earning a year; and his eyes had widened in disbelief when he heard the negligible sum. Deploring the government's niggardly thriftiness, he had hinted smugly that his own income

*exceeded Webb's salary by two or three zeroes—'in back of the
digit, not in front,' he had laughed, hugely amused by his joke.
And he had slapped Webb's thigh, for no apparent reason other
than his own intense satisfaction with himself.*

*Quietly sipping his drink, Webb had wondered how it was
possible that a young dreamer from Hudson Street had evolved
into such a mountainous mass of banality; and whether behind
that noisy surface there was still something left of the generous,
clumsy boy who, for an entire semester, had secretly supported
Eddie Fless from his own sparse earnings. If so, there had not
been the least outward indication; Buster's show of superficial
success had been too flawless to reveal any cracks. Even his generosity had become offensive; Webb had cringed when Buster,
with a loudness that was cruelly out of place in the discreet atmosphere of that fashionable, intimate bar, had offered to buy
a round of drinks for Webb's friends at an adjoining table—a
distinguished circle representing a cross section of the diplomatic
corps in Rome. There had been a moment's startled silence, before Alvarez, the decadent old duke from Seville, had sufficiently
recovered to refuse with thin-lipped politeness. Embarrassed and
angry, Webb had fled. And the next day, when the young attache
from the French Legation had referred to Buster as that horse-
trading barbarian, Webb had felt in no mood to defend his former
friend, and had quickly changed the subject.*

*It was not until three months later, after discovering Buster's
reason for staying in Rome, that Webb found it necessary to revise his opinion of his boyhood friend once more. An American
importer at the club had related some gossip about a pretty
nightclub dancer from Copenhagen, whom Buster had followed
across half of Europe. There had been much chuckling and leer-
ing, in which Webb had not joined, remembering how Buster,
in his youth already clownish-looking and awkward, had always
supposed that he would never be loved by any woman.*

*Another month had passed before Buster had stamped into
his apartment, inviting him to a dance recital given by a lady
friend—a former ballerina from the Royal Danish Opera—cur-
rently appearing at the Bocca d'Ora club. 'Not that she has to
work for money,' Buster had emphasized, when they sat on the
terrace which overlooked the temple of Jupiter, 'but she loves*

dancing. Seems like the only time she really comes to life. There are days when she gets moody and won't talk, not to me or anyone. Just tells me to watch her dance that night, and she'll say all she knows.'

The sun, moving toward the Castello del' Angelo, had got into his eyes when he claimed, at first, that the soiree was completely sold out; and then, shifting his heavy bulk on the wicker chair, he had rather sheepishly admitted that he was putting up the money for the whole thing—'for rental, musicians, advertising—everything expensive as hell—they sure take you for a sucker when they know they got you over a barrel—and you can't haggle—because it's the last thing you'll ever be able to do for a girl with pernicious anemia.'

For a while, as they sat on the terrace, looking down on the roofs and ruins of the eternal city, Buster had given no further indication of anything that went on beneath the veneer of the successful salesman which had so misled both Webb and the young French attaché. And Webb had reflected how difficult it was to make any foreigner understand his countrymen, those blustering, complex, uncouth builders and traders, with their clashing mixture of spontaneous, uninhibited generosity and hardboiled shrewdness, with their unashamed pursuit of material things and their unrealistic attitudes toward life, with their dreams always outrunning their capacity for practical achievement—possibly because, quite unknown to them, they were actually looking for other things than those they were forever trying to grab and to hold.

The following Saturday, attending the dance recital with the French attaché, Webb had watched a thin, vapid-looking girl pirouette on a light-flooded stage. Turning from her to Buster, who was standing alone in the back of the dark concert hall, Webb had wondered how many others in this audience, drawn mostly from the foreign colony, knew that neither the choreography, nor the girl's mediocre talent, nor what she tried to express, really mattered; that what they were watching was an obscure setting inside the heart of an awkward, fat, unlovable boy from Hudson Street, a stage upon which his dreams gyrated and leaped, dreams of a weightless, immaterial beauty, of a tenderness that could not be bought or traded.

After a few waves of desultory, dutiful applause, the curtain had swept down, shutting out the spectators while Buster began bustling around the lobby, as buoyant and boisterous as ever, shaking hands, slapping backs, laughing loud and hard at the insipid jokes he gratuitously made on himself.

The next day Buster had disappeared with the girl; and then nothing further had been heard from them until the French attaché happened to see them again, a few weeks later, in Capri, where he had also learned that she had been in love, all along, with another man, a worthless drifter by whom she had a child, while Buster, who provided for it, had not yet been allowed to kiss the woman even once.

'We were planning to get married,' Buster had told Webb when they met again in New York after several years. 'She kinda liked the idea toward the end—I mean, once that drifter went off with another woman. But then nothing came of it, because she had that accident—'

And as Webb looked up, Buster had shifted his glance. 'Well, accident, or whatever it was ... Just as everything was going along fine. She was appearing in that real low-down cafe in Lisbon. Didn't want to accept any more money from me. To show me that money had nothing to do with it. I mean—between us. And then—anyway, she was losing weight rapidly, and the doctor was afraid that she—. Well, as I said, that's when she had the accident. Wasn't too surprising either with all those medicines in the room. Though I never did find out why she took the wrong pills. Might have done it on purpose.'

And Webb, suddenly remembering the young Frenchman's gradual, almost grudging respect for Buster, had asked: 'What became of her child?'

And Buster's clownish face lighting up: 'Finest little girl you ever saw. Real smart. Best in her class. I get a letter from her every day. Writes like a regular little professor.'

Beaming with pride, Buster had pulled out an envelope, on which Webb had noticed an American stamp, before he read on the letterhead: 'Dearest daddy—'

—Soft murmurs reached Webb from all sides, gradually enfolding Harry's and Buster's altercation, as Webb, after a last glance at the two tall men, started to make his way toward the exit.

How futile it was, he thought, to judge people from surface appearances. In the compact present, every person was like a flattened telescope; to be understood, ring after ring had to be drawn out, time period after time period—just as the truth about Buster could not be known, unless one had been acquainted with the fat boy on Hudson Street—just as Harry's persistance could not be comprehended unless one knew of his loss and the accusations underneath, and, inside of that, still farther back in time, that small innermost tube in which his enthusiasm had glowed at white heat....

Soft murmurs reached Webb from all sides. *If thou art called,* the mountain had since told him, *thou wouldst either follow or rebel, but thou canst not live again as one who was not called.* Perhaps, that is what Buster should have said to Harry, or Harry to Buster—for it would have been far more valid than all their censure and criticizing and tearing at each other, with neither of them fully realizing what the other had suffered, because all they ever saw of each other was the crust over the unhealing hurt of not having been chosen.

Perhaps, that is what should have been said to all those alumni, gathered at that reunion after they had gone their separate ways, traveling across many widely different territories, without ever suspecting that they were all heading toward the same intersection. Perhaps, it could have been said even to Arthur Warren, of whom Webb, at that moment, saw only a blurred smile in a distant group.....

Hushed conversation all around Webb; subdued laughter, nostalgia worn like carnations in buttonholes, forgotten friendships exhumed for the evening, youthful camaraderie dusted off like old suits and worn stiffly and revealing their bad fit. And beneath the jovial clinking of glasses, a guarded scrutiny, a cautious evaluation of others' health, rank, promotion or decline, a secret comparing, each with the other, and occasionally one with himself —with what he had been, or even with what he might have become.

And then Arthur Warren, suddenly near, casually stepping into his way, starting an innocuous conversation. As handsome as ever, by then a popular executive with an airline, Arthur suavely proceeded from small talk to asking: "Have you talked to Eddie?"

And Webb, shaking his head, turned to look toward the long white table, where Eddie Fless stood all alone beneath the huge, fiercely glittering crystal chandelier, a solitary, forlorn figure, with his sloping shoulders as defenseless as ever, and his pinched face still more pallid after his prison term.

"Somebody ought to go over and talk to him," Arthur said, nervously flicking some ashes from his tuxedo lapels. "He's been by himself most of the evening."

But Arthur made no move to join Eddie, and neither did Webb.

"I don't know how the others feel about it," Arthur said, somewhat flustered, "but I certainly don't mean to avoid him because he's been in jail and all that. Makes no difference to me. For all I know, it might not even have been his fault." And Webb: "Maybe not." And Arthur: "Could have been anything—circumstances—bad breaks. Maybe he trusted the wrong people and they let him down. Sometimes it isn't the guy taking the rap who's really to blame."

And Webb: "Not always." And Arthur: "Anyway, whatever he's done, he's paid for it. So there's no reason why anybody should want to avoid him now." And Webb: "Maybe nobody does. I mean—not on purpose. It just isn't easy to talk to someone who's down on his luck."

And Arthur, quickly, almost too eagerly: "That's it. I'm sure nobody means any harm. It's just that he makes you feel so damn uncomfortable."

Others were also watching Eddie; now and then a head turned in one of the nearby groups. And the mountain's words might have been as true for anyone of them as for Webb: *Thou hast persuaded thyself that there was no one to call thee. But there was, and thou hast heard; and one who was called must obey or quarrel, must follow to the end—or refuse and be dragged along, with his heart forever at war with itself.*

Soft murmurs drifting toward Webb from all sides . . . "My wife just had another baby. . . ." . . . . "I tell you, that Clyde Jackson is a man to watch . . ." . . . "If you think Kew Gardens is a growing suburb, you should see . . ." . . . . "I intend to buy some more acreage adjoining the ranch. . . ."

And in the center of all the polite voices and the genteel perambulating—a quiet, forlorn figure, Eddie Fless, his sloping shoulders as humble and picayune beneath the huge chandelier as a memorial plaque overgrown by weeds.

Unable to take his eyes off that small stillness scarcely holding its own in the room's baroque glitter, Webb noticed that Bill Barton and Iris Thor approached Eddie—but then, swerving off slightly, they passed him. And a moment later, Arthur asked: "What do you say, Don? Shall we go over to Eddie?"

And Webb, hesitating only briefly, looked away, quickly gazing at his watch. "I'm sorry, Arthur. But I'm sailing early in the morning. It's rather late, and I—I have to get some sleep."

And so he turned his back on Eddie and walked from the banquet hall, not knowing as yet that some day the mountain would say to him: *Though men may try to destroy the thing they have loved, it will not die by murder. And though thou hast turned to fight it in many ways, it was not possible for thee to live again as one who has never been called.* He crossed the lobby as hurriedly as he could without attracting attention. But near the reception desk, he was intercepted by Iris Thor, who had been one of Esther's closest friends. And, perhaps for that reason, she always looked at him with some sort of reproach in her intelligent and beautiful eyes, as if she felt duty-bound to remind him how much Esther had expected of him.

More irritated than usual by her questioning gaze, he smiled frostily while she told him that she had turned over most of her prosperous law practice to her associates in order to specialize in juvenile delinquency cases. And finally, when he was unable to contain himself any longer, he muttered some excuse, leaving her brusquely. But even then he did not succeed in escaping without further interference. While the hat check girl helped him into his coat, Harry McKenzie stopped by, waiting for him so that they could walk out together.

Not much was said until they reached the corner where Harry took the streetcar. But those few minutes were enough to bring Webb once again into conflict with this hard, immalleable, uncompromising man, whose candor one could only admire or detest.

With his hands pushed deep into his pockets, Harry frankly

admitted that he could have advanced much farther in the chemical laboratory where he worked, were it not for his intransigeance
and lack of diplomacy. "Fact is, I've botched my career. Through
by own fault. They claim I antagonize people," he chuckled,
not at all repentant, while they crossed the deserted square in
front of the hotel. "Just because I refuse to take part in their
office politics." He shrugged with a disdain that made Webb
sympathize at once with Harry's superiors, as if he too had felt
himself included in their great unworthiness. And he drew away
slightly when Harry added: "I see no reason to jockey for position.
There are more important things in life than petty advantage and
their foolish little schemes."

A pervasive fog started to gather around them as they forged
up the street. "I'm still living on Reeper Street," Harry said, referring to the dingy apartment where Webb, in the course of his
first visit, had been introduced to Harry's son, then a rosy-cheeked
baby in an ornate crib. "As you can see, I haven't got very far.
Still living on the wrong side of the tracks."

But again there had been neither dissatisfaction nor apology
in his tone of voice, only the same ineradicable pride which had
provoked Webb as much then as it did now.

"Tommy's getting along well,"Harry said, as if he had guessed
that Webb would shy away from referring to that night in the
hospital. "Grew up to be quite a tall boy. Studying to be a
teacher."

He seemed on the verge of adding something about the consequences of the surgery, but fell silent, and so the core of their
dispute remained unresolved.

"I hear you're doing fine, Don," Harry said when they reached
the streetcar stop. And Webb shifted his glance, looking down
the vacant street and saying almost harshly: "I can't complain."

And Harry, peering at him with those gray, boring eyes below
his bulky forehead, inquired—not contemptuously nor accusingly,
but rather with an extraordinary softness: "I suppose—by now
you've made your peace with the world?"

The streetcar's burning eye loomed up in the depth of the fog,
approached and grew while Webb, trying to look beyond it,
gazed down the deserted street, wondering what was at the end
of it. "I suppose I have," he answered almost aggressively. "And

I'm glad I have. I really am." And suddenly turning, he faced Harry squarely: "What about it?"

And Harry, still unusually gentle and understanding, speaking softly while the streetcar rumbled near: "Nothing. I was just asking." And Webb, irritated by the fog and Harry's open shirt collar and the whole vacant night, burst out: "You weren't just asking. You think I'm a quitter. You think I've left everything by the wayside, all our ideals and everything—"

"I didn't say that."

"But that's what you believe, isn't it?"

"No, Don. Because I don't believe that you can leave anything behind. Like you can't get rid of your shadow by trampling on it. Nor by running from it. The faster you run, the quicker it chases you—and the heavier it gets."

And Webb, inordinately aroused: "Look, Harry, I'm not running from anything. I'm just taking the world as it is. That's all. I'm not fighting it, and I'm not ignoring nor distorting what I see around me, not even to make it fit any sort of desirable theory. I've learned to face facts. I've made up my mind that I've got to live with facts, so I might as well get along with them."

"You mean, bow to them?"

"Yes, Harry, even bow to them. Can you understand that? Can you?"

"And so to resign yourself?"

"For Heaven's sake, Harry, stop it, will you? Don't make it look like I'd just wanted to have things easier for myself. And don't tell me that I've sold out—whatever you mean by that. If I had, I certainly didn't get much of a price. No practical advantage of any kind—not even peace of mind. I would have sold my integrity, without getting anything in return."

And Harry: "One never does."

And Webb, stung and angry: "What about you, Harry? Don't you realize what's been happening to you? That the tide has passed you, and won't come back? Don't you see that it's no use holding out, because nobody cares whether you do or you don't?"

And Harry, a swift spasm shaking his iron face: "It doesn't matter. I'm not going to budge, Don. They'll have to bury me where I stand."

And Webb, hurriedly as he saw the streetcar bearing down on

them: "What are you waiting for, Harry? There's nothing ahead —no reward—no one coming for us. The sooner you face that we got off to a wrong start and wasted the best years of our lives, the better off you are. Draw a line under it. No sense compounding your error by prolonging it."

And Harry, weary but unyielding: "It won't turn into a mistake—until I give up. I'll not admit that those years were wasted. Not ever."

"Whether you admit it or not won't change anything. It's true anyhow."

"You can't be sure, Don. We don't know what was right or wrong."

The flaming, staring light of the streetcar picked them out of the shadows, momentarily holding the two men, who had been called but not chosen, in some sort of flickering scrutiny. At that moment, Webb saw something in his friend's bearing which reminded him of the way Harry had stood in front of the surgery door. And in that instant, he understood why Harry could never give in; how firmly he was tied to the powers which had called for his sacrifice—chained to them as surely by his insistence that they justify the wounds and scars he had inflicted on his son as was Webb, in an opposite way, by his rebellion against the fate which had deprived him of Esther.

The cone of light passed them, forging ahead into endless night. "What are you trying to do, Harry?" Webb asked of the dark figure at his side. "Hold out until you've forced God to His knees? Make Him accept you? Insist that you deserve more than a contemptuous brushing aside, more than a portal shut in your face?"

And Harry, smiling wanly: "At our age, Don, to hold out is as easy as to give in. Either way, we don't have too much to lose anymore."

The streetcar had clanged to a stop. Getting on, Harry said: "And who knows—maybe it was all not in vain. How can anyone be sure that the price one has paid was too high?"

And Webb, stirred more deeply than he had realized, reached for Harry's coarse hand, touching it, pressing it closely. "Good luck," he whispered hoarsely. "Good luck, Harry."

And Harry, the harsh lines around his mouth softening as he

bent down from the top step: "Thanks, Don. If I don't see you again, I want you to know that you've always been my closest—"

The impatient bell cut them off, and the streetcar rolled away on its nightly chore of gathering up human flotsam from moribund streets; and Harry stood on the lighted platform, waving to Webb. And that was the last Webb ever saw of Harry—the square face with the shock of wild, unruly hair—the broad hand waving a final goodbye, just as the conductor stepped up behind him—and Harry turning around, half-astonished, while the streetcar vanished in the languidly floating fog.

For some reason, Harry's expression—at the instant of facing the conductor—stayed with Webb, all the way down to Puerto Carribas. The unyielding head kept floating after him on the waters, forcing him to continue their dispute, night after night, while Webb promenaded along the railing, or stretched out on his deck-chair to look at the stars.

He felt menaced in his resignation, and struck out at the heroic hope implied in his friend's obduracy. Harry was wrong—he had to be wrong. Unlike Webb, who had started early to come to terms with his disenchantment, Harry still insisted on being recognized as one who had been called, implacably holding fate to its promise, demanding that the unknown powers reveal their purpose in calling him—or else be guilty of a monstrous breach of faith.

The foaming wake flared and vanished beyond the ship's light-strewn orbit, passing into a night wherein was hidden the secret which alone could have decided Webb's controversy with Harry. Huddled beneath his blankets, sheltered in a traveling tent of light which flowed ahead, traversed itself and gathered up behind it what luminosity had been spilled, Webb kept moving from one darkness to the next.

As the ship plodded deeper into the southern balm, bearing him along in that calm suspension between two destinations, he felt his quiet despair rise in him like a mist. Having found peace only in hopelessness, he had no choice but to resist any attempt to stir up his dormant yearnings.

It was indeed unfortunate that Harry had crossed his path at this juncture. For it was, after all, not impossible that Harry might be right—perhaps, the undisclosed destiny of one who was called had not come to an end at the moment of his rebuff; perhaps, he still had another appointment with fate—somewhere beyond the next barren stretch of time.

Perhaps, it was not true that he was doomed merely to drag himself to a futile death. Tossing nights in his cabin, sometimes awake until dawn, awake until the porthole gleamed up and he saw the gray waves stream out of the sky's glimmer, he would battle his wish to believe that some revelation, some fulfillment was still waiting for him at the end of his erring about; that someone would yet bend over him and take him into his arms, saying softly: *Fear no more, my son, for it was here that I have waited for thee and not behind the closed door.* And while the tears pressed into the arid hollows of Webb's eyes, the voice would go on to say: *Cry not, my son, for thou wast wrong to believe that I have ever rejected thee. I wanted thee to find thy way to me, so thy search was not in vain. And now that thou hast proven thyself, I shall heal thy many wounds. For although I have tested thee, thou art my son, and thou shalt know how much I have loved thee.*

And, thereupon, all of Webb's pent-up pain and loneliness would brim over. Every sinew in his body seemed to strain toward that voice issuing from a point somewhere just beyond the nearest sky. But by morning, when the commotion in the passageways began, he would still be alone, his bones hurting from lack of sleep. And by noon, when he sat haggard and hollow-eyed in the ship's dining room—with Harry's indomitable head peering at him from the clock above the passengers' chattering and munching mouths—Webb would again try to suppress his futile yearnings.

Day after day, almost step by step, inch by inch, he fought them back. They would be dangerous enough under any circumstances; but since he knew himself to be heading for a remote, primitive bay, his career finished, his youth's impetus spent, his potentialities encompassed, any resurrection of hope could only turn to bitter acid and corrode and mar his days.

Even before the ship veered toward shore, except for an infrequent spasm, he felt that he had won the battle. And as the harbor of Puerto Carribas rose from the ocean, his last presumptions sank to a rest in this palm-lined enclosure, surrounded by the dark impassable forests which held the mountain's bluish glimmer so firmly at bay.

It was not until about a year after he had rented his villa that he discovered the peculiar sheen of the mountain range. And, approximately at the same time, his dispute with Harry was resuscitated for a few short, but poignant days.

Just as he was about to close up his outer office—where Crispian was to wait so humbly later on—a young couple entered the consulate. The young man, handsome and soft-spoken, moved rather peculiarly, as if his shoulder were dislocated. He introduced himself as—Tommy McKenzie.

Harry's son, newly wed. The young couple had just stepped off the boat, intending to spend their honeymoon in Puerto Carribas. The bride, an enchanting, pert, vivacious girl, confessed to Webb, during their first festive dinner, that she had actually wanted Tommy to take her to Florida on their wedding trip, but Harry had insisted that they visit Webb instead. There was, Webb learned, no other message from Harry. And none other was needed, when he looked at the intelligent young man who had just finished his studies, summa cum laude, and had already been offered an excellent position as a research scientist and teacher.

For once in his life, Webb neglected his consular duties. Abandoning his cherished routine, he outdid himself in his efforts to show the young people a good time. The girl's unstudied charm captivated him almost immediately; and, before long, in the course of boat trips, fishing expeditions, donkey rides, she had dissolved the last safeguards of his habitual, formal, cold reserve. Growing more expansive by the hour in their company, Webb showed them all the sights, including the scenic spot at the harbor which, later on, he urged Crispian to paint.

The bride adored the picturesque view. "How I envy you, living in such a romantic place," she exclaimed, delighted by the colorful crowd on the quai. And Webb, for once forgetting his aching solitude, almost involuntarily assented.

That evening, she again expressed her delight at the picturesque environment. They were finishing their dessert—a halved pineapple filled with icecream and rum, when she became fascinated by the guitar players who were singing a melancholy, haunting tune. "Listen," she whispered, "listen to that wonderful animal quality in their voices. If you shut your eyes, you can imagine the whole jungle coming to life—"

And Tommy, chuckling: "What do you know about the jungle?"

And she, wrinkling her pert nose: "More than you give me credit for. Unlike a recent graduate I know, I have imagination. I can see before my closed eyes all the animals trotting around the jungle, peeking from behind palm trees, trying to find the place where the big tropical moon touches the earth—"

And Webb, all keyed up by the young couple's infectious gayety, suggested taking them to a place where they would hear really extraordinary music. "It's not the most luxurious night club," he explained. "Actually, no more than a platform at the edge of the jungle. But the band is remarkable. Untaught men from surrounding villages, who've never learned how to read a note. But they play—they're magicians—it's incredible what rhythms they draw from their primitive instruments. And, of course, if you like dancing—"

He broke off, biting his lips.

Tommy had noticed his embarrassment. "No reason to avoid mentioning it, Mr. Webb," he said evenly. "I can't dance. I could never do any exercise—not since childhood."

And Webb, the blood pounding hotly in his temples, muttered in what was meant to be an offhand tone: "Oh, yes, I remember, some accident—"

And Tommy, quietly: "No, Mr. Webb. It was no accident. And I'd rather you didn't try to hush it up. My dad told me the truth, after keeping it a guilty secret for years. On my seventeenth birthday, he told me how the kids had pushed me under the truck, and how it was all his fault because he hadn't moved from that neighborhood. Can you imagine—his fault! The most wonderful thing any man could have done, and he had felt guilty about it all that time."

And Webb, clearing his throat, groped to express that a father could indeed give no greater gift to his son than the example he set for him; but before he could say anything, the bride laughed: "Want to know something, Mr. Webb? If this hadn't happened to Tommy, I bet he would have ended up leader of a gang, and we'd all have to visit him now in the penitentiary—"

"Oh, be quiet, silly," Tommy scolded, and they burst into laughter, while Webb called for the check, his loneliness a thick lump in him, his heart thumping as heavily as that night when he had stood with Harry in front of the surgery doors.

Perhaps, after all, Harry was right—perhaps the mission of those who had been called was not ended when they were not chosen. Again, he felt the great longing surge up in him; and when, a little later, they sipped their cool drinks at the edge of the jungle, Webb gazed beyond the lighted platform, and there he saw Harry's indomitable head looming up in the black sky above the tree line. Quickly, Webb shifted his glance, disconsolately, panicky, staring at the magnificent mulatto girl who threw herself about on the stage in a frenzy, incited by ferocious rhythms, pursued by the relentless drums, beaten into delirious abandon by the white-teethed musicians, whirled around herself, whipped, twisted into an ecstasy that could not be contained, pulled down, draining resistance into a wide bowl of gyrating earth, sinking, gliding, drawn down and down and down....

The drums reverberated in Webb's mind all night. Day broke, and then another day, and the same ferocious rhythms kept beating in his ears, swelling in wild crescendo whenever his glance passed the cool mountains in the distance. And finally, on the evening of the young couple's departure for the States, the beat became unbearable. As he walked home from the harbor, where he had waved to the youngsters until long after the ship had steamed past the breakwater, he felt that it was better to make an end of the hopeless yearning than to suffer its torment; better to preclude forever its fulfillment than to suffer the indecision of waiting.....

He stopped at a tavern. He drank. He went to another place and drank more. He drifted from one tavern to another, drinking, seeking degradation. He bought drinks for derelicts who, in spite of his freely offered self-abasement, kept a respectful attitude toward the man in the immaculate, white linen suit. And even after he had stumbled, half-blind in a dark street, over a pile of rotting pineapples, soiling his sleeves and his hands on the sweaty pavement, the men in the next tavern would still not accept him as one of their own.

He drifted deeper into lanes which he had never before dared to penetrate. Everywhere, the wild pulse of marimbas beat the air, beat the dust from the pallid chalk, beat inside boarded-up cellars, beat unremittingly behind vibrating windows. He passed beneath the florid, odorous light leaking from cracked shutters. The fever of the tropical night was at last rushing him past the stillness of waiting, the waiting for that voice he yearned to hear and knew he never would, that voice saying: *Cry not, my son, for thou wast wrong to believe that I have ever rejected thee. I wanted thee to find thy way to me—*

Here, among derelict hovels steeped in filth and mire, he could be certain that the voice would never reach him. And as he staggered deeper into the perfume-laden obscurity, he wished to degrade and soil himself, so as to end all waiting for a voice which some day might have said to him: *Thy search was not in vain. And now that thou hast proven thyself, I shall heal thy many wounds. For although I have tested thee, thou art my son, and thou shalt know how much I have loved thee.*

The girls stood in front of the bamboo curtains, or just inside the doorways, so as to let the carmine light shine on their half-naked bodies. They whispered to him, they promised and offered in sultry competition; they snickered as he staggered past, and then they screamed their insults after him. He stumbled ahead, insanely choosing among the painted faces, seeking the one who would make him despise himself the most; because he had to make certain that the voice could never speak to him, that all hope would be stifled in a degradation beyond any chance of redemption.....

She was more than six feet tall, aglow in a half-open dress, her skin aflame, her lips parted in a smile moistened and ripe with unbridled instincts. She stepped aside to let him enter the low-ceilinged cellar room, and then she followed him inside, drawing shut behind her the torn, ruby-colored curtain.

He sat down on the cot and fumbled for his wallet. A baby, which had been asleep in the background, started to cry. She went to rock the crib, stripping off some of her gaudy, tinkling bracelets to let the child play with them. He noticed the reddish streak which ran from her neck to the shoulder, an angry flare like a burn, or perhaps a scar etched into her skin by acid thrown at her in a fight. Then she approached to take the banknotes he handed her, and rushed to hide them in an urn, surprised and overjoyed by the large amount he had given her.

The ferocious rhythms beat on the ceiling and inside his brain. She came dancing toward him, her young body swaying in un-conscious, natural response to the marimbas overhead. She kissed him on the cheek, then danced on to a chair where she put down her blouse. But when she turned back to him, the dance rippled slowly from her limbs. She stood still; something in his expres-sion had perplexed her, and she stared at him, only now beginning to wonder, with almost child-like naivity, why a man such as he should have come to her.

Quickly he looked away, hoping that she had not read the contempt and revulsion in his eyes. But she approached, alerted by some animal instinct. Kneeling down before him, she took his burning face into both her hands and turned it toward her, try-ing to decipher the torment which was written on it in the ancient hieroglyphics of emotion. Apparently, her illiterate eyes could identify only his anguish; and when, accidentally or intentionally, she pressed her breasts against his thighs, there was something in her offering which reminded him of the gesture with which she had dropped the bracelets into the crib to pacify the weeping child.

Her spontaneous and naive charity drove the shame to his head like a hot flame. Convulsed, he drew back. The vibrating hovel reeled in tune with the rhythms overhead. His glance fled along the ceiling; and finally, when he could no longer avoid glancing at her upturned face, he met there, ingrained in her painted features, what he had dreaded to see—the unsoiled sheen of the divine, the sublime promise from which he had sought to escape, the voice he had never heard but which was capable of saying to him one day: *Why hast thou turned from me, my son? And why didst thou hope to hide among those most needing com-passion?*

He leaped up, pushing her away. Sprawled on the mat, she stared at him, at first more bewildered than angry, unable to grasp the cause of the panic and rage which was directed, not against her, but against what he had seen mirrored in her. Slowly, she picked herself up; but when he stepped closer, grabbing her wrist —she repulsed him. Her unexpected dignity, so absurd, so ludicrous in this vile cellar, infuriated him. Intent on debasing in her what he had wanted to blot out in himself, he pulled out his wallet and thrust at her all the money it contained. But his contempt drew from her an unexpected response of pride—an instinctual, battered, useless and yet indestructible pride. Almost violently, she ordered him to leave—

The marimbas beat unbearably inside his brain, beat louder and harder, beat until something in him broke. He could hardly make his way to the exit. When he reached the street, he leaned against the doorpost and looked out into the tropical night. The drummer's beat in his brain had stopped, though upstairs and all along the street the muffled rhythms continued. He did not move —he did not know where to go. When he felt someone tug at his jacket, he looked back, and saw that she had followed him, attempting to push into his pocket the crumpled bills he had given to her.

Humiliated, he stammered that he wanted her to keep the money. Her eyes strayed to the cot, as if she deliberated whether the primitive code by which she lived permitted her to keep a sum she had not earned. And only after he had fully reassured her, did her troubled face break into a smile. She touched his wrist, intent once again on giving him comfort, though now even more uncertain as to how she could soothe in him that raging hurt she sensed but could not comprehend.

And yet, as he gazed at her painted face, he detected beneath the crumbling make-up a bewildered pain—a haunted questioning almost strikingly similar to his own—except that it seemed to alternate, whenever her smile faded, with an instinctive grasp of mysterious why's.

He moved closer to her, absurdly grateful when she did not withdraw as his arm brushed against hers. For a moment, they stood side by side, gazing past the long row of red lights to the sliver of shimmering ocean at the end of the lane. Then a sailor approached from the other direction, and she turned to attract his attention with raucous, bird-like calls, while Webb fled from her door.

After that evening, he no longer attempted to break out in any direction. He would sit on the terrace of his villa, a cool drink in his hand, his eyes on the blue haze of the mountains, knowing that their distant splendor would never be part of his life, and that their unfulfilled lure, on the other hand, could not be eliminated. In the months that followed he perpetuated his attitudes; he knew that he was shrivelling up inside the forced and not-to-be-transgressed routine he had imposed upon himself, but he did not resist. And, gradually, he began to forget that his discipline was actually that of an automaton; he had put a partition between himself and his past, a shell as protective as the fence around his villa, and so was able to persuade himself that his present surface responses were the only ones truly indigenous to him.

Even the distant mountain range was losing its fascination; he actually succeeded in convincing himself that the luring sheen was no more than an optical illusion. There was no change of seasons in this climate; and thus time passed unnoticed, while the congealing process in him affected and imperceptibly adjusted all his opinions to its dry and stifling needs. In the end, seated immobile on his terrace, the cocktail glass chilling the palm of his hand, his eyes on the blue haze of the mountains, he seemed like one of the petrified fugitives caught by the mummifying volcanic ashes in the act of escaping from the eruption, or else like one of the local, pagan, idolatrous statues forgotten in some abandoned clearing of the jungle.

And then, on a day much like all the others, on a day when the blue mountains had been nearly obscured by a thick haze, Crispian had walked into his office.

The wind, in thunderous plunges, cascaded from the jagged ridge, flinging down wave upon wave of massed clouds.

From above and below, the enraged solitude of the mountain pressed harder on the two tiny figures struggling exhaustedly over its bastions; and the approach of evening still further intensified their sense of aloneness. Although the sky was gradually clearing, it was also losing its color; even the black granite all around them was beginning to turn gray in the eerie twilight.

Looking down from a cornice, the Padre signaled that Webb should move faster. "If we don't reach the glacier cave before dark," he called down, "we are lost." And Webb, hurrying up the steep couloir as fast as he could, slipped and fell twice on the sharp stones.

The Padre climbed rapidly toward the top of the ridge—then stopped, only a few feet away from the crest, his shoulders dropping stiffly at the sight which had opened before him.

An icy fear stabbed at Webb. Even before he had reached the Padre, he guessed what was ahead. It almost seemed as if he had known all along that the mountain had been using the storm as a feint, all the while holding in abeyance an even more murderous tool with which to destroy them—

He stopped behind the Padre, his heart pounding. Directly in front of them, the appalling, sheer wall swam out of the mist.

For a while, they stood immobile. The trail, after crossing a short plateau, crawled out into the void, traversing the immense, almost vertical descent. Its thin line seemed to sway like a suspension bridge over the bottomless chasm. Timorously reaching out, it groped ahead, yard after precarious yard, grasping for footholds as it clung feebly to the sheer rock.

The Padre looked all about them for a way out. To their right, they saw the remains of the old trail—blocked by a gigantic rock slide. Buried beneath tremendous boulders, it had become utterly impassable. And the Indians from Zapar, apparently despairing of ever using it again, had hacked that slender ledge across the cliff.

His eyes riveted to the precipice, the Padre seemed to test and re-test it, measuring and evaluating their chances of getting across. "We have no choice, senor," he decided at length. "It is too late to turn back. In another hour, it will be dark. And at night we would never find our way back to Santa Rosa."

Without awaiting Webb's response, he started to move ahead. And Webb, as though deprived of any willpower, followed him across the plateau, strangely unresisting, almost numb.

Only vaguely did he realize that he had to reach some sort of decision. But he could no longer think lucidly; the pale chasm in front seemed to have clamped an iron brace around his brain, the pressure of which increased minute by minute, step by step, as if a screw were being turned.

A deadly awareness of guilt spread in him. He sensed that he was at last heading toward his final accounting with the mountain. The verdict was no longer in doubt; he had been tried, and was found wanting, and his sentence would now be announced.

All his travels from one country to another, all his roaming over the face of the earth, all the wandering of his soul, seemed to have been nothing more than a preparation for the final moment of clinging to that sheer wall. There, on the glaring surface, he would at last meet the truth that was his, and his alone. There, the voice he had yearned for, would finally speak to him. But it would not soothe his anguish as he had hoped. Instead, it would reveal his death sentence amidst a crashing of rocks; it would thunder accusations, while he fell from his last hold on life.

There was not the slightest chance that he could get across the chasm. He could explain to the Padre why he would be unable to traverse the murderous ledge. He could tell him about being involved in that accident when Cliff Williams was maimed by the avalanche. It would be a convincing reason and the Padre would understand. It would sound as plausible as the refusal of an airplane pilot to fly again after a bad crash, or the cowardice of a matador after having been gored. It could be stated simply and concretely, and Webb would not have to delve into the writhing mass of his guilt. He would not have to say: I cannot trust my own reactions in a moment of stress, because I can't foresee what destructive and uncontrollable emotions might shoot up from the past—

Just now, stumbling over a stone, his mind had blacked out momentarily. What if the same thing happened on that wall, if some angry and unresolved conflict surged up to block a split-second response? One misjudged step and he would drop over the ledge....

The abyss was drawing nearer all the time, a glowing midnight blue, as frangible and unreal as a mirage, and yet a persistent, fateful reality that could not be wished or thought away. On that razor-sharp ledge, all half-truths would be cut, all evasions slashed. There would be no concealment, no self-deception of any kind....

The sweat ran down his dust-caked face, as they approached the slope. He saw no way to claw his will into this sheer descent, to arrest the incessant, wild, screaming plunge into the dark chasm. Out there, suspended on a hair's breadth between life and death, his rebellion against the mountain was sure to collapse. All his embittered questions would turn into one last inarticulate scream as he plunged downward, weightless, careening, tumbling....

The trail curved past the last boulders to a small platform, and then swung out into the open, a knife's edge over a glistening, holdless drop. They stood, searching the pitiless wall. Swimming, floating over the void, its surface was polished to a clean blank glimmer. Nothing would soften it, no thought, wish, bribe, persuasion. An unalterable fact of nature, it spread before them in all its glaring, implacable reality. But though it faced them without rancor or fury, it was none the less murderous because it would kill without hatred.

A gust of wind blew up some dust at the far end, and then came gliding along the full length of the smooth surface, like an executioner testing his instrument of death prior to its use. Webb glanced at the Padre, who stood with his eyes half-closed, frowning, lost in thought. His expression did not reveal what the towering wall meant to him—perhaps, something quite different from what Webb had read into it, perhaps the sum and substance of his own past evasions and carefully guarded secrets, which were about to be exposed, ripped open on the cutting edge ahead.

They climbed over the two rocks which had rolled to a precarious standstill at the rim, and then they stepped out onto the narrow groove.

They had already advanced twenty, perhaps thirty feet, when it struck Webb that he had gone ahead without actually deciding to do so. The Padre, pulling up his robe, had simply walked forward; and Webb had followed him, unthinkingly, like an automaton. He now felt that he had to consider his actions, that he could not allow himself to be driven to the scaffold by a set of circumstances, no matter how compelling. But it was already too late; the path had grown so narrow that there was no room to turn around; he had no choice but to proceed.

Escape leaped and broke on the magnetic trail that unspooled before him like a violently shaking ribbon. So far he had avoided looking down. But now the wall bulged out, nearly pressing him from the ledge. For a second only his glance focused on the sinking depth, and at once it tore at him, pulling him into its vortex. Rocks, flats, ravines floated in the pulsating, throbbing waste below, blurring all contours into one mass of terror. An infinitesimally small tree beckoned to him mockingly from the bottom. He swayed and clawed his nails into cracked rocks, waiting to regain his equilibrium, waiting for his vision to clear.

By the time he dared to resume his advance, he had resolved not to look down again. But it was too late; though his eyes now remained fixed on the narrow strip before him, he could not forget the vision of the abyss; it had been too deeply etched into his mind.

He did not know how far they still were from the end of the wall. His consciousness seemed to shrink steadily; it was now confined to the limited circle of his activities: upon the painful raising of a foot, the thousands of minute adjustments necessary to preserve his equilibrium, the testing of each foothold's security before entrusting his weight to it; and then upon the contraction of muscles as he drew the other leg after the first, always in fierce readiness to counteract any sudden change.

And the whole identical procedure repeated time after time—but never becoming automatic, never unconsciously executed, because the fatal consequences, accompanying each move, gave every step a deadly individuality of its own.

He had lost all sense of time. Each yard of the trail stood for immeasurable eternities. He seemed to have left the plateau ages ago; and yet, after he tremblingly raised his eyes, he could still not see the other side. But not far from him, the rainbow-colored spray of a rivulet, pouring down in an almost weightless waterfall, enveloped the Padre. And when Webb, in turn, passed beneath it, the iridescent spray dripped into his eyes, temporarily blinding him.

He tried to blink the moisture away. He did not dare to use his hands to wipe it off, for fear of losing his balance. With his back to the granite surface, he held on to a notch cut deeply into the rock by the rushing waters.

When he was able to open his eyes again, he saw, across the filtering spray, how far they had climbed. He saw the ridge, the canyon, the promontory where the mountain's base fell away to the ravine—fell to the rubble cone below the foothills, to Santa Rosa, and to the blue glimmer of the land below.

At the borders of twilight, he saw the stillness of the ocean in the bay of Puerto Carribas, and beyond it the faint promise of the gulf, and still farther the shores of times long past and forgotten. He saw the years of childhood and growth and maturity, all submerged below the horizons of here and now, all floating up to surround him.

The spray drew its misty veils closer around him. If it were true, he thought drowsily, that a drowning person saw his entire life before him, then he was surely crossing the threshold of death, for he could no longer hold down the many images that swam toward him like colorful creatures of the sea, gazing at him with mutely questioning eyes. There was Harry McKenzie, peering at him with unwavering faith; and there, Don Hernandez; there Tom Sears, trailed by Esther's brother, Joshua. Professor Velliczek came, then Mona; and finally Esther, smiling to him from blue space, inviting him with a gentle gesture to join her—

He drew back, at the last moment. His heart fluttered wildly when he realized that he had started to edge toward the abyss. With a ferocious effort, he broke the spell of his hallucination.

No more than a few seconds could have passed. The Padre had advanced only five or six steps since Webb had last seen him inching along the ledge. Following him, but now with his back pressed against the wall, Webb moved sideways, at an excruciatingly slow pace.

Below him, the abyss throbbed avariciously, a ghostly, skeleton-littered waste that was quiveringly alive. After each step, Webb had to take a deep breath; then his heart would roar up, and his lungs pumped for air too long withheld, and his nerves ran wild, until he managed to subdue them again.

The wind had almost entirely died down. There was a great stillness around him, a paralyzed silence in which the scraping of their shoes grated harshly. Suddenly, leaping across the mute distance, Cliff Williams' scream roared up, rising to a high pitch; at the same time, his crutches came spinning toward Webb, revolving like the arms of windmills, striking at Webb as they rolled closer and closer, just barely missing him at each turn—

He leaned against the wall. The obsessive states came and went in waves, threatening to submerge his consciousness like an angry flood licking up the shores of an island. Now he would see clearly the smallest crack and mound on the ledge; then again he would hazily imagine that another self, his exact double, was approaching from the other side. They would meet in the center and embrace and finally merge into one—before tumbling down from the ledge, before dropping, skipping a few times on the hard shields, bouncing out into the air and circling downward in free fall....

He no longer dared to raise his glance, not even as far as the Padre. He could hear him, however, and so he knew that the mountain priest was still near; he kept listening to the crunching of the heels on the stone, to the agonizing tests of surface, the slow feeling out of leverage and safety. And then—

The crunching had stopped. After an endless wait, Webb looked up. The Padre had come to a halt at a point where the ledge, instead of proceeding horizontally as before, looped down, declining steeply for about twenty feet before swinging up again.

For a long while, the mountain priest stood still. Apparently, he had decided that they could not advance. Slowly pivoting around, he looked past Webb, his face ashen, his chafed lips trembling, whispering something incomprehensible—and in the middle of it breaking off.

A ragged cloud drifted past them, momentarily enveloping them in a dark mist. Webb waited until it had floated away, and his waiting made him realize that there was nothing to wait for, nothing to expect, no change, no help from anywhere.

The Padre, gradually stiffening, moved closer to the side of the mountain, and took his first step down the loop.

Webb gasped, stifling an outcry. Freezing to absolute stillness, he watched the Padre disappear by degrees. By the time the mountain priest had vanished from sight altogether, Webb could no longer endure the uncertainty. He edged his way forward to the spot where the ledge declined—and then stopped, growing dizzy as a sick feeling spread from the pit of his stomach. Not only did the ledge loop down more steeply than he had been able to observe before, but, in addition, a section near the bottom sagged so badly toward the abyss that it was unthinkable to cross without slipping in one direction or the other.

The Padre was approaching the bottom. With his hands clawed into the smoothness of the rock, he half-lifted himself across the sagging ledge—slipped—regained his balance—and, after an interminable suspension of time, managed to move on, more rapidly ascending the other side of the loop, and finally reaching the top where the ledge levelled out.

He leaned against the wall, exhausted, limp. He could not turn to watch Webb; the ledge was too narrow to let him pivot around. All he could do was to wait until he would hear the scraping and crunching of Webb's steps—

But all of a sudden Webb knew that he would never descend that loop. A clouded faintness arose in him, while the abyss, roaring up to claim its prey, snapped at the last strands of his willpower. Across the chaos of screaming rocks, he saw the end approaching. And suddenly he knew that he was about to meet death—and, in death, himself.

He knew that in another moment he would fall from the ledge and crash thousands of feet below. And he no longer hoped to resist. Instead, a weird fascination for death took hold of him, making him yearn for that glacial embrace of something vast and peaceful in which no memory could survive.

At that moment, the Padre, without waiting for him any longer, straightened up and moved on toward the next obstacle— a heap of rubble on the ledge about thirty feet away. A triangular sheet of rock had crumbled from the overhanging wall; its shattered remnants now lay on the trail, blocking the passage. After he had reached the deadly barrier, Padre Paolo gazed beyond the rubble, as though evaluating the possibility of jumping over it and across—but evidently was forced to abandon the plan.

Cautiously bending one knee, he lowered his heavy frame, and started to brush the rubble over the edge. For a while, he made good progress; a steady trickle of dust and stones went skidding and clattering down the slope. But then, as he leaned forward, his shoulder caught in the protruding wall. In his half-crouched position, this slight pressure was enough to tip him toward the abyss—and only at the last moment was he able to save himself by dropping on both knees.

Webb had cried out, frantically, insanely. For several seconds, the mountain priest remained immobile. But then, after slowly recovering, he crept forward again, and proceeded with his lethal work.

He had cleared away about half the rubble, when he encoun-

tered a heavy slab, partly concealed beneath a layer of dust and
wedged into the wall at the near end. The effort of prying it
loose upset his balance, this time even more dangerously. With
his bulky shoulders see-sawing wildly, and his back heaving in
vain to re-distribute his weight—

Webb rushed ahead. A blind impulse swept him onward. He
was only dimly aware that he was moving down the loop. He had
to reach and hold the Padre—in that single intent his whole being
was galvanized and encompassed. He did not measure his steps.
The need for the swiftest unconscious calculations had swept
aside his rational powers. His brain seemed to have surrendered its
authority to subordinate nerve centers, which took charge, communicating among themselves without supervision, collaborating,
functioning smoothly.

There was no more hesitation, no trace of doubt or fear in him.
If he was at all conscious of death, it was only in regard to the
Padre. As for himself, he had accepted it; it no longer concerned
him. Whether or not he now slipped mattered only in so far
as it would keep him from getting to the Padre. That was why
he had to throw his weight back, then toward the wall, and
forward again. And now, as he passed the sagging section, the
ground gave way under his feet, but his momentum carried him
on and up....

His momentum carried him even beyond the point where the
ledge levelled out. He saw the Padre bending down again to his
work; and Webb moved toward him, as rapidly as possible, forgetting danger, almost recklessly.

As he sidled along the ledge, he suddenly had the odd sensation that something tremendous had happened. He could not
make out what gave him the impression that he had shed a thousand leaden weights in crossing the loop. But he distinctly felt a
rising and soaring in him, an inexplicable exuberance, as he
reached the Padre and held him fast, clutching at the black sleeve
while supporting himself on a horn-like mound in the wall.

Some awareness of danger was returning to him. But it could not
squelch the strange, jubilant ringing in his ears, which was now
joining with the chorus of the rocks around him. Once again he
heard the granite voices near and far singing their archaic hymns

in praise of men and their noble spirit and all the good in their hearts. *Men are born good,* they called to him, *and so wast thou.* As his great dispute with the mountain was thus renewed, he expected himself to rebel again, but found that all his denials had crumbled and vanished. And instead of setting him apart, the ringing in his ears merged with the chorus of the rocks, linking him triumphantly to the immense strength emanating from the mountain....

A strong blast of wind passed the two small figures glued to the towering wall. Beneath the Padre's coarse cloth, Webb could feel the muscles strain, grow hard and relax—but no sound of falling stone followed their exertion. Looking down, he saw that the slab was still on the ledge, too heavy to be moved, though part of it was now rearing out into space.

The Padre straightened up. No more than about twenty-five feet away was the end of the ledge, where a broad terrace beckoned to them with a tantalizing promise of safety. Almost impulsively, the mountain priest advanced; but as he set one foot upon the slab, it started to rock so ominously that he had to withdraw at once.

Padre Paolo's shoulders tensed. Gently, he pulled Webb's hand from his robe. And then, after bending to a slight crouch, he suddenly leaped forward, jumping just high and far enough to clear the slab. At the instant of landing, as he counteracted the shock by spreading his arms, he looked like a dishevelled bird perched on a wire. But at once, without even waiting to regain his balance, he tumbled ahead, straightening up as he moved along, and so reached the terrace at the end of the ledge.

The jubilant chorus in Webb's ears swelled up. He felt so free and unburdened that he imagined himself capable of reaching the terrace without setting foot on the ledge. Without any trepidation, he stepped on the massive slab, experiencing a curious thrill as he noticed its rocking beneath his feet. He lost all awareness of weight while his body was thrown forward in a swift arc; and then he was propelled ahead more rapidly, and he could no longer arrest his flight. For now he was running along the ledge with quick, mincing steps—not so much to keep himself from falling, but to soar higher and higher. Because just above the terrace, he saw Esther, floating toward him from the blue void, holding out her arms to pull him up, to embrace and draw him into that great forgetfulness—

A fierce pain shot through his exhilaration. Something brutal had clawed into his arm. There was a violent pull; he saw the Padre dragging him over the rim, with one leg braced against a rock. Then he dropped on the terrace, skidded, rolled over. He still felt a throbbing hurt in his knee—then the dark waves inundated his brain, and he blacked out.

PART FOUR

ZAPAR

CHAPTER XIV

THE THROBBING pain in his knee broke through his sleep. There was a light somewhere, and he felt the warmth of a fire. Above and to his right, he saw strangely elongated rocks, like stalagmites in a cave, aglow with an eerie radiance. Then his eyes closed again and he was borne away on a slow river of exhaustion.

The hurt in his knee pulsed through his dream. It pursued him as he was gliding over a bizarre landscape; it overtook him while he sought refuge in a tree, and there, once again, awakened him.

Dazedly, he looked about. The moist, glistening walls seemed unfamiliar; he felt sure that he had not seen them before. He had no recollection of reaching and entering this cave. He remembered the terrace on which he had blacked out; then their weary climb up to the moraine in the fading twilight. He remembered how the glacier had glowed above them in a searing blue, which had gradually cooled in the gathering gloom. He remembered that, for a long while, it had gleamed like a dying face turned up to the sky. But then, sinking almost abruptly into an ash-white pallor, it had melted into the night; and they had crawled on blindly, seeking their way in total darkness.

He noticed the fire in the center of the huge cave. Through slitted, swollen eyelids, he saw the Padre drop a twig on the flames. The sparks shot up; and then, as he watched them float down, he believed himself gliding back into his dream. But the fire held him fast; he was kept straddling the threshold between wakefulness and sleep.

Drowsily, he recalled how he had crossed the ledge to rush to the Padre's rescue. An almost bewildered joy lifted him momentarily above his exhaustion; in retrospect, his unselfish deed appeared even more startling. He felt that he had to explore himself anew, like he would a stranger who had always kept his face averted; and now that it had finally been turned, one saw on it no mark nor scar—and no reason ever to hide it.

321

He shifted his weight on the straw, relaxing in an almost pleasurable lassitude. Some harsh, constraining anguish had been cut on that ledge, liberating a great many unknown facets of himself. Watching them spread, he felt himself unfolding like a Japanese paper flower he had once dissolved in a glass of water, as a child. Then, too, he had watched in awe as the small kernel grew and spread, waving, opening, and releasing from its tightly folded substance a miraculously large amount of hidden surfaces....

Gliding back across the shadowy borders of sleep, he imagined that he saw primitive figures dancing along the smoke-stained walls of the cave. Then the dream widened and soon absorbed all of him. He rose from the cave and soared over the glacier and flew over mountains higher than El Soledad, mountains so high that no man had ever climbed them. But he did not have to scale them, for he was already so far away that the peaks appeared as low as the plains....

He did not sleep very long, and when he awoke again he saw that Padre Paolo was still sitting up behind the fire, a ghostly apparition undulating in a column of smoke.

Rocking back and forth, the mountain priest seemed to be in a trance-like state. Moving his lips in silent prayer, he did not hear Webb prop himself up; nor did he see him shift closer to the fire, though at that moment his eyes were open, staring past Webb with a vacant gaze.

Webb broke a twig in two and dropped it into the flames, hoping to attract the Padre's attention. But the staring eyes did not budge. Instead of narrowing a gap, Webb's approach seemed to have widened a gulf between them. For in the simmering silence of the cave he was growing aware that, even if they were to talk, the mountain priest would be unable to express in words his inner experiences, just as Webb could not have conveyed his own. They had reached a point where the symbols of speech were as inadequate as the mathematical sign for infinity; where a person was as alone as at the moment of dying; where no signal could bridge the ultimate solitude of men.

He watched the smoke drift in front of the Padre's blank stare. They were as far apart as if they were separated by a thousand light years. It seemed cruel enough that they were the only living beings within a wide radius of ice and rock; but that the two sole survivors in a frozen waste should be still further divided, isolated by a lack of communication, was a stricture too hard to endure.

Like a shroud, the fabric of human loneliness descended on Webb. The compulsion to communicate with someone or something almost drove him from the cave. But he had no idea where he would turn in a forlorn and endless universe. Whether he staggered across the glacier or stayed inside this cave, he would have to cope, in some manner, with his aloneness.

Along the walls, he suddenly re-discovered the dancing figures he had noticed before falling asleep. Evidently, he had not just imagined them; they were ancient drawings scratched into the rock, their style characteristic of the prehistoric hunters' uncanny artistry. The colors were so faded as to blend with the stone in many places, but form and movement had retained through the millennia an almost electrifying freshness.

With an immediacy which seemed to have banished time altogether from the prancing hoofs and frozen leaps, a wealth of images came streaming toward Webb. He visualized how the primitive tribesmen might have crowded into the cave, thousands of years ago, bending close to the wall while they etched, by the light of a similar fire, their magic messages into the rocks for themselves and future generations. He imagined their intent scowls as they contributed, in the infinitesimally short span of individual existence, a lasting record to the human race as a whole. And when he endeavored to decode the riddle of the drawings, he felt how something of their ancient magic reached him below the surface of time, infiltrating his aloneness, setting off echoes too diffuse to be grasped.

Pursuing a procession of bisons and horses across the ceiling, he noticed that some of the drawings appeared to be more recent than others. He wondered whether they had been sketched by the ancestors of the Indians now living at Zapar, perhaps within the last few centuries, or even by the present generation, still upholding the sacred trust and carrying farther into the future the spark handed down from the past.

An unbroken chain, extending from the darkest beginnings to a still unshaped tomorrow, ran through this cave, involving Webb as its latest link.

Fatigue clouded his sight, blurring the drawings and enlarging the confines of the cave. The spectre of solitude was still streaming from the smoking fire, wrapping itself around him like a shroud. But now there was no need to ward it off, for inside of him he could no longer experience himself as a separate entity. His individuality was actually a surface phenomenon, a luminescent aura surrounding a dark globe. The greater part of his being was inherited from countless generations, each of which had passed on to the next all it had received, together with all the new it had brought into the world, ceaselessly selecting what was of value. And in the end, the accumulated achievements of all his antecedents had been deposited in him, the present protagonist, whose turn it had been to bob up to the light from the dark stream of progeneration.

He pushed an ember back into the fire, watching it flare up again. Even so ordinary a movement as the raising of his arm was a task he could not have performed, were it not for the immense labors of evolution. There was greater wisdom in the pulse of his heart, in the ability to distinguish shapes or the color of the Padre's robe, than he could have ever learned by himself. Whether he became aware of it or not, in all his thoughts and actions he was aided by ancient support.

A million ancestors had made him what he was. While the streetcars clanged around the maternity ward where he was born, a fantastic assembly of forebears had converged upon that modern building in the center of Philadelphia. An astounding array of cave men, primitive hunters, desert tribesmen, medieval knights, of artisans, tradesmen, and pioneers had gathered around his cradle, each to deposit his gifts. And they were still acting in him, never leaving him altogether to himself, never quite unassisted, nor as alone as he had believed himself to be only a short while ago.

Donald C. Webb, born in Philadelphia, twentieth century. He watched his enormous, hulking shadow flicker along the moist walls, framing a large, black area. Its indistinct outlines did not reveal what he was like within. In that blank space, there was a mysterious continuity, an uninterrupted succession which defeated time by telescoping forever the past into the present. There was in him an undefinable continuum which had overcome the disintegration of matter by evolving the miracle of death and birth.

Donald C. Webb, consular official. The succinct biography in his files stated where and when he was born, what schools he had attended, how many years and in which countries he had worked. It did not state that he was also the bearer of a torch first lighted in primordial days, the custodian of ancient possessions entrusted to him. It did not say that he was endowed by such tremendous evolutionary achievements that his personal deficiencies could never outweigh them; that, even at worst, he was never as worthless and futile as he had believed in moments of utter despondency.

Donald C. Webb, a minor civil servant, often overlooked by those who did not stop to consider that he might be more than just an expendable functionary; that there acted in him the unconscious genius of mankind, developed, perhaps blindly, over millions of years, pushing him, as it did all others, toward an ever greater destiny, which had never been planfully formulated by either an individual or a generation, but which nevertheless flowed of necessity from a billion successful selections in the past.

Donald C. Webb, a frail man huddled in a cave—but also a focal point in time and space upon whom immense forces were acting; a trustee for treasures accumulated since the dawn of time, whose seed was full of implications directed upon an even greater future. Heir to a universe and bequeather of life, he was time-bound in a timeless design, playing an undefined part in an immortal scheme, assisted by ancestral wisdom developed through the ages—

The Padre stirred; his massive hands dropped from his lap. But the sunken eyes were still staring past Webb, scanning inner horizons, and perhaps there finding Webb, as Webb had found the Padre in the eerie depths of solitude—in those innermost regions where they were joined as trees growing on the same soil, as waves rippling on the same stream.....

His head sank to his chest; he was losing ground in his struggle with sleep. He felt the heat of the fire singe his hand and drew back. Lying down, resting his cheek on the straw, he thought of tomorrow's ascent. For a while still, he gazed at the swaying figures which moved across the ceiling in a broad stream. The prehistoric processions of mammoths, deer, and prancing horses danced in the smoke as if their spirit were still alive after thousands of years. He wondered what Crispian might have thought of them, while spending the night in this same cave. As his heavy-lidded eyes closed, he recalled the rearing horse in Crispian's painting; and then other images welled up, drifting toward him from far away...a golden chariot...a winged man flying to the sun...a centaur, half-human and half-animal, leaping across a shoreless river....

The moonlight seeped into the cave, past the rock-sheltered slit at the entrance. Its diffuse beam flowed toward Webb; and when it touched his face, he awoke.

The fire had gone out; the Padre was asleep. Half-leaning against the wall, with his head sunk to one shoulder, he looked as if he had been overcome by exhaustion in the very act of struggling against it.

Webb got up as quietly as he could and tiptoed outside, taking care not to disturb the Padre.

When he arrived in front of the cave, the moonlit and moon-like landscape received and absorbed him in its frozen stillness. The wind had ceased altogether; nothing stirred in the frosty glitter of the luminous globe suspended from absent galaxies. Below Webb, embedded between dark moraines, the glacier gleamed in a deep, rich, milky white, sheltered and gently rocked between the arms of the mountain. Behind and above it, El Soledad's shadowy head loomed up in all its wise and pristine beauty.

Only now did Webb see what heights still had to be scaled to reach the peak. He saw the grandiose tower rise from the icy river, its base covered by white, foamy sheets of snow. He saw the black cliffs guarding the approaches to the ramparts which protected Zapar. He saw the glistening spires above Zapar, the spiraling ledges swirling toward that field below the crown, the tapering columns swept up to the ultimate consummation.....

He had to close his eyes against the dizzying heights, and then he sat down on a flat rock near the edge where the moraine fell off to the glacier. He knew that he could not climb the peak; but he also knew that he could not refrain from attempting it.

Along the eastern horizon, the first flickers of dawn shot into the sky. Before long, the Padre would come out and join him. Together they would look at the mountain; and then they would eat and go toward death, because there was nothing else they could do—because they could not resist the mountain's unearthly lure.

He dropped a pebble on the glacier, and heard it slither over the ice. At the lower end, the glacier shot out into the night and vanished, beneath a shower of sparks, like a waterfall dropping over the edge. As he watched it disappear in the direction of Santa Rosa, he was reminded of the gusts of glacial air which had chilled him in the streets facing El Soledad. And when he recalled the people seeking shelter in the ghastly tavern, he could not help wondering whether he would ever return from these heights to the blind alleys of that lost town.

The glacier sparkled all around him with an opalescent glitter. It did not seem likely that this pale landscape in the heart of death's own domain would ever surrender anyone who had penetrated its recondite splendors. But if it did, if he were allowed to return, he would merely be passing through Santa Rosa; he would not be pinned down again at that midway point. Descending from El Soledad, he could not possibly lose his way in that maze of dead end streets, which had so shockingly mirrored his life in Puerto Carribas.

For here, amidst this icy radiance, he could not even evoke the dispirited reasoning which had marred his days in the lowlands. Crouched at the feet of moonlit giants, he found it difficult to believe that he had wasted so many years in futile preoccupation with petty upsets, with senseless habits and debilitating fears.

And yet, he also realized, this period of enforced stillness might well be a stage everyone reached; perhaps, every person had his own Santa Rosa, a place somewhere in the foothills of the mountains, higher or lower, according to how far the ascent had carried.

For this was the point beyond which no one could carry his unresolved conflicts, where even the swiftest runner found himself overtaken. It was the place from which no one ever broke out to go higher—until he had retraced his steps to retrieve the vital energies he had left behind at various stalemates. It was the cemetery where the living buried their hopes, and then waited—waited without further expectations, waited among dead yearnings that could not be revived, waited in a graveyard of decomposing dreams, waited and stared into empty days, fearing extinction—and yet unable to do more than endure life in agonized dread of death's unhurried approach.

He dropped another pebble on the ice below. He knew only too well that he, too, might never have broken out from his routine in Puerto Carribas, if some new pressure had not been added to the precarious equilibrium of his interlocked defeats.

Across the idly spinning disk of time, he had seen a figure approaching, vague at first, distant enough, but slowly revealing itself as the skeleton which signified an end to all his habits. Mocking the obsessed repetition with which he attempted to secure a feeling of permanence, the grinning skull had drawn closer, bearing down on his comfortable villa. And in the course of its relentless approach, it had cracked open even his resignation— that last safeguard with which he had hoped to defend himself to the very end against any demands life might yet make on him.

He gazed at the sheen of slippery rocks endangering the descent to the glacier. He no longer had to ask why he, who in recent years had become so concerned with self-preservation, had sought out these murderous surroundings. For by now he knew that, if he had escaped from the security of his villa, it was because he had feared extinction so much that he could not indefinitely endure its threat. Rather than await impassively the dread moment of execution in a jail of his own making, chained by his unresolved conflicts, he had sallied forth to meet the enemy; he had rushed out to meet death.

His glance recoiled from the glowing skyline. The frozen landscape simmered quietly beneath the moon's amber light, its bizarre shapes casting no shadows. Here, in the valley of the glacier, he had at last tracked death to its lair. As far as his eyes could see, he was surrounded by space without life, by the bulwarks and castles of death. And this, he finally admitted, had been the true goal of his journey. This was the reason why he had crossed the jungle, hesitating, turning back and then climbing higher, fearing and seeking death, avoiding and craving it.

His insight had come too late; there was no possibility of escape from the glacier's realm. He was encircled by death; it watched him from behind the grotesque cliff to his right; it awaited him below the slippery moraine; it had set its traps on the crests guarding the approaches to Zapar. The end was near—so near and inescapable that it no longer seemed to inspire any fear, but rather a strange kind of tranquility.

He turned—a sudden roar had thundered across the glacier, followed by a protracted rumbling. He scanned the broken, cracked surface, but failed to detect any change in the fissures, and assumed that, deep down below, under the pressure of thousands of tons of ice, some crevasse had buckled and collapsed, allowing the inert stream to push forward another inch.

Gazing at a bend in the moraine from which a great many crevasses fanned out, he wondered if Padre Paolo would find a way around or over those treacherous gaps. Without a rope to secure them, if one or the other should slip—there would be no chance of being rescued.

Against his will, he imagined himself trapped in the depths of the frozen maelstrom, wedged in at the bottom of a blue grotto, slowly freezing to death. It would be an angry death; a death scorching his limbs with icy claws, congealing the blood in his veins, drawing cries of pain from one nerve cell after another before numbing them; a death that would slowly cross his whimpering body until its icy hand touched and stopped his heart—

He looked up—his astonishment meeting the glacier's pale glimmer. He had expected a resurgence of the terror with which the prospect of annihilation had haunted his nights in Puerto Carribas. But here, for some reason—here where he was surrounded on all sides by concrete dangers—he could contemplate every facet of a fatal accident with an equanimity that would have seemed inconceivable on the terrace of his villa.

Such immunity was not to be understood, yet neither could he deny it. Now that death was upon him, it simply evoked no fear. It almost seemed as if the image of death which he had conceived in the plains had disintegrated at his approach—he no longer knew where to find it.

Bewildered, he scanned the glacial landscape. The grinning skull had disappeared; it was certainly not in the gleaming ice; he found no trace of it in the frozen cascades at the glacier's source. A strange, unknown relief surged through him. Almost joyously, he looked higher, searching the upper regions where softer mounds shone quietly in the pale light. And from there his glance rose to the shadowless, deathly-white basins from which the glacier's inert stream was fed its eternal snow—and still there was no hint of death as extinction, of the death he had feared as an absolute end.

Old, encrusted anguish, deprived of its cause, dropped from him like shackles broken. He felt like a man who had been told all his life that the circle of chalk he had drawn around himself could not be transgressed; and then, after he had at last stepped beyond it, rushed ahead to explore the triumph of unexpected liberation.

Apparently, in the course of the ascent, his attitude toward death had undergone a continuous change; his fear, unfathomably, had decreased in proportion to death's proximity. It was as if a black wall had steadily receded while he came closer, melting away, and finally, at the very moment when he expected to touch it, disappearing altogether, as if it had never been more than an optical illusion, an imaginary boundary projected by deceived and deceiving senses.

And beyond it, now that the obstruction had been removed, a limitless distance had opened. His eyes rose higher to the intoxicating sight of El Soledad. He longed to reach the trackless, shimmering slopes above Zapar; more and more passionately did he wish to immerse himself in that unearthly radiance illuminating the night. And his yearning grew yet more intense when he sensed that no living being had ever stepped on these pallid fields —no man alive would ever reach that sublime, feathery, unsoiled whiteness.

On the sharp needle point of every graceful spire he saw dancing both death and desire, opposites miraculously united and indissolubly embracing each other. On the sparkling beds of untouched snow he saw Eros and Thanatos joining in what had once appeared to him as an illicit and guilty union, but was in truth the affirmation of the ultimate oneness of death and desire, the revelation of death as the offspring and goal of all desire.

For here he saw Eros demanding fulfillment, and, in its craving to reach the objects of its desires, project and envision consummation—thus creating the human fiction of finality.

He saw Eros spur the child's drive for wish fulfillment, thus ingraining upon the still unformed brain the concepts of goals and ends. He saw the early habit established and intensified as a mode of thought, until it culminated in the adult's harrowing projection of death as the sum and substance of all goals and objectives—the end of all things—the greatest finality of all.

Thus he saw Eros give birth to Thanatos—and desire its offspring in incestuous confusion. Thus he saw the origin of a human illusion—of death as an absolute end—a concept as erroneous as the earth-bound perception of a three-dimensional world, a mere figment of man's imagination as unreal as the shadow brought forth by light.

A cold breath of wind touched his feverish face, and then whirled on. The moon was moving along the glacier as Webb got up; the flickering dawn brimmed over the eastern horizon more forcefully. Nowhere in the icy wastes was a trace of death to be seen. In the whole gigantic panorama, in the soaring crests and dancing spires, in the immense glacier and the vast fields of eternal snow, Webb found not the least knowledge of death. The heavy shadow, which had obscured his view from inside his eyes, had never existed outside; and now it dissolved and vanished in the glow of the divine summit.

The sun, having swept the sky clear of dawn and its last uncertainties, heated the glacier with a flaming stream of glare and brilliant, molten light.

There was no refuge from the glitter on all sides. It met them in the granular substance beneath their feet; it was in the incandescent blaze on either side, and sometimes even overhead, when they passed alongside a piled-up mass of snow.

Before long Webb's eyes hurt unbearably. Already swollen from the strain of the previous day, they defended themselves against the stabbing glare by squinting and blinking; overwhelmed by avalanches of frenzied light, they started to deceive him by projecting dark spots and shapes where there were none.

Time and again, he would still see the Padre's black robe in front of him, though the mountain priest had already stepped aside to circumvent an icy crag. Or he would believe himself running into non-existent walls. And twice, when his vision blurred, he nearly stepped over the edge of a crevasse. He clawed into the

green sheets of ice that dropped below the surface; he saw the glistening depth where a mysterious light glowed as unfathomably as
death. And then he drew back and caught his breath and felt himself overcome by the wonder of that indescribable radiance in the
glacier's heart.

Death was alive, it was aglow in the blazing day, and a song
in the endless night. Death could not die, he thought on a perilous
snow bridge—and thus there was no extinction, and the great
fear which had fed at his insides was at last scattered into endless
space.

Death was no end; there was no end anywhere in nature; all
finality was a human illusion, imposed on the brain by life's impassioned desire to reach ends. Death was transfiguration and
change and immortal continuation.

He opened his inflamed eyes, drinking heady draughts from the
brilliance all around him, losing his sight in the glitter of eternal
snow and ice. The rarefied atmosphere at that altitude had an
inebriating effect. All fear and terror of the mountain had fallen
away. And in its place a subtle enchantment descended from the
summit, drawing him along the glacier, enticing him ever higher.
He felt released from fatigue, from any perception of obstacles.
He was striding forth with the unbounded faith that he was ready
to scale the heights.

Death is no more, his heart sang out; death has been abolished.
He tried to resist the exhilaration of his new freedom; he tried to
think logically; he traced back the gradual disappearance of absolute ends from primitive man's view of the world. Everywhere
the man-made concept of finality had retreated, from the notion
of the earth as a flat disk, from the sky as a star-spangled bell, from
the belief that matter simply disappeared. And instead, as nature
had revealed itself more distinctly, the secrets unveiled were endless time, distance without end, and continuous transformation.

Death is no more, he kept repeating to himself; death was the
ghost which had never existed in the empty room. How curious
it was that rational people deprived themselves of the belief in
continued survival. The more honest they were, the more guiltily
they refused the faith in an immortal soul. Distrusting it as a
mere wish projection, they grew more incredulous in proportion
to their yearning to believe. And yet, paradoxically, their very

logic should have taught them the opposite; for the atavistic concept of death as an absolute end was derived from primitive notions, which reason had every right to dispel.

The blazing white of the snow all around them became more intense with every step. Even the black moraines were now covered with sheets of ice; and behind the crest toward which the Padre was heading, long, glaring ridges poked skyward, past fields aflame with torrid light.

They climbed steadily. Rising higher and higher, Webb felt as if he had become part of the mountain's orchestration. He could hear the thunderous harmonies of choral multitudes, exulting in the upward cascades of El Soledad's eternal fugue, with wave after wave driving toward gleaming and yet shrouded heights from which none ever returned.

More and more frequently, Webb's eyes failed to distinguish contours. His sight dissolved into one mass of turbulent fire. Sometimes, he still discerned in it the tower of El Soledad, covered with streaming yellows and swathed in red proturberances shooting out from its bastions.

But now the awesome vision no longer inspired either fear or the resentment of helplessness; nor the impotent rebellion against that imperious grandeur. For his revolt had collapsed amidst the great love which, he now sensed, the mountain felt for him. So that, if he still hoped to reach the heights, it was not to conquer, nor to overcome his weakness, but to join that which he now loved with all his heart.

They climbed; they toiled and forged ahead. The hours passed; and still they rose, they strained, and climbed.

To go higher, and higher still. To have felt the rocks melting, to have reached a point where the weight of cliffs turned into circling heat—and to go higher still.

To go higher. To see the peak dissolve in the sky, and the sun tumble over a slope and break and flash away—and to go higher still.

To rise beyond all human limitations. To unlock the sky. To reach Zapar. He did not care what might befall him, once he had penetrated that shadowy citadel. He had to find Crispian, if he were still alive; and if not, he had to obtain whatever was left of the painting.

The blaring, soaring ice, arrested in its motion, reared up in ever higher blocks. Once or twice, after they had left the glacier far below, the Padre had to bend down and pull him over a crag.

His vision failed him so alarmingly that he felt in danger of going blind altogether. But he did not dare to call it to the Padre's attention, for fear of being forced to turn back.

Several times, after they had passed the crest, he had the impression that he could see some parts of Zapar, vaguely rising above a high ring of cliffs. From the glittering bastions, a myriad eyes seemed to be peering down, relentlessly watching their approach. He knew that what he saw was the sparkle of ice, and yet he trembled at the thought that he would not be allowed to enter Zapar.

Truculence arose in him once again. If necessary, he would force his way past those guards. There was, he told himself, a rare work of art at Zapar, a masterpiece that would be lost forever, if he did not bring it down. It was his duty to prevent that Crispian's greatest achievement should have been created in futility, and would never be seen by the many who were parched for some of the primordial beauty that had become so rare in present-day, mechanized culture.

His sight became so clouded that he could only grope his way forward. There was so much he would never know, and some of it might be contained in Crispian's painting. If Crispian had really attacked the impossible, how far had he been able to advance before he was stopped? What distant beauty, what mysterious affirmations had he concentrated in the smaller area he had cut out of the vast canvas? What transcendental truths, dimly seen at the outer reaches of human understanding, had he left behind at Zapar?

Lost echoes of his former rebellion continued to pass through him. Nothing could ever again touch his faith, but there was also the human wish to know. He wanted to look beyond death. He wanted to see beyond his eyes, think beyond his brain, know beyond mortal knowledge. He wanted to believe and know and get to Zapar—and his eyes grew clouded as he climbed higher and the mountain withdrew from his sight the gleaming visions surrounding him on all sides.

His hand on the Padre's robe, he groped blindly through the gates of Zapar.

He listened intently for any sounds in the portentous silence; but there was neither alert nor greeting. Only gradually there arose a shuffling of feet, of men approaching and passing, while the Padre continued to climb wearily up the street.

Once or twice he forced open his snow-blind eyes, and then he believed to discern a great number of squat, heavy-set men, small but powerfully built, with broad chests and short legs, with wiry, gray hair and bushy eyebrows over peering, unmoving gimlet eyes.

But none of them approached. Eerily indifferent to the intruders, they passed into the outer darkness of Webb's failing eyes. And when blindness closed in again like an opaque fog, there remained only the indistinct murmur of many men scurrying about on ceaseless errands; a murmur of unintelligible communication, a murmur both song and lament, of reverence as much as of repentance.

There was only that murmur, and not the voice saying: *Here I have waited for thee, my son.* And yet, he knew that El Soledad was near; the mountain's crown was surrounding the village in awesome proximity, with the peak towering directly over the ice-thatched roofs.

But he could hear only the murmur and no words of greetings; there was no voice welcoming the weary traveler, the battered, bruised wayfarer, the survivor of life's harsh tests and trials, the believer who had dragged his broken body and hurt soul all the way up to Zapar, to the highest perch before El Soledad's summit.

There was no one to take from him the unwept tears, the lostness of a thousand lonely nights, the injuries suffered, and all the pain—the hidden pain—the pain never confessed for fear of showing weakness. And yet, if not at Zapar, where would his soul ever find the comfort withheld in all the destitute, disinherited days?

But even here, he was still alone, still blindly led on by the Padre, his hand on the coarse robe.

The snow crunched under his feet. A myriad icy crystals blew past him on brittle gusts of wind. Even with his eyes sightless, he was aware how near he was to the peak. That last diadem of rocks, shaped like a dome, rose before him in all its overpowering reality. He could no longer doubt its immense existence; there was no questioning its truth, no more than he could still pretend that life was futile. For here, below the gigantic summit, it was impossible to believe in the senselessness and ludicrous injustice of the human comedy. Here, at Zapar, it was certain that fate was real, and fate had meaning. And thus, he sensed, as pain lost its futility, it also lost its sting.

It had started to snow. The wondrous flakes dropped gently on his upturned face, melting on his cracked, torn, burning skin. He felt cold; he shivered. But inside the dark orbit of his eyes, there flared the fire of his sun-scorched soul; surrounded by outer obscurity, there gleamed the memories of glaciers, of splendorous ridges and spires, of all the glory which had become forever etched into his substance—a knowledge of miraculous existence never again to be eradicated.

The Padre slowed down, then stopped, swayed, and suddenly collapsed, broke to his knees, felled by utter exhaustion. Webb tried to raise him up; but the mountain priest's heavy body hung limply in his arms. Holding him by the waist, Webb swung one elbow over his neck and lifted his friend from the ground, at the same time shouting for help. But no one came, though the busy shuffling of countless feet continued; nor was there any change in the incessant murmur. And so Webb had no choice but to stagger ahead blindly, with the Padre's inert weight dragging him down.

He climbed; he stumbled ahead, not knowing where to, unguided, unseeing—until he suddenly ran into an obstruction, a wall, a pillar, perhaps a fountain—

And at once, four of the murmuring men approached, forming a circle around them. They pulled at the Padre. But instead of offering their aid, they demanded his help. Their murmur coagulated into an Indian idiom with which Webb was vaguely familiar. One of their women, they said, was in the labors of a difficult birth and required the Padre's assistance. And with that, they padded away; they did not even help Padre Paolo to his feet.

And the mountain priest, though half-unconscious, near fainting, weary unto death, set out to follow them. Although he no longer had the strength to stand upright, he yet freed himself of Webb's support and lurched away. But after a few steps, he fell; and then Webb heard the scraping of the cloth on ice, as the Padre crawled after the men on his hands and knees.

The snow floated softly upon Webb's flaming eyes. He stood

alone amidst the ceaseless murmur and could not see where he was. Shadows as of great birds flitted past him, and he thought he could hear their raucous screams. And suddenly he, too, screamed and ran ahead, screamed and ran up the street, screamed and shouted Crispian's name.

The murmurs stopped. A man approached, and then a boy. They both passed hastily; but soon an old woman came and put her bony hand into his and led him ahead. She hobbled alongside, while he alternately screamed and whispered Crispian's name. And in the same cadence, she laughed and cackled; she told him that her house, in which Crispian and Mona had stayed, was the highest in all Zapar; she told him that they had lived with her, until they had gone their separate ways.

She chattered; they climbed. Before long, their steps lost their echo. Apparently, there were no more houses on either side to reflect the sound; they had reached the upper boundary of Zapar.

Her bony hand tugged at his; she pulled him up some stairs, and then across the threshold of her house which, she said, faced the summit. It was so high up, she cackled, that some nights the stars floated across the rooms; and when one of them burst, she and her sister had to wipe the floor for weeks.

Inside, her sister came from the steaming stove and touched his face with an even older hand. His eyes, she said, were bleeding. The two women bustled about, and then rubbed some salve on his lids which was to restore partial sight, although, they chuckled, it would not alleviate his pain. The salve burned like acid. He felt warm droplets roll down his cheeks, but when they touched his lips, he could not tell whether he was tasting blood, tears, or both.

And still his vision did not clear. When the two women led him up the stairs to the attic where Crispian and Mona had spent their last days together, he lashed out at red blobs and speeding triangles which, he knew, did not exist. And after he had reached the end of the stairs, he believed himself met at the unhinged door by a cold wind that undulated in scintillating waves past his tormented eyes.

He stumbled over a broken chair; he ran into a musty bed; the softness of dust on wood touched his probing fingers. He felt himself surrounded by dilapidation and decay, by the ravages of time and the erosion of the elements, by the struggle of mortality against its own passing.

Nowhere else but in this pit of corrosion, he suddenly knew, could Crispian have forged the incorruptible core of his painting; nowhere else could Mona have found the strength to leave him whom she loved and return to sustain life ever-fading.

The two sisters chattered incessantly, but never once referred to the painting. He groped along the walls, feeling his way in the hope of finding the canvas, crying out when nails and splinters tore into his flesh. Once he tried to pry open his eyes, but the pain was insufferable. And yet, after his blind search proved in vain, he tore open his clogged eyelids, looked about—and screamed when he saw Mona's head gazing down on him from the ceiling.

Paroxysms of pain forced him to shut his eyes at once. He stood petrified, trembling. The canvas had been used to cover a hole in the ceiling.

While the two women burst into peals of laughter, he stepped with one foot on the broken chair and pulled the painting from the gap. And after he had thus cleared the hole, he saw above the roof, for one moment, a black sky streaked by lightning and flowering suns.

He laid the destroyed painting on the floor, sobbing. Around the rims, where the canvas had been most exposed to rain and snow, the fabric was moldy, the colors had streaked—the coarseness of earth had taken its revenge on the beauty achieved. Defeated, driven back briefly, unable to hold down the supreme energy evoking the vision, it had surged back to eat into the dead matter, into the vulnerable base of the sublime—and so the coarseness of earth had yet been victorious.

Flattening the crumpled canvas on the floor, Webb kneeled down beside it. Light flowed from the painting, from secret sources within, from behind forms and colors, from Mona's face, from the Cross. As his wounded fingers went gliding over the pigment, he knew that he touched a merging of the human and the divine; that it was not willfully produced, but inspired; that the hand which had drawn these lines was touched by grace; that the man who had perceived the lasting truth behind these forms had not offered himself to the task, but had been chosen, at some point of his life, to bridge two worlds, so that the invisible could flow through his mind into the hearts of those who wished to perceive and could not otherwise see.

The coarseness of earth had yet taken its revenge—a soft patch of canvas, rotten and moldy, dropped off at Webb's touch. But the radiance of Mona's head had not been impaired; nor had the soiled spot in her hair achieved a darkening of its sheen and lustre. For there was in her skin, in her shoulders, neck, and outstretched arms, a glow as iridescent as if the source of light could never be extinguished.

He blinked the pain from his eyes, unable to keep them open longer than a few seconds at a time. Imagination thus mingled with remembrance, blending the figure of the woman by the Cross into one superb embodiment of love, of love felt and given, of love received.

The two sisters shrieked with laughter. Whether his eyes were closed or open, Mona did not vanish. More and more lucidly she stood before him, the enigma of why she had left Crispian impregnated in her loins, in her breasts, in her body's round forms. Her eyes pale with the anguish of parting, her lips trembling with the sacrifice of love, she had already half-turned away from the Cross, leaving, descending, returning, returning to life—returning to give life.

The sisters guffawed and cackled and hopped on the musty bed, nearly breaking its last supports. Their gibberish revolved around a child, or pregnancy; they chattered on about Mona leaving, and Crispian staying, and painting, painting, painting Mona's likeness, as if he could bring her back, or breathe life into her portrait. And then Crispian leaving, too. To the tool shed, they laughed. To the abandoned tool shed, the tool shed, tool shed.

The canvas rolled and heaved under Webb's hands. He pressed it down, here, there, but it kept flapping up wherever he released it. Here was the central panel, the central truth, and he could not unfold it. In flashing, squirming patches, he saw Mona, and the Cross—the bottom part of the splintered beam with Christ's tortured, slashed, bleeding body—then his sight gave way again.

On both knees, he crawled toward the upper part, blindly, giving his eyes a rest. He smoothened the canvas as he went along. Suddenly, his fingers groped into the void. He reached back, alarmed; and then, as his hand ran along the uneven edge, he felt that a section of the canvas had been cut away or ripped out. He opened his eyes and saw a horrid gap—above the chest and shoulders a part of the painting was missing—the head of Christ had been taken away.

The two women shrieked and laughed as he leaped up. They blithely ignored his incoherent questions. But in any event there was little they could have told him. He knew what had happened. To reach the summit of achievement, Crispian had still further reduced the painting. In an inevitable culmination of intensity, to penetrate the core of all mystery, Crispian had discarded everything around the Christ head. He had gone beyond Zapar.

The sisters stepped aside when Webb stumbled toward the unhinged door. They neither warned nor stopped nor helped him when he fell on the landing and then tumbled down the narrow stairs.

Bruised and battered, he reached the street. He knew where he would find the Christ head. He knew that he had to go to the abandoned tool shed. But there was no one to show him the way. The murmur of the squat men flowed past him impassively; no one stopped to lead him to the shed; no one listened to his calls.

The black fog had closed around him once again. He lurched ahead; he climbed; he had no doubt that the tool shed was still higher, higher than Zapar. He slipped on the snow and scrambled to his feet, and fell again and went on. He ran into an icy spire; and while it disintegrated with a tinkling of many bells, he thought he could hear the Padre shout a warning from far below. But he did not heed it; he went ahead; and, almost directly, he was met and halted by two of the squat men.

Their murmur, at first unceasing and unintelligible, sounded like argument, then like quarrel and indecision. Finally, one of them walked ahead, pulling him along, ostensibly offering to accompany him to the tool shed—as a guide, but more likely as guard.

He was, the man murmured, the tool shed keeper who had been Crispian's last warden. Every day, he had gone to the shed, taking up food. Sometimes he had watched Crispian daub paints on the canvas; he had seen him stand by the window and gaze at the summit. On several occasions, they had talked; but more often Crispian had not even noticed that he had arrived with the food.

Too absorbed to look up, he had stared at the Christ head; and there was no way to break into the spellbound silence between him and the radiant eyes he had created, the eyes holding him captive, the eyes that glowed.

The tool shed keeper paused, then relapsed into his unintelligible murmur. He was short and stout, and there was something about him that reminded Webb of the fat man in the tavern at Santa Rosa.

Every day, he wheezed, he had been obliged to climb up to the shed; every day, it had become more unnecessary. For Crispian had hardly touched the food. He had moved about less and less. Even when he did not paint, he would gaze at the canvas—from nearby, from the window, the cot, the wall. And finally he could not leave the radiant eyes at all; he was held fast by the eyes he had created, the full, rich, transparent eyes, the eyes that glowed.

The snow fell densely on Webb's palpitating lids. Across the whirling flakes, he discerned the silhouette of the tool shed, a tiny shell dancing on swirling snow, glued to a sheer cliff, floating over the ultimate border between here and beyond, the absolute outpost of human striving—before shedding the ballast and bondage of coarse earth.

The tool shed keeper slipped on the round edge of the deep channel hacked into the snow; he fell, rose, and wheezed on. Every day, he murmured, he had been obliged to climb this steep path, the icy trail beyond Zapar, the tragic road to triumph. He had slipped, crawled, staggered up to the shed; he had knocked, entered, deposited the food, and left. Except one day, when a snow storm had forced him to remain in the shed. Then he had watched Crispian in front of the Christ head. All through the night, Crispian had added no more than one or two brush strokes; and yet, the face on the canvas had continued to change; by morning it had seemed larger, brighter, more luminous still.

The snow grew dense; it blew into a wall, it condensed into a white impasse. The tool shed keeper murmured excitedly. He tumbled about in the wind; he cried hoarsely to the shadows of great birds winging past on raucous screams. He had, he shouted, carried up food; more he had not been told to do; he had punctiliously executed orders. And so, whatever had happened, he was not to blame; he had left enough food on the shelves, on tables and boards, to nourish Crispian for weeks. But when he had found the door to the shed locked, he had not attempted to break in. He had simply left the last bowl on the threshold, and had not returned.

The wind rose; it overthrew the squat keeper; he rolled in the snow. He crept after Webb, but kept gliding back. He clutched at Webb's arm; he gripped, clawed, and had to let go. Sliding back, he yelled after Webb, warning him to climb no farther; he begged and screamed and fell behind the white impasse, while the wings of the great birds passed directly over him.

The snow muffled his screams; the snow whirled busily inside the rising silence, inside a coming peace of silence, the radiant silence.

With his steps wondrously muted, Webb stamped through the deep snow. Exultantly, he passed through the bright obscurity, following the glimmer of distance embedded in shadowless light. He felt freed from all strain; and in a frenzy of hope, he suddenly believed that Crispian was still alive and would meet him in the shed above.

On thinning veils of snow, the dark shell of the hut danced nearer; it withdrew to the cliff as the flakes thinned and subsided; it clung to the black rock and yet reared out and floated on the brilliant light streaming from a cleft in the clouds, from clefts in the mountain and the torn horizon.

Approaching, Webb started to feel the blaze of the painting's eyes from within the shed; he felt their radiant stare penetrate the dark hull, felt it swing near and sweep past, and then return and focus on him.

Illuminated in every obscure recess of his soul, he staggered up the elliptic path. Blind and stumbling, he bridged the last gap separating him from the eyes which had rested on him all along, watching him below the neon dust of large cities, drawing him from Puerto Carribas, guiding him through the jungle and supporting him on the foothills and the high slopes of El Soledad.

He left the white channel; he climbed up steeply. When he rounded the last spiral, he saw that the door to the shed was open—

...it flapped slowly in the wind...and in the empty grinding of its hinges, his wish to find Crispian alive was foiled—

...but not ended—it raced on, passing itself, passing its earlier limitations, passing beyond the roof of the shed to the white snow on the summit....

He hurried ahead. He pulled himself up along the railing which curved around the misty void; he kept sliding on steps hammered into the ice....

The wind had ceased; the door flapped to a halt; there was only a great white stillness of light as he approached the entrance.

He climbed over the snow drifts which covered the threshold.

He stepped inside.

Beneath the low ceiling, he stood motionless. At first, he hardly recognized scant contours; and he heard no sound other than his own heart beating.

Nothing stirred; only the snow kept sifting quietly along the floor, coating untouched bowls of food with a thin glaze, covering scattered paints, brushes, tubes, rising and sinking in a slow drift toward the window.

Nothing stirred; only the white flame of the summit burned quietly in the window, a geyser of light, a shining victory in the sky, a presence so bright, so true, so near that it seemed not outside but part of the dark room.

The door moved, screeched, and hung immobile again.

In the stillness, Webb felt the gaze of the eyes almost directly behind him. He turned; he stepped back; dimly he recognized a shelf shaped like an easel—but without canvas, snow-dusted and vacant.

Yet the blaze of the eyes, more and more distinctly, came from that direction.

He approached; he passed the tripod chair, which Crispian might have used while painting; he imagined him seated on it, facing the Christ head, absorbed, spellbound in growing stillness, forgetting time and place, drawn ever deeper into the orbit of the radiant eyes—until, in the end, he no longer added to his creation but solely communed with it....

The spell, like a laming frost, took hold of Webb...or was it the unbearable cold wafted through the door...time was slowing down...it would stand still altogether, if he did not shake off the paralyzing cold....

He stirred free; he advanced, he reached the table. And there, tumbled down from the shelf, he found the canvas, draped in heavy shadows, untouched by the sifting, drifting snow....

The room had grown darker...there was no light...he saw no more than a white blur on the canvas, a pallid face, singularly indistinct. The features continually withdrew into rich and strangely luminous darkness; they kept retreating; they lapsed from sight. And only by following them into the mysterious shadows was it possible to discern the contours of the face...a face no longer tormented, released from pain...a face still human and yet so far removed from all suffering that its serenity knew neither smile nor.....

His hands shook; he could not hold the canvas; he had to put it down....Here was the prize—the end of his search....In its compressed and intensified space, it reaffirmed all the truths he had grasped in the course of his ascent...it affirmed the truth of man's greatness....It affirmed.....

He drew closer...even in this reduced surface, he sensed, Crispian had heightened the core...if he had let the contours of the face sink into the shadows, it was to light up the eyes in the center—

Time was slowing down around Webb until it froze...the laming cold encircled him, clinging to his skin...he could not stay much longer at this altitude...he would have to descend before he lost the wish...all desire to return...to leave.....

While the pallid face continued to disappear in the night, it grew more luminous in its highlights...the light gathered in the center...the eyes drew all the light into themselves...they grew wider...they glowed with an incandescent brilliance... they flared up in a white fire—

Blinded, he staggered back...the altitude drained his balance ...he was both plunging and soaring, whirled into holdless vertigo...he was plunging into the orbit of the eyes...and he made no attempt to resist...he wished to pass through the eyes into the world that opened behind it—

He clutched at the table....For a moment, a golden beauty, a golden unknown light had shimmered inside the eyes—

But the light had passed...and he was unable to follow it... he was held outside, and the cold air flowed around him, laming him.....

Vertigo...a dizzy swerving and rolling....He resisted, he must not succumb....The canvas...he had to...he had to share its beauty with others...not alone...he wished to let others see that pallid face floating over the table....He would take it down to the millions of men and women for whom it was painted.....

He fought against the laming cold...he drew himself up... he staggered toward the canvas, staggered along the circling shed —and fell back against the window....

The shadowy face gazed at him from the far wall...but now there was also another glance...other eyes staring at him from somewhere nearby.....

The cold ate into his skin, the cold melted his flesh...he longed to surrender...he was sliding down slowly from the wall, sliding onto the snow piled high beneath the window....

And there—he was met—met by that other gaze from inside the snow...hollow eyes buried under the powdery surface....

A hand in the snow, an emaciated arm—he drew back—beneath transparent veils of crystal whiteness, like a drowned face below water level, loomed Crispian's gaunt cheeks, the pale mounds of forehead, the empty sockets in which the transitory beauty of earth's many images had once been collected....

The snow came sifting, drifting from the door, adding its tiny crystals upon the abandoned shell, covering and closing the empty hollows of absent, vanished eyes....

The door screeched in the wind—a hoarse cry lamenting man's fate—soon silenced in the radiant stillness—the stillness in which the great fugue of human striving had rushed to its triumphant conclusion.....

Clutching the canvas with frozen hands, Webb descended through the white impasse. And as he approached the gates to Zapar, he was met and again surrounded by the murmur of many men.

The murmur was angry and loud; but there was still not the voice saying: *Thy search has not been in vain; and now that thou hast found thy way to me, thou shalt know that I have never rejected thee.*

The voice had not spoken to him in the shed above, nor outside when he had stood at the edge of the misty void, nor afterwards as he returned through the bright obscurity of eddying snow and shadowless light.

And now that he was descending through Zapar, there was no more hope. For here, there was only the angry murmur of many men, and the raucous screams of great birds, and the black night of his bleeding eyes.

But this time the squat men did not pad about impassively; they started to follow and surround him in a growing cluster.

Holding the canvas with frozen hands, he protected it against the buffeting crowd. And suddenly he heard the Padre at his side; the Padre whispered that they would not be allowed to take the canvas out of Zapar; that the squat men could not let it pass from their shadowy citadel.

But Webb would not surrender it—not even when the Padre whispered that the leaders of the squat men had offered to guide them safely as far as Santa Rosa, and even beyond, provided Webb left the canvas behind.

Webb slipped, fell, stumbled on, and so descended, sightless and weary, through Zapar. But he would not give up the canvas, for he knew that if he did not take it down to the cities below, the great fugue would have soared and passed unheard, and there would only remain the hoarse dirge of the screeching door at the grave of a man buried beneath sifting, drifting snow.....

The Padre warned him; the Padre implored him; he reasoned with him all the way to the lower gate. And though Webb knew him to be right—knew that he could not return unguided—he would not surrender the canvas.

The angry murmur ceased at the gate. The Padre lagged behind. He had done his duty; he had tempted and tested Webb, and would be rewarded and led back to safety by the squat men.

Utterly alone, Webb walked through the hushed silence, and stepped outside into the snowy wastes. Alone and forsaken, he stumbled down the blind slope, clutching the canvas with frozen, aching hands.....

He would not give it up, no matter what would be done to him, for he was no longer thinking of himself, but of others; of all the others to whom he had to bring the canvas, so that they could see and know the glowing eyes.....

He had not gone far when he felt an arm around his shoulder, firmly holding and guiding him. He did not know who had so come to his aid; but he knew then that he had never been rejected, nor had he ever been alone. He knew then that here it was that he had been awaited; here it was that he who had been called was chosen, and would never again lose his way......

If you wish to share the experience of this book with others, please use the convenient coupon for ordering from your local bookstore or directly from the publisher.

Jubilee Press, Inc.
7906 Hillside Ave.
Los Angeles, Ca. 90046

ORDER FORM

I wish to order . . . . copy(s) of THE THIRTEENTH APOSTLE @ $7.95 plus $1.00 for postage and handling. I will send check or money order —no cash or C.O.D.'s.

Signature . . . .

Name . . . .

Address . . . .

City . . . .

State . . . . Zip . . . .